BRITISH IDEALISM:
A GUIDE FOR THE PERPLEXED

CONTINUUM GUIDES FOR THE PERPLEXED

Continuum's Guides for the Perplexed are clear, concise and accessible introductions to thinkers, writers and subjects that students and readers can find especially challenging. Concentrating specifically on what it is that makes the subject difficult to grasp, these books explain and explore key themes and ideas, guiding the reader towards a thorough understanding of demanding material.

A selection of Guides for the Perplexed available from Continuum

Aristotle: A Guide for the Perplexed, John Vella
Bentham: A Guide for the Perplexed, Philip Schofield
Berkeley: A Guide for the Perplexed, Talia Bettcher
Deleuze: A Guide for the Perplexed, Claire Colebrook
The Empiricists: A Guide for the Perplexed, Lauernce Carlin
Habermas: A Guide for the Perplexed, Lasse Thomassen
Heidegger: A Guide for the Perplexed, David Cerbone
Hobbes: A Guide for the Perplexed, Stephen J. Finn
Hume: A Guide for the Perplexed, Angela Coventry
Husserl: A Guide for the Perplexed, Matheson Russell
Leibniz: A Guide for the Perplexed, Franklin Perkins
Locke: A Guide for the Perplexed, Patricia Sheridan
Pragmatism: A Guide for the Perplexed, Robert B. Talisse and Scott F. Atkin
Relativism: A Guide for the Perplexed, Timothy Mosteller
Rousseau: A Guide for the Perplexed, Matthew Simpson
Schopenhauer: A Guide for the Perplexed, Raj R. Singh
Socrates: A Guide for the Perplexed, Sara Ahbel-Rappe
Utilitarianism: A Guide for the Perplexed, Krister Bykvist

BRITISH IDEALISM:
A GUIDE FOR THE PERPLEXED

DAVID BOUCHER AND ANDREW VINCENT

Continuum International Publishing Group
The Tower Building   80 Maiden Lane
11 York Road   Suite 704
London SE1 7NX   New York NY 10038

www.continuumbooks.com

© David Boucher and Andrew Vincent 2012

All rights reserved. No part of this publication may be reproduced or transmitted in any form or by any means, electronic or mechanical, including photocopying, recording, or any information storage or retrieval system, without prior permission in writing from the publishers.

Author has asserted his/her right under the Copyright, Designs and Patents Act, 1988, to be identified as Author of this work.

British Library Cataloguing-in-Publication Data
A catalogue record for this book is available from the British Library.

ISBN: 978-0-8264-9677-5 (hardcover)
978-0-8264-9678-2 (paperback)

Library of Congress Cataloging-in-Publication Data
Boucher, David, 1951-
British idealism: a guide for the perplexed / David Boucher and Andrew Vincent.
p. cm. – (Guides for the perplexed)
Includes bibliographical references (p.   ) and index.
ISBN 978-0-8264-9677-5 (hardback) – ISBN 978-0-8264-9678-2 (pbk.)
1. Idealism, British. I. Vincent, Andrew. II. Title.
B1616.I5B68 2011
141.0941–dc23   2011016506

Typeset by Amnet International, Dublin, Ireland

To Clare and Mary

CONTENTS

Acknowledgements	viii
Introduction	1
Chapter One: The Coming of British Idealism	7
Chapter Two: Absolute Idealism and its Critics	38
Chapter Three: Monism and Modality	57
Chapter Four: Political and Ethical Philosophy	76
Chapter Five: Idealism as a Practical Creed	102
Chapter Six: Nationality, Imperialism and International Relations	130
Notes	155
Bibliography	178
Further Reading	189
Index	193

ACKNOWLEDGEMENTS

The authors have, for more years than either wishes to acknowledge, been engaged in common endeavours as friends, colleagues and collaborators. We have contributed to that wider movement of scholars, spanning several continents, who despite being dismissed as necromancers of the philosophy of the day before yesterday, have established the place of British Idealism in contemporary political thought. We warmly welcome this opportunity offered to us by Tom Crick, if not to dispel completely the perplexities of understanding the Idealists, at least to make them a little less mysterious and a little more intelligible to the uninitiated. In this endeavour, we hope that we will escape the unkind remark bestowed upon James Hutchison Stirling when he was purported to have revealed the secret of Hegel. We will be relieved if it cannot be said of us that if the authors have discovered the secret of the British Idealists, they have kept it uncommonly well.

Our debts are considerable, not least to our contemporaries, and to the younger generation of scholars who have seen much to value and extol in British Idealism. They are too numerous to mention, but our gratitude to them is limitless. This community of scholars would be far less than it is and much impoverished if it were not for the personal inspiration and stimulus of the examples of the late W. H. Greenleaf and Alan Milne. Raymond Plant, Rex Martin and Peter Nicholson continue to contribute to promoting the study of British Idealism. To Peter we owe a special debt of gratitude for once again demonstrating his generosity of spirit in reading through and commenting on the chapters in this book. It goes without saying that the infelicities that remain are our sole responsibility.

David Boucher and Andrew Vincent
Cardiff University, Sheffield University

INTRODUCTION

Idealism is a much-maligned word. In ordinary language, it is pejoratively labelled unrealistic, or unduly optimistic. Philosophical Idealism has nothing to do with the ordinary sense of Idealism. It is not about ideals, or utopias, but about ideas and particularly consciousness. Consciousness cannot be separated from the reality of which it is conscious. In other words, the mind is not a passive receptor of external stimuli, but an active element in constituting that very reality of which it is conscious.

There are versions of Idealism to be found in Ancient Greece, especially in Plato who posited a realm of immutable ideas or forms outside of the transitory reality we experience. In its modern form, it was influenced by Berkeley whose ideas were directed against materialism. Berkeley wished to reveal the ultimate spirituality of experience behind our sense impressions. Despite his scepticism, he was convinced of one thing: the reality of the self in self-conscious activity. Berkeley's "subjective" Idealism, which privileged the experiencing self, was challenged by Hegel who began with the postulate that experience is one indivisible whole, in which there is no sense of the self until consciousness begins to differentiate the *I* from the *Thou*. This is known as Absolute Idealism, which critics suggested is in danger of consigning the self or the individual to oblivion. Berkeley to some extent provided stimulus to the revolt against Absolute Idealism by the so-called Personal Idealists or Personalists. They maintained that finite selves, or individual people, whatever else they may be, had to be central to any account of experience. The whole cannot be understood except from the standpoint of the experiencing individual. While agreeing that everything is spiritual, the contention is that the content of spirit must be encompassed by a self.

The opposite of Absolute Idealism was not materialism but Realism, which eventually proved to be its undoing. Oakeshott captures the essence of the dispute between Idealism and Realism when he contends: 'Thus the "driving force" of Idealism is the belief that the known cannot be independent of the knower; and the "resistance" of Realism is the belief that what is known must be an antecedent reality'.[1]

All the forms of Idealism have at least one common element; they refuse to acknowledge that the material process is the ultimate character of reality – to the extent that reality is known or knowable.[2]

Idealism was not refuted, despite G. E. Moore's extravagant claim to the contrary; it was though frequently rebutted until such time the key proponents were no longer alive to respond. However, there were many lesser Idealists conducting a campaign of guerrilla warfare against the likes of Bertrand Russell, John Cook Wilson, G. E. Moore, Wittgenstein and Ayer well into the early twentieth century. A younger generation of Idealists, principally R. G. Collingwood at Oxford and Michael Oakeshott at Cambridge, also carried the banner well into the twentieth century, but understandably they were often reluctant to be too ostentatious about proclaiming their allegiance. Indeed, Collingwood believed himself to have gone beyond Idealism, especially in logic in that he rejected propositional logic common to both Idealism and Realism in favour of a logic of question and answer, which ultimately rested on statements that were not propositions.

The guiding principle of Idealism may be encapsulated in the following manner. All of reality, that is, all that is and appears, is for and in consciousness. To suggest that there is anything outside this fundamental principle of consciousness is unintelligible or meaningless.

British Idealism by the end of the nineteenth century had taken deep roots in the society because it fulfilled a number of social purposes. The consequences of rapid industrialization and the expansion of world trade caused immense social and personal dislocation and degradation for certain sectors of the society. Idealism was not merely a philosophical movement, but primarily a reforming force. It counterbalanced the individualism of utilitarianism, offering a philosophy that emphasized social cohesiveness, social justice and equality of opportunity. It was a philosophy that emphasized social responsibility through the greatest of all social levellers, universal access to education. It was also a philosophy that stood out against the degradation of man and God in naturalistic theories of evolution. Nature and Spirit were integrally and inextricably related. Spirit was the potential in Nature, and Nature was intelligible only to Spirit or Mind. For

INTRODUCTION

many of the British Idealists, poetry, religion and philosophy were at times indistinguishable; each offered the same insights through different routes into ultimate reality, the Absolute, Spirit or God. For many, God was present in the development of freedom in the world and expressed Himself through individual lives.

At a time of obscene social exploitation, appalling working conditions and disregard for safety, escalating levels of drunkenness and rampant and virulent disease, the consequence of unimaginable social squalor, British Idealism was an intensely moralistic and judgemental philosophy. It condemned all social evils, including the evils of drink, as impediments to self-realization, that is, to the realization of what is potential in oneself as a worthwhile human being. It advocated the removal of everything that hindered this attainment. The role of the state in all this was to ensure that the obstacles to self-realization were removed.

While most British Idealists were committed liberals, they nonetheless advocated the "right" kind of socialism, which eschewed class antagonism and emphasized social responsibility. The criterion for the extension of state activity always had to be the enabling of individuals to attain greater freedom. Thus, compulsory education did not diminish the freedom of choice but actually enhanced the capacity of individuals to develop their talents. British Idealism emphasized both the responsibilities of individuals to seize the opportunities to make themselves more virtuous, and of the owners of capital to act responsibly by transforming their workshops from schools of vice into schools of virtue.

Utilitarianism, in the view of the Idealists, was a philosophy incapable of accounting for, or encouraging social cohesiveness, because of its failure to account for moral actions, which could not be simply reduced to the pursuit of pleasure. Morality, for the Idealists, is fundamentally social, and acting morally necessarily means reciprocal concern for others and not merely a desire to attain a private state of mind, namely happiness or pleasure. Morality is equated with self-realization, which, unlike pleasure, is the goal of moral action. Self-realization is a moral duty. We have a duty to realize our best self.

British Idealists also associate self-realization with the common good. The common good is viewed as unachievable apart from the membership of a society,[3] and the self that is to be realized through moral activity is 'determined, characterised, made what it is by relation to others'.[4]

British Idealism, as it crystallized in the 1870s, was unquestionably something of a peculiarity in a culture characterized by an instinctive utilitarianism and the hard-edged empiricism of Thomas Hobbes, David Hume and Jeremy Bentham. In many ways, after the interlude of Idealism, a comparable form of empiricism and instinctive utilitarianism returned to prominence in Britain in the 1930s. Empiricism, particularly in the shape configured by Bertrand Russell, and the early Ludwig Wittgenstein, pressed ethics virtually beyond philosophical sense and appraisal into the realms of emotivism. Moral judgements were seen as neither based on fact, nor capable of being truthful. Morality thus had no position in the world of Wittgenstein's *Tractatus Logico-Philosophicus* (1921) or Alfred Jules Ayer's *Language Truth and Logic* (1936). This dismissive form of argument was subsequently replaced by much more sophisticated and morally sensitive forms of neo-Kantianism and consequentialism in the 1970s and 1980s. However, suffice it to say that British Idealism nonetheless visibly and unequivocally generated a profound and subtle interrogation of this utilitarian instinct from the 1870s up to and during the early part of the twentieth century. It also precipitated a deep philosophical and practical reconsideration of the utilitarian instinct's role in personal and public life, which shaped several generations.

British Idealism was a social philosophy that exuded optimism at a time of extreme social dislocation and pessimism. In summary, it acted as a profound interrogation, critique and metaphysical counterbalance to the individualism of the variants of an instinctive British utilitarianism and naturalistic evolutionism. It offered a philosophy that gave the much-needed orientation to social cohesiveness and to the closeness of the relation between individual and collective responsibility. Its emphasis on the importance of active social citizenship subsequently became an important theme in early twentieth century politics and welfare theory. In this sense, Idealism was a "working philosophy", which certainly for a significant moment in British cultural history set the course of moral and political thinking and delivered a resounding, if nonetheless temporary, rebuttal of the utilitarian ethos.

British Idealism, in addition to being conceived in a turbulent domestic world, contributed to the understanding and resolution of problems in an uncertain and explosive external environment. The age of Imperialism was at its height; jingoistic nationalism at its worst; and the willingness to go to war was at its peak during the ascendancy of British Idealism. In all of these areas, the British Idealists opposed the pernicious forms of the doctrines they were all too often accused of supporting. Social Imperialism, premised on exploitation, was abhorrent to them, but it was a fact that had to be faced. Those nations enmeshed in the affairs of different and alien cultures had a moral duty to elevate the lives of those individuals by imparting to them the skills and abilities to achieve self-government and attain a higher level of civilization. The British Idealists rejected the forms of nationalism that were insular and inflammatory. The nation, for them, was an ethical ideal and the sustainer of a moral community. Yet, as the sinews that hold people together became more extensive, the nation could be superseded by a higher and more expansive moral community, until ultimately the whole world may become our neighbour. War for them was not a necessary instrument of policy, but the manifestation of the failure of states to fulfil their purpose of enabling each individual to become the best he or she can, which for them was necessarily a moral ideal.

In the chapters that follow, we set all of these aspirations and ideals in the context of the real achievements of British Idealism in the realms of philosophy, politics and social policy. These achievements were to enrich the debate in all these areas with their emphasis upon the spiritual reality of existence and the irreducible role of consciousness in conceiving of and responding to a reality that had no independent existence apart from the minds that know it. The optimism exuded by the exponents of this philosophy cannot be overestimated. It was always the human potential for good that they emphasized and not the capacity for debasement and evil.

This book is therefore addressed to the reader who may have been initially put off persevering to understand the British Idealists. For some critics, it is the erroneous views of the British Idealists and for others their impenetrable style and unfamiliar language, which act as deterrents to a clear understanding of their work. It is indeed, for the most part, the language and style of argument that is unusual to the modern reader, especially among Anglo-American philosophers. The strangeness of the language, and manner of argument, of the British Idealists may easily be mistaken for obscurity if one does not persevere, and one is unlikely to persevere if what one is reading already has a poor reputation. British Idealism is not, however, completely alien to the modern world, having its roots in continental philosophy and resonances with some contemporary thinkers such as Richard Rorty, as well as modern constructivists. Ironically, such British Idealists as R. G. Collingwood and Michael Oakeshott have attained considerable contemporary popularity, without their admirers invoking their undeniable Idealist credentials.

What we are doing to allay perplexity in this book is to introduce the reader to the full range of the British Idealists' philosophy, elucidate their overall approach, explain and exemplify their main terms, outline their general conclusions, and comment on the value of all the foregoing issues. The book is distinctive in that it includes serious discussion of the Idealists who carried its ideas forward into the middle and late twentieth century. We also make comparisons of more recent writers with whom the reader is likely to feel more at home. The principal claim is that if one gets behind the unfamiliar style (which is only that, a style), then the British Idealists have interesting and significant things to say and in some cases what they say may contribute something of value to current discussions.

CHAPTER ONE

THE COMING OF BRITISH IDEALISM

British Idealism emerged slowly and intermittently over the course of the nineteenth century in the United Kingdom, gaining momentum in the last quarter. Its most towering figures, T. H. Green, Bernard Bosanquet and F. H. Bradley were all English. They were born in Birkin, the West Riding of Yorkshire; in Alnwick, Northumberland; and, in Clapham, London, respectively. Their prominence has served to understate the extent to which Scotland contributed to this philosophical tendency, and was indeed evangelical in spreading the news abroad to Canada, Australia and South Africa. Among the Scottish Idealists Edward Caird, who succeeded Benjamin Jowett as the Master of Balliol, Oxford is probably best known. The movement was almost religious in its fervour and counted among its members more than its fair share of sons of the manse, who themselves sometimes turned their hands to lay preaching. The personal impact of the most religiously zealous of them cannot be underestimated. The likes of T. H. Green, Edward Caird, and Henry Jones personally enthused generations of students to devote themselves to "good works" in the slums of Glasgow and London.

In this introductory chapter, we indicate how and why German philosophy came to have a foothold in a country with apparently antithetical philosophical traditions. Secondly, we explore the way in which British Idealism countered two of the most powerful scientific and philosophical movements of the time, namely the naturalism of evolution and utilitarianism. Against both tendencies Idealism emphasized the ultimate Spiritual character of reality, for which neither could adequately account.

THE ALLURE OF GERMANY

Early in 1770, Kant had made a vital distinction between knowledge acquired through the senses and that attained through pure thought. The latter he believed could reveal the fundamental character of things and relations, which are not themselves present to the senses. It was the revelation that such a metaphysics was in need of justification that set the problems of philosophy for subsequent generations. Kant's *Copernican revolution* in philosophy was presented in his *Critique of Pure Reason* some 11 years later in 1781. He contended that instead of thought having to conform to reality, that is, as it is traditionally conceived as representing its objects, it is reality that has to conform to thought apprehended through *a priori* categories such as space, time and velocity. The world does not conform to whatever we may believe. Instead, it conforms to our cognitive capacities. In other words, reality is intelligible to us, as interpreted through *a priori* categories of thought. Kant contends 'Before objects are given to me, that is, *a priori*, I must presuppose in myself laws of the understanding which are expressed in conceptions *a priori*. To these conceptions, then, all the objects of experience must necessarily conform'.[1]

In Britain, German philosophy became the route through which aspirant intellectuals could establish their own credentials. It was the royal road to liberation from Scottish empiricism and common sense philosophy and a counter to the dominance of utilitarianism and naturalism in England. While the Germans were greatly admired, it was not without reservation and some considerable modification that they became domesticated. Both Thomas Carlyle and Samuel Taylor Coleridge visited Germany and, in their own idiosyncratic way, enmeshed the German Spirit with that of Great Britain. Coleridge travelled to Germany with Wordsworth. He stayed first at Ratzeburg and then at Göttingen, where he spent almost a year to effect 'a more thorough revolution in his philosophical principles and a deeper insight into his own heart'.[2] Coleridge confessed, however, that his disposition was already somewhat formed before coming to Kant and Schelling, but that the Germans nevertheless helped him to gain clarity. Carlyle, however, proved to be the greater inspiration for succeeding generations, including the doyens of Scottish and English Idealism, Edward Caird and T. H. Green, respectively. Neither Coleridge nor Carlyle, however, could claim any great expertise in the works they purported to admire.

In the early part of the nineteenth century, the Scotsmen William Hamilton and Frederick Ferrier visited Germany and learnt the language in order to acquaint themselves first hand with the revolutionary ideas to be found there. It was James Frederick Ferrier (1808–1864) who first elevated Hegel above Kant and Schelling and urged his fellow countrymen to take the trouble to gain a greater understanding of the Hegelian position. He travelled to Germany in 1834 to acquaint himself with the growing tide of German philosophy, which he described as 'that mighty stream of tendency towards which all modern meditation flows, the great gulf-stream of Absolute Idealism'.[3] Although it is clear that Ferrier was not a committed Hegelian and adopted a more sceptical and eclectic position.[4]

Ferrier's complex relation to Scottish Common Sense philosophy remains still a matter of contention, but he certainly developed his own position with reference to it and became an opponent particularly of the intuitionist version, associated with Reid's disciples. He thought the latter was too susceptible to appropriation by religious obscurantists. However, the German pilgrimage, which Ferrier initiated, gradually became almost obligatory for younger intellectuals. Both T. H. Green and Edward Caird were inspired by Carlyle's example, and they in turn inspired others. Caird went to Dresden to improve his German, and T. H. Green was a regular visitor to Germany during the early 1860s.

Just before his election to a fellowship at Balliol in 1860, Green took up an intense study of the German theologians of the Hegelian-orientated Tübingen School, such as F. C. Baur. He also decided to consider the work of Kant, Fichte and Hegel in much greater depth. In effect, he satisfied himself, with the aid of their philosophies, that much of what he found of permanent value in Christianity could be preserved by their methods. In 1874, Richard Burdon Haldane also studied at Göttingen where, instructed by Herman Lotze, he acquired a deep love for the work of Kant and Fichte. Haldane extolled the virtues of Lotze as a teacher and subsequently influenced both Andrew Seth[5] and John Henry Muirhead in their decisions to visit Göttingen.

In summary, Germany exposed young British intellectuals to a new philosophical and literary landscape, yet none adopted Kant or Hegel wholesale. Indeed, J. H. Muirhead contends that British Idealism owed as much to the indigenous revival of Platonism, as it did to Kantianism and Hegelianism. The transcendental element in all such trends tended to function though as a generic antidote to both naturalism and empiricism. By 1883, the year after the death of T. H. Green, the aim and purpose of British Idealism did momentarily crystallize into a common endeavour, which thereafter, until the 1920s, developed in a number of directions, including, as we shall see in Chapter 2, the overt rejection and modification of Hegel by the Personal Idealists.

Essays in Philosophical Criticism, edited by Haldane and Seth, was published in 1883.[6] The volume was dedicated, in a strongly symbolic way, to Green whose noted *Prolegomena to Ethics* was to be published posthumously in the same year, just after F. H. Bradley's *Principles of Logic*. Both Green and Bradley, in effect, prepared the way for the development of Idealism to become the dominant philosophy in the English-speaking world in the latter part of the nineteenth century. Green had published his introduction to Hume, in particular, in 1874. This cleared the philosophical ground for the reception of Kant's and ultimately Hegel's work. F. H. Bradley had also published his groundbreaking *Ethical Studies* (1876), in which he attempted to transcend the limited conceptions of ethics associated with both utilitarianism and Kantianism.[7]

The author of the preface to *Essays on Philosophical Criticism* was Edward Caird, the leading figure among Scottish Idealists. The authors of the essays, Caird contended, all agreed that the line philosophy must follow had been inaugurated by Kant and carried forward by Hegel. The task the contributors set themselves was therefore to discern, in the philosophers they studied, the core principles that could throw light on the pressing questions of the day.[8] Andrew Seth, who 4 years later would lead the revolt against Hegelian Absolutism, set the scene by emphasizing the importance of identifying exactly what Kant's critiques had destroyed. What Kant destroyed was the notion that any metaphysical structure could be built upon an uncriticized dogma, whether it be the rationalism of Christian Wolff, or the Empiricism of John Locke.[9]

How the philosophies of Kant, Fichte, Schelling and Hegel came rapidly to displace the Scottish Common Sense philosophy (and the utilitarianism and naturalism of England) is nothing less than remarkable. The English context of utilitarianism and the evolutionary organicism of Herbert Spencer is reasonably well known, but the extent of the influence of Idealism in Scotland has been ignored, a casualty of the scholarly obsession with the work of Hume, Reid,

Fergusson and Hamilton. Idealism, nevertheless, came to dominate British philosophy in general for more than 30 years.

THE RECEPTION OF KANT AND HEGEL IN SCOTLAND

One of the reasons why the contribution of Scotland to Idealism has not been adequately acknowledged is that it was rather alien to the Scottish philosophy that preceded it. Further, what gave it a distinctive quality – a heavy emphasis upon poetry and literature – was not itself philosophical. Thomas Carlyle, for example, used Hegel's thought freely, adapting it to his own somewhat mystical style. The empiricism of Dugald Stewart and his colleague Thomas Brown at Edinburgh University was, in Carlyle's view, a mere preparation for philosophy, and in particular, a preparation for what was to be found in Kant. In his essay 'Signs of the Times', he encapsulated in the phrase 'the Mechanical Age', his pejorative characterization of the main features of the time.[10] The problem in his view was that from Locke onwards metaphysics in Britain had been both empiricist and mechanistic, obsessed with the origins of consciousness and the genetic history of the content of the mind. This task had been done at the expense of exploring the mysteries of freedom and our relations to God, the universe, space and time. Unfortunately, Carlyle sometimes gave the impression, not wholly justified, that he was uninformed about philosophical systems. Even someone sympathetic to Carlyle could argue that 'something more thorough going than the literary methods of poetry and prophecy was called for to meet the intellectual demands of the new time'.[11]

Ferrier had expounded his ideas in opposition to Thomas Reid and William Hamilton. Although Hamilton was critical of Kant and Schelling, his philosophical negativity was, nonetheless, itself important in introducing their ideas to Scotland.[12] Ferrier's version of subjective Idealism was largely inspired by Berkeley. He was at the forefront of interpreting Berkeley not as a mere transition between Locke and Hume, but as the discoverer of the spiritual nature of reality.[13] Ferrier was severe in his judgement of Scottish Common Sense philosophy. He noted that: 'Dr Reid, in the higher regions of philosophy, is as helpless as a whale in a field of clover'.[14] Ferrier, nevertheless, thought his own philosophy was, at root, Scottish. He recognized the need for a rational philosophy expounded as a deductive system of necessary truths that could overcome the division between the mind and its objects that reason created.[15] This he saw as the *reconciliation* of philosophy and common sense.[16] He identified the key to his philosophy in two propositions, to be found in *The Institutes of Metaphysic*. The first is the principle of self-consciousness. Thus, there is an intelligence that knows itself as a foundation of knowledge.[17] He denies false dichotomies, such as the distinctions between subject and object, the real and the ideal, sensation and intellect. In relation to the subject/object dualism, upon which Common Sense philosophy depends, he maintains that there cannot be an object without a subject, nor a subject without an object. They are inseparable and both presuppose each other. Knowing can neither consist in a pure object, nor, a subject.[18]

The second of the two propositions is the claim that we can be ignorant only of that which can be known. Ignorance is a defect, and there can be no defect in not knowing that which cannot be known.[19] Anything that is unknowable or unthinkable is also unreal. Ferrier claims, as the culmination of his argument, that: 'All absolute existences are contingent *except one*; in other words, there is One, but only one, Absolute Existence which is strictly *necessary*; and that existence is a supreme, and infinite, an everlasting Mind in synthesis with all things.'[20] He nevertheless still often admitted to his colleagues that he understood little of Hegel.[21]

Alexander Campbell Fraser was a student of William Hamilton at Edinburgh University, and succeeded him to the chair of logic in 1856. He was another interpreter of Berkeley and Locke, and an admirer of Reid. Yet, he was personally influential in encouraging his students, including Andrew Seth, to take Hegel seriously. He was, in fact, an acknowledged expert on Berkeley.[22] It was his Berkeleyan theism that enabled him to declare, towards the end of his life, a deep faith in an immanent Divine Spirit. He set himself the task of reconciling J. S. Mill's and Herbert Spencer's emphases on agnostic scientism with the metaphysical and spiritual philosophies of Spinoza and Hegel. He felt he could to do this through Berkeley's philosophy.

Fraser found in Berkeley a nascent theism able to counter contemporary attacks on the spiritual conception of the universe. Although he leaned towards the scepticism of Hume, he had no doubts about one thing: the reality of the self in self-conscious activity. Yet he rejected Hegel's Absolute Idealism, because it attempted to explain, by abstract reason, the concrete things of sense. He began with Berkeley's concrete things of sense. Instead of gravitating towards the empiricist and scientific naturalist tradition, Fraser, following Berkeley, emphasized the ultimate spirituality of the universe. His inclination was, in point, towards Personal Idealism,[23] preferring instead the term 'Spiritualism Realism' which, in addition to affirming the spiritual reality of the universe, also affirmed the commonsense reality of the world of sense.

This was not a shallow Realism. It did not stop at the visible and tangible world of phenomena and scientific laws. It rather penetrated more deeply until it reached the spiritual world, which underpins physical phenomena and from which we derive scientific significance. What Berkeley teaches us, Fraser maintains, is 'that the material world has its being and agency in Spirit.'[24] What he does not teach us, however, is the moral character of the universe. In order to avoid universal pessimism we must presuppose that the 'directing Spirit is morally perfect'.[25] Overall, it was Fraser's reluctance to accept Hegelian Absolutism and his embrace of personal or subjective Idealism that impressed Andrew Seth. Seth went on to develop a personalism that did not rely on Berkeley, but which nevertheless did not lose sight of the experiencing self.[26]

James Ferrier's admission of failure to understand completely the argument of the German was not shared by James Hutchison Stirling, a gentleman scholar from Glasgow, resident just outside Edinburgh, who somewhat recklessly claimed to have found the secret of Hegel. His now infamous book, *The Secret of Hegel: Being the Hegelian System in Origin, Principle, Form and Matter* (1865) included rather terse translations of the *Logic* and a commentary presented in a Carlyleian style.[27] Stirling was indeed an admirer of Carlyle. He believed, in effect, that Hegel's secret was to be found in Kant's idea of *a priori* categories and in Hegel's idea of the concrete universal. Kant's importance was to demonstrate that thought was constitutive of things. Where he was remiss was in believing the categories were mere representations of things in themselves. The central idea, implicit in Kant, was of a universal that determines its own particulars. Hegel's advance on Kant was the insight that the categories saturate subjective experience, while at the same time being wholly objective. In Stirling's view, Hegel believed that the universe is the creature of God's thoughts. In knowing the world, we know the thoughts of God.[28]

The book's novelty ensured it attracted a wide audience. It was, however, equally, if not more impenetrable, than Hegel himself. Even

Stirling's admirers found it 'almost as difficult as the original'.[29] If Stirling had found the secret of Hegel, it was suggested, he had kept it very well.[30] Despite its idiosyncratic style, *The Secret of Hegel* is widely regarded as the first book in English to make Hegel more accessible to the English-speaking world.[31] Hegel's popularity was such in Scotland that most of his major writings were subsequently translated by Scotsmen into English in a steady persistent flow. The principal translations were: *The Logic of Hegel* (1874), and *The Philosophy of Mind* (1894) by William Wallace of Cupar, Fife; *The Philosophy of Art* (1886) by William Hastie of Wandlockhead, Dumfries; *Lectures on the History of Philosophy* (1892–96) by E. S. Haldane of Edinburgh, the younger sister of the Idealist Richard Burdon Haldane; and *The Phenomenology of Mind* (1910) by J. B. Baillie of Edinburgh University.

The role of Robert Flint in introducing continental ideas into Britain should not be overlooked here. Flint took up, against T. H. Green's candidature, the chair of moral philosophy at St. Andrews University in 1864, on the death of James Ferrier. Flint was a Scottish disciple of the Italian eighteenth-century thinker Giambattista Vico, the author of *The New Science*, who argued notably that the civil social world was far more intelligible to us because we are its authors, than the world of Nature (the author of which was God). Flint was particularly important in making the English-speaking world aware of unfamiliar continental ideas in the philosophy of history. He was the first to write a book on Vico in the English language, in which he contended: 'The star of Vico shows no sign of paling before those of Comte and Hegel; it rather appears to derive from them additional brightness'.[32] He meant here that Vico may be understood as the precursor of both Comte's positivism and Hegel's Idealism. Flint was not merely a reporter of ideas. He distinguished between the clear exposition of a doctrine and its critical analysis, both of which he regarded as important.

Carlyle, in addition to impressing Stirling, was a formative influence on the most formidable of the Scottish Idealists, Edward Caird, as well as on Henry Jones, his protégé, and ultimate successor to his chair of moral philosophy at Glasgow. Caird's judgement was that Carlyle was the first in Britain to discover the full significance of the German literary revival and in particular how poetic and philosophical Idealism provided support for a declining faith.[33] Jones came to Carlyle independently while a young man at Bangor Normal Teacher

Training College, and he claimed that his early admiration 'deepened with the years'.³⁴

THE RECEPTION OF KANT AND HEGEL IN ENGLAND

Just as a literary figure, such as Carlyle, brought German literature and philosophy to the attention of the intellectual classes in Scotland, England also had its champion in Samuel Taylor Coleridge, now more famous for his poetry and literary criticism than philosophy or politics. He was, at first, like the young William Wordsworth, a radical in politics, but disillusionment with the French Revolution inclined him towards conservatism.

Hegel's influence was, however, felt independently from literature, in Oxford and Cambridge. Benjamin Jowett, the Master of Balliol, was one of the few men in Oxford to read German and knew the works of Kant and Hegel personally. He also acquainted himself with the German historical school and its new methods in philology and biblical criticism. Exposing Oxford to these tendencies helped to widen its horizon to broader intellectual movements. He was also influential in the revival of interest in Plato's philosophy by lecturing on and translating his works. Although he was tired of Hegel in his later life, Jowett encouraged Green and his contemporaries to study the German theologians and read the texts of the German Idealists in the vernacular. Direct contact with the text elevated the level of scholarship far beyond that which could be found in the paraphrases of Coleridge or Carlyle.³⁵

One of the earliest and most important of the Oxford Idealists was T. H. Green. Like contemporaneous fellow Idealists he had no great interest in just replicating Hegel's method. British Idealists all realized the significance of Kant in paving the way for Hegel, but in order fully to appreciate the significance of Hegel's philosophy a great deal of philosophical waste had to be removed. Green's constructive philosophy was preceded by a thorough interrogation of the assumptions and inconsistencies in the systems of Mill and Spencer. Green concluded that their errors could be traced back to Hume. In exposing the catalogue of inconsistencies in Hume, Green appealed to Englishmen to put away their Mill and Spencer and take up their Kant and Hegel.³⁶

With Jowett, Green and Caird at Oxford, joined in 1866 by William Wallace, F. H. Bradley had much encouragement to take up Kant and Hegel. The famous chapter in *Ethical Studies*, 'My Station and its Duties' was largely a restatement of Hegel's notion of *Sittlichkeit*. This is the strongest statement of a communitarian point of view to emerge from the Idealists. The individual is nothing without society, and morality is through and through social. However, as we will see later, Bradley was dissatisfied with this formulation of morality and superseded it with what he called, "ideal morality". Bradley's health did not permit him to contribute to John Henry Muirhead's edited volume *Contemporary Political Philosophy*, first series, and his death intervened before the publication of the second series, which was nevertheless dedicated to him. Muirhead's dedication attributed to Bradley the impulse that revived philosophy in the latter part of the nineteenth century.[37]

F. H. Bradley (1846–1924) was born in Clapham, London, and attended Green's lectures while at Oxford. In 1870, he became a life Fellow of Merton College, on condition he remained a bachelor. He took little active part in the intellectual life of Oxford after 1871 because of severe ill health, which plagued him for the rest of his life. Bradley's initial encounter with German philosophy is not altogether clear. It has been suggested that Bradley's second class in *literae humaniores* was due to the critical Idealist stance he took towards the prevailing empirical orthodoxy. What we do know is that, apart from some earlier essays, Bradley's first systematic foray into academic writing was his *Ethical Studies* (1876) and this work shows his wide-ranging and immensely sophisticated grasp of eighteenth- and nineteenth-century German philosophy. In many ways, *Ethical Studies* is the most directly Hegelian of Bradley's works. This was also a work that he viewed with some ambivalence, resisting its republication until shortly before his death in 1924 (although he never lived to see its appearance in 1927). In later books, such as *The Principles of Logic*, he took a quite overtly critical stance to Hegel (repudiating the idea that he was Hegelian) and if anything seemed more sympathetic to the work of Lotze and Sigwart. In consequence, Bradley's work was unique among the British Idealists and occasionally caused some puzzlement and anxiety among his philosophical contemporaries, such as Caird, Bosanquet and Jones. He undoubtedly retained his very critical views on empiricism and naturalism and he clearly still shared many of the core philosophical arguments of Idealism. His work on logic (with that of Bosanquet) is, in many ways, the high point of British Idealist contributions to Idealist logic. He is also often classed with Bosanquet (who remained a close friend throughout his life) as one of the foremost representatives of Absolute Idealism – with the proviso that works such as *Appearance and Reality* remained highly idiosyncratic within Idealism. A second philosopher often linked with Bradley under the rubric Absolute Idealism was Bernard Bosanquet (1848–1923). He was a student of T. H. Green at Balliol. He was born at Rock Hall, the family estate, near Alnwick, Northumberland, and was educated at Harrow and Balliol College, Oxford, where he gained firsts in Classical Moderations (1868) and *Literae Humaniores* (1870), the same year as Bradley. As an undergraduate he was greatly influenced by both Benjamin Jowett and more particularly T. H. Green. Green thought him as one of the ablest students of his generation. It was at this point, primarily under Green's influence, that Bosanquet developed his lifelong interest in both Hegel and German philosophy. From 1870 to 1881, he was a fellow of University College. He did not find Oxford much to his liking and went instead to live in London where he became a prominent figure in the activities of The London Ethical Society and the Charity Organisation Society, of which he became chairman of the Council in 1916. Bosanquet was also president of the Aristotelian Society from 1894–1898. In 1903, he succeeded D. G. Ritchie to the chair of Logic, Rhetoric, and Metaphysics at the University of St. Andrews where he stayed until 1908, when he returned to Oxshott, where he had bought a house in 1899, in order to devote his energies to writing. He delivered the Gifford Lectures at Edinburgh in 1911 and 1912, which remain a systematic statement of his Absolute Idealist position. Bosanquet was, with Henry Jones, one of the most Hegelian thinkers among the British Idealists, and the most prolific writer of the school on all aspects of philosophy and politics. One important facet of his writing is that, despite his reputation as one the foremost Hegelians and representatives of Absolute Idealism, he nonetheless embodied a much broader and more eclectic philosophical position, particularly nearer the end of his life in works such as *The Meeting of Extremes in Contemporary Philosophy* (1921). He was also a prolific correspondent with leading philosophers of his day, such as Benedetto Croce, Giovanni Gentile and Edmund Husserl.[38]

There were, of course, many lesser know Idealists at Oxford, such as J. A. Smith and Harold Joachim, whose importance may be gauged by their influence on the younger generation of Idealists. Joachim's *The Nature of Truth* was formative in the development of Michael Oakeshott's thought at Cambridge, whereas at Oxford, Smith directed the young R. G. Collingwood's attention towards Italian Idealism of which Smith was a major expositor in England. Smith, at first, immersed himself in Aristotle, but later came to study Descartes, Spinoza, Leibniz, Kant, Locke, Berkeley and Hume. Such reading did not dissuade him from subscribing to something like a realist theory of knowledge in which the object known is unaffected by the knowing subject. In other words, the object is what it is independent of consciousness of it. Yet, it was a chance encounter with the work of the Italian Idealist Benedetto Croce, while on holiday in Italy, that was formative in the development of his philosophical position.

Smith first read Croce, and broadened his knowledge of the wider philosophical context, which included the work of the Italian Idealist Giovanni Gentile. He was unable to accept the full autonomy of the forms presented by Croce, such as aesthetics and history, but nor was he able to accept the Absolute of Bradley and Bosanquet. Both Croce and Gentile put a great deal of emphasis on history as a form of experience. Indeed, Gentile identified philosophy with its own history. Deriving inspiration from this source, Smith contends that the whole of what is *Real* is constantly in movement. It is a process of change. There is no static or inert background against which this process takes place. Being is existence and not something that transcends it. To be is to exist, happen or occur. The Real is for Smith history, and every part of it is historical. The implication is that he rejects the doctrine that the Absolute includes within itself all histories and therefore has no history, thus parting company with Bradley and Bosanquet. This history, he believes, is spiritual throughout, and the Reality of which he speaks is activity. This spirituality realizes itself in self-consciousness.[39]

Unlike the Italians who inspired him, Smith never put the philosophy into practice by demonstrating what his view of philosophy implied when addressing particular problems. Gentile, de Ruggiero and Croce all undertook extensive historical investigations. Their philosophical conclusions were formulated by embedding the questions in their historical development. In emulating the Italians, it was R. G. Collingwood who ultimately shifted the focus of Oxford away from the Germans.

In Cambridge, the stirrings of Idealism begin with John Grote, who in 1865 published *Exploratio Philosophica*, the culmination of many years of engagement with indigenous and German philosophical ideas. While regretting Ferrier's system-building, and rejecting his abhorrence of ordinary language, Grote generally agreed with Ferrier's views on knowledge. The general character of Ferrier's thought he took to be philosophical Idealism, which was suggestive of his own work.[40] Grote was largely eclipsed, in Cambridge, by the work of J. M. E. McTaggart and to a lesser extent William Ritchie Sorley. Cambridge Idealism in the twentieth century, however, was epitomized by the indomitable Michael Oakeshott, who was not unmindful of Grote.

Sorley was one of the original contributors to *Essays in Philosophical Criticism*. His contribution was 'The Historical Method' in which he identified the parameters of the range of questions to which the method was appropriate, and the limits beyond which it had nothing to offer.[41] The rejection of speculative philosophy of history and a turning towards critical philosophy of history, that is, the examination of the postulates of historical understanding, while pioneered by F. H. Bradley, became a major preoccupation of the latter day British Idealists, that is, Oakeshott in Cambridge and Collingwood in Oxford.

In *The Moral Life,* Sorley argued that religion provides the unity for the diverse expressions of morality: temperance, courage, wisdom, justice and benevolence.[42] The view that religion is somehow the completion of morality seemed to Oakeshott preferable to the alternatives, that is, the view that there is no relation between the two or that they are identical.[43] In this respect, he is much closer to Bradley. Sorley was though largely preoccupied with the debates of the latter part of the nineteenth century, particularly with the relationship between evolution and ethics, and the ethics of naturalism in general.[44]

McTaggart taught an 'Introduction to the Study of Philosophy' at Cambridge, and Oakeshott was a pupil of both him and Sorley.[45] Oakeshott's notebooks show that he was an avid reader of a wide range of non-philosophical and philosophical books, many of them written by Idealists. The notebooks show that he was familiar with the work of Caird, McTaggart, Bosanquet, Jones and Mackenzie, in addition to Bradley and Hegel. His tendency was to copy quotations rather than comment on them, but the quotations often resonate with a content that was later to become his own. In 1922, his selection betrayed the value he was to place upon activities or practices. He quotes extensively, for example, from Henry Jones *A Faith That Enquires*; 'A thing is what it does. ... A thing that does nothing *is* nothing. Strip an object of its activities, and see what remains: You will find nothing'.[46] The same idea is expressed differently in Oakeshott's selection from McTaggart's *Introduction to Ethics*: 'The inside of two empty boxes are no doubt singularly alike. But the unity of this sort may possibly be over-valued'.[47] This emphasis upon unity, which so characterizes *Experience and its Modes*, is replicated in the notes Oakeshott took from a review of *The Life and Philosophy of Edward Caird* (edited by Muirhead and Jones) in the *Hibbert Journal*, October 1922: 'At the basis of his whole thought lay a single idea, reaching not by reasoning but by insight, expressed better (letter 1891) in the words "to me difference always seems to presuppose and replicate unity – which is the fact below all other facts"'.[48]

By 1933, while still able to muster new recruits, Idealism was under siege from all sides. In that year two of the younger generation of Idealists published works that were to ignite the steady flame that continues today with increasing brightness. The publication of Oakeshott's *Experience and its Modes* in 1933 was in the same year as Collingwood's *An Essay on Philosophical Method*. There is an affinity between Collingwood's *Speculum Mentis* (1924) and Oakeshott's *Experience and its Modes*, in that they constitute the last truly comprehensive British Idealist studies of the variety of forms of experience. Collingwood's *An Essay on Philosophical Method* is a defence and justification of the method he employed in *Speculum Mentis*, which focuses on establishing the differences between philosophical and scientific concepts.[49] Oakeshott's *Experience and its Modes* combines the exemplification and justification of philosophical method. It is an exploration of the idea of unconditional knowledge, manifest in interrogating the conditionality of abstract arrests in experience, where the unconditional is an unachievable ideal towards which the philosopher is always en route.

AGAINST NATURALISM: THE ALLURE OF EVOLUTION

The discussion now moves on to two issues of late-nineteenth-century Britain, aiming to exemplify the way in which Idealism responded to prevailing norms of the time. The issues are evolution and utilitarianism. These examples are simply illustrative of the way Idealism functioned as a mode of philosophical critique.

Evolutionary theory is rarely included in introductory philosophy books these days, so it is difficult to conceive of the impact that this form of naturalism had on all aspects of intellectual life. It came to dominate ways of thinking throughout the second half of the nineteenth century because, unlike the other sciences, it was intelligible to a wider audience, and it held out the possibility of being the foundational unifying explanation for all of the sciences, including philosophy. David George Ritchie, probably more influenced by evolution than any of the other British Idealists, contended: ' "Evolution" is very generally looked upon as the central idea of modern scientific and philosophical thought'.[50]

One may wish to argue that evolutionary theory has nothing to offer philosophy. Wittgenstein, for example, argued that no form of naturalism, including Darwinian evolution, contributed anything to philosophy. The role of philosophy was logically to clarify thoughts, and therefore an empirical theory such as Darwin's was an irrelevance.[51] Idealism, however, was not only a logic seeking conceptual clarification, but also a metaphysics and ontology, which assigned to philosophy the role of rationally accounting for what is given in experience. Naturalism contends that explanations of human activity should take the form of explanation offered for any other aspect of nature, because humans are part of nature.[52] The appropriate method is scientific, because scientific explanation is the most appropriate way to understand the natural world.

Darwin certainly aspired to conform to the methods of modern natural science, particularly those inspired by Newton's astronomy, and developed by the empiricist astronomer John F. W. Herschel and the neo-Kantian and strongly anti-evolutionist philosopher of the inductive sciences, William Whewell. They differed considerably on metaphysical questions, as their primary loyalties would suggest, and also in the extent to which they disagreed with Darwin, but all three concurred at a fundamental level on what a scientific explanation should look like. They saw scientific theories as hypothetico-deductive systems. This entails a distinction between fundamental, or universal, laws, and derived or empirical laws. What the scientist must aim for, in Herschel's and Whewell's views, is not contingent causes identified to explain a particular phenomenon, but instead the relation of phenomena of different kinds, explicable by means of an all-sufficient cause or mechanism, quite likely reducible to some sort of force.[53] The hypothetico-deductive model and the attempt to explain disparate phenomena by means of one overarching cause are features evident in Darwin's methodology throughout his scientific endeavours. The hypothetico-deductive model is exemplified, but not always very successfully as many critics pointed out, in the way Darwin argues the case for the struggle for existence as the driving force for natural selection, which is the mechanism that facilitates evolution.[54] Natural selection was the fundamental cause or mechanism by which problems in diverse field could be related and explained from geology, classification and comparative anatomy to embryology and so on.

Darwin's influence on social evolutionists has been exaggerated,[55] and ignores the fact that long before him evolutionary ideas were being proposed and taken seriously by many leading scholars.[56] In 1809, for example, Jean-Baptiste Lamarck contended species developed and transmuted, by means of the mechanism of use and disuse. Animals that once spent many hours in daylight, but which for survival took to spending most of their time underground, lose over time and through inheritance the faculty of vision. Use and disuse of the organs lead to modifications in their powers to act effectively. Environmental factors could lead to physical changes and spontaneous transmutations in organisms. The changes, including those of moral character, were then inherited by subsequent generations. This is the doctrine of inherited characters.

Sir Charles Lyell not only formulated the hypothesis of the struggle for existence, but also attacked the argument for use and disuse inheritance in his famous *Principles of Geology* (1830–1833). Darwin, while not completely in disagreement with the doctrine of use and disuse, put forward the doctrine of Natural Selection as the principal mechanism of change. Lyell came to accept Darwin's idea, but not until after the 1867 edition of the *Origin of Species,* some 7 years after its first publication. Herbert Spencer is probably the most notorious of the social evolutionists, but he was in fact inspired by Lyell's attempted refutation of 'Use and Disuse', rather than Darwin's initial positive endorsement. Spencer was though tremendously accessible to a wide reading public with his populist biology (philosophically conceived, but not well grounded in empirical research) and extended by analogy to society.

On the surface of it, Idealism shared with evolution a propensity to understand a problem or an event as it unfolded. J. B. Baillie contended: 'For a time it seemed possible to interpret all forms of experience in terms of the central fact of knowledge regarded as an evolution of thought'.[57] Idealism, however, was not a naturalistic philosophy and therefore felt compelled to challenge the naturalistic postulates of evolution and provide a more satisfactory theory based on Hegelian principles. While agreeing with naturalistic evolutionists that humanity is continuous with nature, the Idealists still contended the *first* must be explained and understood in terms of the *last*, and not as Darwin posited, the *higher* must be explained with reference to the *lower* in the evolutionary process. W. R. Sorley encapsulates the Darwinian contention succinctly: 'What we call the higher forms are in all cases developments from simpler and lower forms'.[58] Herbert Spencer similarly contends: 'we must interpret the more developed by the less developed'.[59]

In this respect Idealists do not go as far as to suggest that humans are so different in kind from the rest of nature that they require completely different forms of explanation. It is nature that has to be explained in terms fitting of human beings. The contention is not that nature is intelligent, but that it is intelligible *only* to the mind that knows it, that is, the human mind. Because humans are self-conscious we should explain their behaviour in terms of values, principles and ideas rather than instincts.[60]

Charles Darwin and Alfred Russel Wallace's theories were first revealed, in the absence of both authors, at a meeting of the Linnean Society in London on 1 July 1858. The occasion was inauspicious and the sponsor of the papers, Joseph Hooker, thought the whole subject under discussion rather ominous.[61] At the end of the year, the President of the Society thought the proceedings for the session rather uneventful. On first sight, Darwin thought Wallace's conclusions were almost identical to his own. Wallace had even isolated natural selection as the evolutionary mechanism. It transpired, however, that there were significant differences between their theories. The mechanism for eliminating the unfit differed: for Wallace it was the environment, while for Darwin the emphasis was on a merciless competition among individuals.

Ideologically, they were wide apart and it influenced the way they interpreted evidence. In studying the Dyaks, for example, as a committed socialist, Wallace viewed them in egalitarian terms. Darwin, a committed conservative, understood the Fuegians as savage and bestial.[62] They also differed on the question of the ultimate purpose of Natural Selection. Darwin rejected the question altogether, while Wallace was convinced that the end was the achievement of a more just society and the gradual perfection of man. The outline that Darwin received from Wallace in 1858 gave no indication of these differences.[63] Wallace's findings as Darwin understood them in 1858, panicked him into the publication of *The Origin of Species* in 1859. Consequently, the account was far less detailed than Darwin would have liked. This elicited a good deal of criticism along the lines that the argument was too hypothetical and not deductive enough.[64]

In *The Origin of Species*, Darwin put forward three main contentious hypotheses. The first was that new species emerge as a result of modifications that take place in other species, that is, the transmutation hypothesis. Secondly, species emerge in a manner that resembles branches of a tree, therefore at some point all species share a common ancestor in the evolutionary process. And, thirdly, the principal, but not exclusive, mechanism for change in this process was natural selection.[65]

Despite Darwin deliberately avoiding the issue of Creation portrayed in the book of *Genesis*, and expressing his ideas in as non-provocative a manner as possible, readers drew their own conclusions.

The context against which Darwin was judged was, for example, the affirmation of the religious hypothesis by the eighteenth-century zoologist, Linnaeus, who contended that species are immutable, irrespective of the fact that there were frequent anatomical resemblances between different species.[66] Darwin denied that each species was "independently created". He contended that there is a common ancestry from which each species develops, many had become extinct, and few would transmit progeny unchanged to a distant future.[67] The implications were clear. Darwin's theory was a denial of the Creationist theory and a challenge to the natural theology of the likes of William Paley. Paley proposed an example that was to become famous and inspire the title of one of Richard Dawkins' books.[68] Paley asks us to think of the universe as a watch, with its immensely intricate mechanism, requiring a watchmaker, or creator, namely God, the artificer who designed it to fulfil a specific purpose. Paley applies the same principle to plants, animals and human beings. An artificer designs and creates each with a purpose to fulfil a particular function, the beneficiary of which may not always be the organisms that possess the qualities.[69] A second implication of Darwin's theory to cause consternation was the unwarranted belief that he contends that man was descended from the apes. What he actually claimed was that the apes and man have a common ancestor. But in either case the implication was that the absolute distinction between Nature and Spirit, or animal and human nature, was denied.

Although derided by many for being a poor biologist and an even worse philosopher, Spencer captured the popular imagination. Richard Hofstadter says of Spencer's work: 'it was not a technical creed for professionals. Presented in language that tyros in philosophy could understand, it made Spencer the metaphysician of the home-made intellectual, and the prophet of the cracker barrel agnostic'.[70] Because of its practical and reforming character, the British Idealists could not allow Spencer's form of naturalism to appropriate evolution. Spencer had to be discredited if Idealism were to put forward its positive evolutionary reforming doctrines. Henry Jones, Andrew Seth Pringle-Pattison and Bosanquet, to mention only a few, were harsh in their judgements. They variously believed that his whole project, premised on an unmoved mover, was sheer madness, and his ideas were common place, and lacking sensitivity on intellectual and moral issues. Furthermore, Spencer was held accountable for importing conceptions and fashionable analogies drawn from anywhere, except experience of the phenomena to be explained. The result was crude distortions of fundamental truths obvious to us for 2,000 years.[71]

Idealists gave little credence to the Lamarckian principle of inherited characters, while at the same time stressing a strong, but not exclusive, environmental influence upon human personality. The theory of inherited characters seemed to Idealists, such as David Ritchie, surplus to requirements. There are no instances of heredity that could be explained by the theory of inherited characters which could not be explained by other means, such as natural selection, habit, training and imitation. The case for inherited characters was simply "not proven".[72] Natural Selection was indisputable.[73] We should not therefore revert to dubious or unknown causes, Ritchie argues, when there are known causes that are sufficient. Natural Selection, for him, works in both nature and society.

The capacities that we inherit genetically are capable of being developed or hindered by the social environment or civilization into which the individual is born, and which we may say is likewise inherited by successive generations. The facilitator for such social inheritance is language. Language, self-consciousness, and the ability to reflect, make it possible to transmit experience that is not biologically inheritable. The explanation of how we come to possess such advantages in the struggle for existence, Ritchie claims, is the hypothesis of Natural Selection.[74] We inherit biologically the capacities for self-realisation, but without an environment conducive to their flourishing our capabilities would come to nought. As Henry Jones colourfully suggested, you can place a canary in a cage in the most depraved and debauched dens of iniquity and it will suffer no moral harm. A child, however, placed in the same environment suffers irreparable damage.

We tend to think of nineteenth-century evolution as one theory, or dominant paradigm, to use Thomas S. Kuhn's words, which "normal" scientists then apply to a wide sphere of natural and human activity. It was, when released on the world in 1859, a highly speculative theory, and as with all scientific revolutions much needed to be accepted on faith or trust.[75] It was a theory ripe in itself for spawning different strains. The British Idealists themselves developed a distinctive form of evolution based on Hegel's notion of emanation. We may call this "Spiritual" evolution, and it is distinct from its contemporaneous competitors, naturalistic and ethical evolution.[76] Each type had different postulates and no necessary political or social conclusions followed from any. Each could and was used to justify political programmes from the extreme left to the extreme right.

However, the issue of ethics, religion and evolution continued to open up deep divisions in late Victorian Britain. Orthodox Christianity posited a distinct break between nature and spirit. Humans thus occupied a different sphere from that of animals and were distinct in possessing moral characters uniquely bestowed upon them by God. Naturalistic evolution appeared to posit a fundamental challenge to this deep social convention. It postulated a continuity between Nature and Spirit, in which the former was explanatory of the latter. This is what Darwin meant by suggesting: 'When I view all beings not as special creations, but as the lineal descendants of some few beings which lived long before the first bed of the Silurian system was deposited, they seem to me to become ennobled'.[77] Spencer was similarly explicit: 'we must interpret the more developed by the less developed'.[78] Debates on this issue raged across late nineteenth century Europe.

However, Darwin's friend and admirer, T. H. Huxley, opened up a sweeping divide between Nature and Spirit. Physiologically, and on zoological criteria, he classified humans with the apes. Both had a common origin and had undergone similar evolutionary processes. Darwin, in fact, relied heavily upon Huxley's findings to substantiate his own arguments in the *Descent of Man* published in 1871.[79] There was more to human existence than zoological categories and explanations could comprehend. The pursuit of natural rights, in Hobbesian terms, undermined society and benefitted only the successful individual. Naturalistic-based rights have no correlative obligations. The carnivorous tiger has a natural right to eat meat, but humans have no correlative obligation to submit themselves to its appetites. Moral rights do have correlative obligations conducive to social progress.[80] It was Huxley's view that the survival of the fittest could not constitute an ethical standard, because fitness is circumstantially related to the variability of nature. Ethics are not 'applied Natural History'.[81] The evolution of Nature and moral evolution were for him two *different* and *discontinuous* processes. Within the cosmic process, which governs the evolution of nature and human organisms, the idea of the survival of the fittest was appropriate. The attributes and capacities required for success in nature (red in tooth and claw) are exactly those that destroy social existence. The emergence of morality did not begin until the cosmic process had been checked, starting with a concern for the opinions of others, developing into shame and sympathy. Feelings of approval and disapproval generated moral rules. On their acquisition we gradually became accustomed to thinking about conduct in terms of them. This was what Huxley called the artificial personality, or conscience, which countered the natural character of man. W. R. Sorley summarizes the position admirably: 'The cosmic order has nothing to say to the moral order, except that, somehow or other, it has given it birth; the moral order has nothing to say to the cosmic order, except that it is certainly bad. Morality is occupied in opposing the methods of evolution.'[82]

Huxley inserted a proviso, however, which introduced an ambiguity. This subsequently gave ammunition to his critics. 'Strictly speaking', he argued, 'social life, and the ethical process in virtue of which it advances towards perfection, are part and parcel of the general process of evolution.' What is more, Huxley contends, the 'general cosmic process begins to be checked by a rudimentary ethical process, which is strictly speaking, part of the former.'[83] The dualism he posited between Nature and Spirit is undermined.

As always, when faced with a dualism, British Idealism takes the antithetical points of view and synthesizes them into an understanding that brings out the positives on both sides. Evolution is no exception. Evolution is nothing other than another name for the development of Spirit. Naturalistic theories of evolutionary ethics explicitly assert the unity of the cosmos. The unity is not as such a proposition to be proved, but instead an inescapable assumption, a colligating hypothesis or absolute assumption.[84] Evolution is the hypothesis that provides 'the methodizing conception which we employ to render intelligible to ourselves the process which spirit follows in becoming free'.[85] The Idealists reassert the unity of Nature and Spirit, but reverse the explanatory power of naturalism. The higher accounts for the lower. Nature is infused with Spirit and intelligible to the mind that knows it.

Huxley's argument particularly became the focus of much attention, providing a corrective to those who posited nature as the criterion of moral conduct. The responses of Idealists were various, ranging from Bosanquet's dismissal of the theory as a "fatal misconception",[86] to Jones's argument reaffirming the unity of Nature and Spirit, while at the same time acknowledging the error of ignoring or understating the difference between naturalistic processes and rational moral activity. For Huxley, nature is incapable of knowing or thinking and therefore lacks the capacity of morality. Knowing and thinking nevertheless presupposes nature. Nature presents us with the data. Intelligence interprets it, but an intelligence that nature herself has evolved. The product of intelligence, namely knowledge, belongs just as much to nature as to man. Intelligence is the instrument through which nature is expressed, and although nature is not itself intelligent, it is intelligible only to the mind. There is an interdependence between nature and mind, neither capable of existing without the other, and far from being opposed to morality, nature is a willing partner in its development.[87] The unity of nature and spirit is maintained by arguing for the all-sufficiency of natural selection. It can easily account for both moral progress and organic development. Ritchie maintains recognition of the spiritual principle at work in the universe is the condition of our understanding nature.[88]

British Idealists thus reaffirmed the unity of Nature and Spirit, but differentiated themselves from naturalistic evolution by denying the explanatory power of origins in any theory. Agreeing with Hegel they maintained that: 'Nothing can be more certain than that all philosophical explanation must be explanation of the lower by the higher'.[89] For Hegel, we understand a part only by looking at it as part of a whole. The origins of something are properly understood when they are comprehended as the early stages of something more fully developed. This applies to all specialist fields of knowledge, including the attempt to conceive the universe as a whole.[90] Caird thus maintains: 'in the first instance at least, we must read development *backward* and not *forward,* we must find the key to the meaning of the first stage in the last.'[91] Although acknowledging the unity of Nature and Spirit, Spencer's evolutionary theory failed because it did not acknowledge Aristotle's dictum that the true nature of a thing is to be found not in its origin but in its end.[92] Spirit cannot be explained in terms of matter, and that matter itself is intelligible only in the context of the Spiritual World.[93]

In summary, evolution in the mind of the Idealists was therefore an affirmation rather than a denial of religious and moral experience. Evolution bridged the divide between the present and the past, revealing the unity in the diversity of humanity by distinguishing 'the one spiritual principle which is continuously working in man's life from the changing forms through which it passes in the course of its history'.[94] Evolution, understood in this manner, intimated the solution to the dualism between the mind and its objects, and held out the promise of undergirding moral and religious experience.[95]

THE REVOLT AGAINST UTILITARIANISM

Bernard Williams observed that 'morality is not an invention of philosophers. It is an outlook, or, incoherently, part of the outlook, of almost all of us'. For Williams, we live morally before, during and after reflection and the important business is living, not so much the reflection.[96] Moral practice is not something therefore that flows necessarily from a philosopher's premises. There is though a complex and subtle relation between moral philosophy and moral practice. This comment in the 1980s echoes a comment from the British Idealist philosopher T. H. Green in the 1880s, namely that, on many occasions, conventions, institutions and tradition embody an implicit reason and 'actuate men independently of the operations of the discursive intellect'.[97] Morality is not primarily an abstraction; it is integral to human institutions, communities and social practices. We can make it an abstraction in philosophical reflection, but that can sometimes have quite a limited role in human affairs. Greater knowledge of morality cannot always be gained by moving away from practices and impersonalizing or abstracting them. We learn morality continuously in concrete contexts.

One important pervasive aspect of the *concrete context* of late nineteenth- and indeed twentieth-century Britain, was a deeply instinctive commitment to utilitarianism as a mode of value appraisal. One might almost see it, at points, as a metaphysical presupposition. As Iris Murdoch remarked in 1993, 'Some form of utilitarianism is probably now the most widely and instinctively accepted philosophy'.[98] This would be as true of the Victorian era as today. Henry Sidgwick (1838–1900), the very quintessence of late Victorian intellectual utilitarianism – and a committed philosophical opponent of Idealism – sensed this underlying instinct. In both his *Method of Ethics* (1874) and *Elements of Politics* (1891), he assumed that utility was indeed the underlying customary ethics and common sense of British culture *in toto*. For Sidgwick, common-sense utility embodied a neutral standard. It needed therefore to be continually referred to and indeed cast (for Sidgwick) in a scientific format. He argued that all the practical common-sense virtues we use in everyday practice are therefore, in essence, utilitarian. Ordinary practice provides what Sidgwick referred to as the "middle axioms" for utilitarianism. When carefully criticized and refined these axioms provided a purified ethical guidance. Utilitarianism was therefore seen as the "adult" morality of the British people in the 1870s and 1880s, infecting their personal lives as well as their public policy.

Sidgwick unexpectedly claims that the decisive background influence in formulating this perspective was Aristotle. He comments that Aristotle's *Ethics* provides 'the common sense Morality of Greece, reduced to consistency by careful comparison: given not as something external to him but as what "we" ... think, ascertained by reflection'. Sidgwick continues, 'Might I not imitate this: do the same for our morality here and now [in Victorian England] in the same manner of impartial reflection on current opinion'.[99] Utility thus embodied the ethos of an historical community.

This was, however, a utilitarianism, as has been remarked, 'grown sleek and tame'.[100] Sidgwick thus used Jeremy Bentham (in his *Elements of Politics*) to justify, in effect, the political principles of Edmund Burke.[101] The upshot of this position, in Sidgwick, was, as many have noted, both theoretically and practically conservative. Sidgwick, by the late 1880s, had moved on a practical level from Millian liberal radicalism to a Burkean conservatism. However, Sidgwick's utilitarian ethics in the 1880s, in the final analysis, lacked the strident self-confidence of Bentham or the positivistic yearnings and liberal radicalism of J. S. Mill. His utilitarianism was more eclectic, sceptical and wavering, yet still committed, in the end, to utilitarian calculation, consequentialism and policy recommendation.

There are two further features to note, on the above analysis: first, utilitarianism in the nineteenth century was not one singular thing. Sidgwick, J. S. Mill and Jeremy Bentham all had markedly different perspectives, both morally and politically. Utilitarianism was a hydra-headed creature with deep and diverse allegiances among, for example, classical liberals, some new liberals, classical political economists, evolutionary theorists, anarchists, socialists and conservatives. In this sense alone, it would be difficult to see precisely what kind of moral, social and political philosophy could arise *necessarily* from utilitarianism. Secondly, one important idea that could be easily missed in identifying utilitarianism as the "concrete context" of British culture during this period is the element of self-criticism and reflexivity. Although humans develop within certain concrete contexts, they do not simply abdicate reflection. The human self is both shaped and shaping continuously within conventions and social institutions. The crucial question is whether we remain within them or alternatively convert to another mode of value appraisal. Humans thus have the continuous open possibility to interrogate themselves and others about the demands of their native or adopted traditions. In this sense, it is important to realize that what Sidgwick thought of as the concrete context of British culture did clearly come under sustained criticism from the British Idealist movement, on a number of levels. In a vital sense, for a considerable time, Idealism initiated a major reversal of utilitarian fortunes.

In recent years, some scholars have seen elements of utilitarianism within the philosophical domain of Idealism itself, and indeed, Idealists themselves did not deny the efficacy of such notions of value, nor as we have already seen the values of evolution, suitably incorporated into its own spiritual conception of the world. For example, consequentialist motifs have been identified in the philosophy of T. H. Green, although many other scholars vigorously contest the efficacy of this claim. However, less problematically with Idealists such as David G. Ritchie, there was clearly a subtle adaptation of a form of "social" utilitarianism to Idealism. For Ritchie, utilitarianism was clearly not without its merits, but it took the doctrine of evolution, particularly natural selection, together with Idealist social theories, to correct its errors and vindicate its truths.

In a very different manner, a philosopher such as R. G. Collingwood also integrated utility into a much broader value scale with both right and duty.[102] Every action, he contended, was the embodiment of all three values, and each could be justified because it was useful, right, or my duty.

On the most general level, though, what did utilitarianism represent to British Idealism and what were the key flaws in the doctrine? This is a complex and multi-faceted issue that can only be briefly glossed. Many domains and arguments overlap. On the most general level Idealism responded critically to utilitarianism on metaphysical, epistemological, moral, social and political levels.

Metaphysically utilitarian arguments were seen to rely on the idea of an aggregation of 'single sentient individuals' to make any case for morality or politics possible. British Idealism saw this as exemplifying an underlying metaphysical abstraction. On one level utilitarianism was seen to have failed to articulate the underlying nature of the individual self, a point that is as true today as it was in the 1880s.[103] For Idealists there was no way that any of us could really imagine (except in our wildest flights of fantasy) being utterly alone (atomized) and still thinking morally – especially in abstracted utilitarian terms. As F. H. Bradley ironically commented on this metaphysical spectre within utilitarianism (in this case in Sidgwick): 'Figure yourself then, reader – your imagination, not like mine, may keep pace with author's – figure yourself as a single sentient being in a non-sentient universe, and tell us, would you not believe in "a real end of Reason, the absolutely Good or Desirable"?'[104]

Epistemologically, Idealists associated this atomistic and individualist theory (within utilitarianism) with a deeply empiricist account of knowledge. In this sense, knowledge was derived from sensations, perceptions and experiences, via an engagement with an external world. Truth claims therefore entailed correspondence with this external world. For Idealists, in very general terms, the self could not be identified with any series of discrete perceptions, experiences or sensations, since the self, as such, was seen as the presupposition to there being any sensations, perceptions of experiences, particularly sensations or experiences which were identified in terms of a series. For Idealism (following Kant), knowledge of the world exists in the context of the conscious subject. There could be no experience of things antecedent to the conscious subject. Thus, a consistent empiricist account of knowledge (characteristic of utilitarian thought) would literally be speechless. A series of sensations, feelings or experiences (such a pleasures or preferences) would be meaningless unless they presupposed a conscious subject as the ground for such a series. Further, the idea of a "sum" of any such feelings or experiences would be conceptually meaningless. How could the utilitarian agent (epistemologically) *know* a sum of infinitely passing unrelated pleasures, feelings or sensations, which were still continuously mutating? In a similar way, how could one gain any clear interpersonal comparisons of, say, utilities (whether it was preferences, pleasures or welfare)? The greatest sum of utility, in any of these formats, remained for Idealists purely fictional and rhetorical. Could one, for example, actually compare the pleasantness of diverse, transient, unrelated pleasures? Could one actually *know* a sum of different pleasures? Could there be any quantitative grasp of pleasures, that is, a cognitive science that collated passing ephemeral sensations? These questions contain their own substantive debates which will not be pursued here. However, for Idealism, the utilitarian did not really provide adequate answers to any of these questions. Consequently, its account of human knowledge was seen as completely epistemologically flawed. For Idealists, knowledge of the experiential world (and nature) could *not* explain the nature of knowledge. Utilitarianism – a philosophy focused largely on empiricism and a form of sensationalism – was thus considered to be epistemically defective from its very inception.

Morally, utilitarianism was also seen as a deeply problematic doctrine insofar as it was linked, once again, in the minds of most Idealists, to the same unsubstantiated abstract atomism. Utilitarianism was thus seen to treat human individuals as, more or less, self-enclosed homogeneous moral atoms, with similar feelings which could be mechanically quantified, and among whom a quantity of pleasures could be distributed. Its demand on institutions was that they justified themselves in terms of their conduciveness to the general happiness. For D. G. Ritchie, for example, Benthamite utilitarianism was open to many of the criticisms of the theory of natural rights. The appeal to nature tries to reconcile the abstract individualism of the multiplicity of isolated instincts with an abstract universalism concerning humanity. Like the bogus appeal to nature, utilitarianism assumed a narrow uniformity of human nature over time and place. It combined the abstract individualism of treating every person as a discrete unit, with the abstract universalism concerning its view of happiness, which is taken to have an existence divorced from the concrete individuals who are singularly capable of experiencing it. Once again there is a battery of Idealist arguments here on the question of morality, but at the most basic level, pleasure (in classical utilitarian theory) was seen as far too abstract and contentless to be of much use in any process of serious valuation. Pleasure and pain were both viewed, once again, as transient feelings. The concepts were abstractions from these vague feelings – feelings which were regularly coming into being and then perishing. A series of pleasures, in diverse sentient individuals, could not function as any guide to conduct. The idea of "greatest possible" happiness or pleasure was a pure moral fiction – an infinite quantity of pleasures was utterly incoherent if postulated as an end. Consequently, the idea of any moral calculus of pleasures or interests (or preferences) struck most Idealists as meaningless.

Furthermore, pleasures may not always be good and pain not always bad. Some pleasures and pains may, in fact, be neither good nor bad. Pleasure, in other words, is not coterminous with morality. If pleasure is the end, it would appear to be even more significant than virtue. Virtue becomes merely a means. In addition, virtuous acts, as we commonly recognize them, do not always conduce to happiness.[105] The greatest good and most virtuous acts do not necessarily therefore lead to the greatest pleasure. This would appear to be a mundane observation on moral experience. Thus, for Idealists, hedonism and utilitarianism could clash with ordinary morality. Morality may include pleasure, but it was not the end of moral action. Pleasure may supervene on morality, but was not coincidental with it. Further, utility did not tell us how to act. To think of pleasure as a motive was to confuse a "motive" (the object before the mind) with a "psychical stimulus" (which is not an object before the mind).

Finally, one of the key critical concerns of Idealism with utilitarianism was that it tended to view society in the same odd dogmatic manner, namely, as an aggregate of separate isolated atoms. There were some variations though on this issue among utilitarian thinkers. Both Herbert Spencer and Leslie Stephen – although utilitarians – thought individualism was deficient if it did not take account of the social factor and understand society as an biological organism. Both, therefore, simultaneously attempted to sustain the organic metaphor for society; but, for Idealist critics, both failed to liberate themselves from empiricism and naturalism.[106] For Idealists, they neglected the real nature of the social organism, which is neither mechanical nor biological, but instead depends upon the complex recognition of the relations in which each person stands with every other. The sinews and ligaments of society are the moral ideas and personal relations, without which a society would be a mere aggregation.

In effect the communitarian-inspired British Idealists saw themselves in profound opposition to the social and political ideas of utilitarian individualism, not only in Mill and Bentham, but also in the evolutionary individualism of Herbert Spencer and Leslie Stephen. In the language of modern communitarianism, the moral self is seen to be constituted through a community. There are no 'unencumbered selves' standing outside a community frame. There is thus no sense that moral issues or moral vocabularies can be addressed independently of a community. Morality and politics are not invented, but interpreted from within a particular community. We therefore read off an existing tradition of moral discourse. The community is constituted by such internal pre-understandings.[107] As F. H. Bradley argued, the child is not born 'into a desert, but into a living world, a whole which has a true individuality of its own, and into a system and order which it is difficult to look at as anything else than an organism ... the tender care that receives and guides him is impressing on him habits, habits, alas not particular to himself, and the "icy chains" of universal custom are hardening themselves round his cradled life'.[108] The community thus represents what Hegel called "objective mind". As Hegel argued, the individual can be viewed as part of an "ethical substance" that consists of "laws and powers",[109] where 'these substantial determinations are *duties* which are binding on the will of the individual'.[110] Agents place the rules of the communal ethos before themselves. The community is quite simply a larger and more systematic whole, containing sedimented rules and social functions, which most humans assimilate and posit to themselves.

CONCLUSION

This chapter has aimed to show how, during the nineteenth and early twentieth century, aspects of German philosophy became an intellectual refuge for those students, initially in English and Scottish universities, who sought to escape from the stultifying atmosphere of an all-pervading empiricism, naturalism and individualism, which some commentators still see as a more indigenous form of philosophizing to Britain. In fact, it is important to realize that the present generation of philosophers in Britain, share a view of philosophy developed in the 1940s and 1950s which, constructed their own vision and indeed myths, against the background of Idealism, a movement which they have often tried in crude ways to dismiss. This has affected the understanding and genuine scholarly appraisal of British Idealism until the present day.

The key German Idealists admired in Britain were Kant, Fichte, Hegel and subsequently Lotze. Schelling was probably less influential, although nonetheless still deeply admired. One important aspect of their thought was its sheer range; their philosophical interests (and overall systems) encompassed religion, art, poetry, literature and science, as well as covering, in their unique way, all the more conventional components of philosophy. This fact alone broadened their appreciative audience in Britain. Such comprehensive rich systems of thought, when practised and thought through, actually responded very effectively and positively to many of the deep problems and anxieties that affected late nineteenth- and early twentieth-century Britain. The integuments of the Idealist theory were used to address issues in morality, politics, religion, science and arts. As we have stressed, this did *not* mean that British Idealism simply blindly adopted German Idealism. On the contrary, they rigorously adapted often severely modified and blended Idealism with existing components of extant British philosophical thinking. Thus, the latent traditions were not abandoned, but often subtly integrated. This makes British Idealism different in substance and style from German Idealism and also makes it stand out as a unique and idiosyncratic philosophical movement. We have also stressed – as will become clearer in subsequent chapters – that British Idealism itself was not one thing. It was a constellation of broad-ranging, sometimes philosophically antagonistic components. Again, critics often miss this simple fact of internal complexity. What British Idealism tried to achieve was a counterbalance to the one-sidedness of certain existing norms and philosophies. In so doing, many stressed the intricate, but ultimately spiritual aspect of reality, although what was precisely meant by "Spirit" needs to be clarified.

We have aimed briefly to illustrate this latter point in the manner they responded to two profound issues of late-nineteenth-century Britain – evolution and utilitarian moral theory. In subsequent chapters, we will explore and illuminate the metaphysical and epistemological dimensions of British Idealist thinking; its unique and influential reading of ethical and political philosophy; its distinctive attempt to practice philosophical thinking; and finally, its idiosyncratic approach to international affairs.

CHAPTER TWO

ABSOLUTE IDEALISM AND ITS CRITICS

INTRODUCTION

As was stressed in the previous chapter, British Idealism was not one thing. In this chapter, we therefore distinguish between Absolute Idealism and Personal Idealism, giving first the basic world view of Absolutism, followed by the critique that Personal Idealists brought to bear on it. Aspects of both are further elaborated, as we explore some of the Realist rebuttals and Idealist responses.

ABSOLUTE IDEALISM

The sheer enormity of the scale on which Absolute Idealism operates – the universe is its subject matter – opens it to a great deal of misunderstanding and confusion over its central tenets. Its comprehensiveness and inclusivity are not only a virtue, but also the source of its problems.[1] When Absolute Idealism tries to characterize the totality of experience, it is indicted for a multitude of crimes. It is accused of losing God in man, or man in God; dissolving things into thought, and matter into spirit; abolishing all right and wrong; and conflating truth and error. In the face of such wild accusations, Henry Jones defended Idealism in terms of its refusal to make simplified contrasts and demanded that justice be done to the complexity of reality. Its achievement was 'to hold difference *as difference* within its own unity, and to be able to manifest its own nature only in a self-externalizing process, and by fortifying its opposites against itself.'[2]

The British Idealists found in German philosophy two ideas that were to form the basis of their critiques of empiricist and sensationalist theories of knowledge. First, they contended that understanding is always contextual, and that which is to be understood has to be related to wider terms of reference, until ultimately the whole of experience or the Absolute is implicated. Put simply, there can be no isolated entities, facts or individuals. All have to be understood in their essential relatedness. This has been termed monism, although it is an internally complex monism. Ultimately, experience is an undifferentiated unity that has become fragmented. For Idealism, what needs explaining is not the unity but how it has become differentiated into all of the elements with which we are familiar.

Secondly, the historical method, or emanation, as it was known in the context of the evolution debate, was their preferred mode of explanation, although what they meant by it differed among them. Unlike positivism, or the Realism that was to revolt against it, Idealism did not privilege natural science above other forms of knowledge. The historical method had the merit of identifying the genesis of a problem and its evolutionary development as pointing the way to its resolution. Thirdly, unlike empiricists, utilitarians and Realists, the Idealists denied the possibility of a reality independent of mind. This has often led to a great deal of confusion and the accusation that they believed that nothing exists except mind. They did not think that a table, for example, ceased to exist as soon as you turn away from it. Whatever the carpenter says of the table is likely to be empirically true, about the type of wood; the run of the grain; the joints that hold it together and its function. The carpenter's understanding does not exhaust what is to be said or understood about the table. The scientist, the artist, the historian will all appreciate different dimensions of it, and in that respect it ceases to be the object that the carpenter sees. It is not that reality is independent of mind, but it is dependent on mind, because without it reality would be unintelligible. Similarly, the Idealist contention that nature and spirit are continuous is often misunderstood as meaning that nature is intelligent, differing only in degree from mind or spirit. It would be absurd to suggest that water or rocks think, and no British Idealist ventures to suggest this. It is not that nature is intelligent, but that it is *intelligible only to mind*. Without mind, it just as well does *not* exist.

Fourthly, because there is no object independent of the experiencing mind, truth cannot be a matter of correspondence. The truth of a statement does not rely on how closely it corresponds to an external reality because that reality is integrally related to mind and dependent on it for its intelligibility. There are two principal versions of the correspondence theory of truth. The one version requires that one of the corresponding entities must be a mind that makes a judgement about an object, and believes that it has formulated a true description of its object. The description is said to correspond with what it describes. The alternative version contends that two separate factors are believed to correspond for a mind. The mind deems one of the two factors as a true statement about, or representation of the other.[3]

Instead, for the Idealist, it is the world of ideas, or broader context of propositions and ideas that provide the reference point for the truth of a statement. The coherence of a proposition, in relation to the world of ideas in which it belongs, is what determines its truth. Each judgement is not in isolation the affirmation or denial of a proposition, but instead the invocation of a whole world of experience in the designation of a fact. A fact is not something given in experience. It is a conclusion reached. All thoughts are related to the whole and implicate each other. Truth and meaning derive their authority from the whole to which each judgement belongs.

Both Realism and Idealism posited forms of propositional logic, but the truth of the propositions rests on different criteria: in the former on an independent reality, and in the latter on the coherence of a world of ideas. R. G. Collingwood later criticized the propositional logic of both in formulating his response to the contention of logical positivism, particularly as formulated by A. J. Ayer, that metaphysical propositions are meaningless nonsense. He contended that metaphysical statements are not propositions at all, they are absolute presuppositions upon which knowledge is built, and the question of truth and falsity does not apply to them. Truth relates only to the contention whether such presuppositions were absolutely presupposed.[4]

Fifthly, there were differences among Idealists over the level at which experience begins. F. H. Bradley, for example, argued that we have experience of the undifferentiated whole, and this he calls sentient experience.[5] However, it is at the level of thought that proper experience begins in the process of differentiating or mutilating the unity. Differentiation requires abstraction and mutilates the reality that belongs to the one and indivisible whole. Abstraction is nevertheless necessary. Without abstraction we would not be able even to distinguish between the *I* and the *Thou*.

T. H. Green and Michael Oakeshott, however, reject the idea of sentient experience because in their view all experience is thought. Nevertheless, Bradley, Green and Oakeshott agree that to think at all is to judge, that is, to differentiate a *this* from a *that*. Oakeshott, for example, contends that pain is not simply a sensation. We are aware of it in thought or judgement. This view is exemplified in the statement 'there is ... no experiencing which is not thought, and consequently no experience which is not thought, and consequently no experience which is not a world of ideas'.[6] The implication of this for R. G. Collingwood was that 'all history is the history of thought',[7] by which he meant all human artefacts are the product of thought and the result of intelligible, intelligent and purposive practices.

Sixthly, the Idealists viewed the world of experience modally. This is the implication of beginning with the principle of unity, or the undifferentiated whole, and then having to account for the variety of experience. How the modes arise and their relationship to each other and the Absolute or the whole of experience is a matter of contestation among the Idealists. What is important, however, is that the modes are the arbiters of truth and falsity. It is not only their coherence that gives rise to the veracity of the truthfulness of our statements, but also their comprehensiveness.

It was Bradley who most systematically formulated this view of the criterion of truth as the union of coherence and comprehensiveness. The more self-subsistent, consistent and complete a mode, or world of ideas, the greater its share of truth. Truth and reality for Bradley are a matter of degree. Bradley contends 'truths are true, according as it would take less or more to convert them into reality'.[8] Because these worlds or modes of experience fall short of the Absolute, or reality as a whole, the ideas that we are compelled to use are all more or less imperfect in varying degrees.[9]

This does not mean that we arbitrarily create our own truths. The social character of experience requires that we are inducted into these worlds, which delineate sense from nonsense. Broadly speaking, the material presented by each world is given and compulsory, and out of my power to change. In other words, 'reality is not what I happen to think: it is what I am obliged to think'.[10] While all of these appearances of reality are defective, they are nevertheless useful, and hold sway in their own domain. Nature, Bradley argues, has little reality, but it is nevertheless an 'ideal construction required by science, and it is a necessary working fiction'.[11] We have no alternative outside philosophy but to accept the appearances that, in relation to the whole of experience, are unintelligible. Each mode of understanding is at liberty to use whatever ideas serve its purpose best, and within its limits each must be allowed the liberty to pursue its own business.[12]

Finally, the relationship between philosophy and the modes has implications for the relationship between theory and practice. The issue revolves around whether philosophy, having interrogated and exposed as wanting the various claims to truth presented by the modes, has anything to contribute to the way each conducts its affairs. We can detect among the Idealists a variety of points of view, one of which is shared with Realism.

Hegel was of the view that philosophy comes onto the scene after the event, and can contribute nothing to the activities it interrogates. Hence the infamous line: 'When philosophy paints its grey on grey, then has a form of life grown old. The owl of Minerva takes flight only with the coming of dusk'.[13] This view is embraced by both Bradley and Oakeshott.

The opposite of this view of philosophy's relation to practice is expressed in the title of Henry Jones's book *Idealism as a Practical Creed*.[14] Here philosophy does have a role in exposing the deficiencies and contributing to the better conduct of the activities it criticizes. Edward Caird, Jones's mentor and teacher, and Collingwood exemplify this position. Collingwood, for example, argues that all problems arise out of practice and return to practice in their resolution.[15] A synthesis of both positions is put forward by Bosanquet and Green. Here, it is acknowledged that the business of philosophy is distinct from the activities in which practitioners of various kinds engage, but the latter often encounter difficulties and perplexities, the resolution of which may be contributed to by the former.

THE ABSOLUTE VERSUS THE PERSONAL

When L. T. Hobhouse criticized the metaphysical theory of the state, which he attributed in different degrees, to the Absolute Idealists, but in particular to G. W. F. Hegel and his English follower Bernard Bosanquet, he in fact was complaining about the idea of a unity above and beyond the individuals who comprise it, and which has a will of its own; the capacity to deliberate; and to act morally. More pejoratively, it was referred to as the God State. The danger of such a diminution of the individual and subordination to a 'higher' entity was, in Hobhouse's view, connected to both German militarism and the conflict of the First World War.[16]

A number of Idealists, while not in full sympathy with Hobhouse's attack, had many years before expressed concerns about the almost complete absorption of the individual in the Absolute.[17] These critics of Idealism became known as the Personal Idealists. Among them is a good deal of internal variety. The most prominent Personal or Subjective Idealists were Andrew Seth Pringle-Pattison, Hastings Rashdall, Henry Sturt, W. R. Boyce Gibson, the American Brand Blanshard and the idiosyncratic James M. E. McTaggart, who taught the latter day Absolute Idealist Michael Oakeshott.

Idealism was consistent in emphasizing that there could be no thought without a thinker, and no thinker without thought. The point at which they parted company was over its implications for the idea of the finite individual. The question of finite individuality was at the heart of both Absolute and Personal Idealism, and was a central metaphysical concern. The "individual" in Bradley and Bosanquet is used in a logical sense. It signifies a comprehensive unity, or totality, self-subsistent and coherent, implying non-contradiction. Only reality as a whole, the Absolute, possesses this character. Bradley's scepticism is most evident in his treatment of the finite individual and personality. The individual 'only exists through an intellectual construction'.[18] This ultimate reality, or the Absolute, is beyond our comprehension in discursive thought. The individual self – the person – is not real, but merely an appearance. The finite individual, or self, exhibits a greater degree of reality only insofar as it contains within itself more of the "total Universe", that is, insofar as it becomes transmuted, comprehensive and self-consistent. By implication, this means that a self becomes more of a self to the extent to which it becomes less distinct from other selves.[19] The individual self is more real and less abstract as part of a community. The idea of an isolated individual is thus regarded as an unsustainable abstraction, and the claim that only this individual is real is a "mere fancy". A person is a person only insofar as that person is 'what others are'. A person is simply not 'real' outside of a community. Self-realization is the realization of something beyond the self, 'and so must be called a universal life'.[20] Bradley provocatively maintained: 'There is nothing which, to speak properly, is individual or perfect, except only the Absolute'.[21] Individuals or persons have value only insofar as they express or manifest features of the Absolute. Bosanquet summed up the argument in contending: 'All the great contents of the developed human self – truth, beauty, religion and social morality – are all of them but modes of expression of the Ideal self.'[22]

Caird and Jones, fellow Absolute Idealists, while agreeing with the monistic unity of the whole, do not subscribe to the more extreme views of Bradley and Bosanquet. The Scotsman and the Welshman give much more emphasis to the *reality* of the *appearances*. For Caird and Jones, the unity embodies the principle of rationality, which is expressed in and through all the differentiations of the whole. Jones argues that while Idealism repudiates the psychological method of beginning a philosophical inquiry from the inner life of the subject, it cannot do without that inner life. Activity, emotions and purposes are all incorporated, but what is denied is any ultimate distinction between subject and object. They are merely distinctions within a real ontological unity. This ontological unity, Jones argues, is not incompatible with 'their equally real difference'.[23] Jones's problem with Bradley and Bosanquet was that their conception of the Absolute was too static and monistic, impelling them to ignore (what Jones took to be) essential differences. In direct criticism of Bradley, Jones contends: 'A unity which in transcending the differences obliterates them is not their unity. A unity which becomes itself unknowable, or lies beyond the reach of predication, holds no differences together, but sinks itself into an empty affirmation of the all-in-allness of everything.'[24] For Jones, the Absolute is a unity in difference, and Idealists should avoid putting all the stress on unity and infinity and by implication relegating all claims to finitude.

The debate reached its zenith in 1918 at a meeting of the Aristotelian Society, which addressed the question: 'Do finite individuals possess a substantive or an adjectival mode of being?'[25] The Personal Idealists differed from the Absolutists over the issue of the denial of the distinction between subject and object. They feared that denying the distinction put the self at risk of being completely absorbed into the Absolute.

It is the problem of finite individuality that Michael Oakeshott is still grappling with throughout his 1933 book *Experience and its Modes*. He does not ask what is real in a mode of experience. Instead he asks what in each is an 'individual' or a thing. It is in the practical mode that we hang on most tenaciously to the idea of the autonomous self or person. In practical life, as in other modes, the thing, or the individual, is designated and presupposed, not defined. Completeness is not the criterion of designating the individual, but instead the individual is designated by what is separate and self-contained. The practical self, the person, is the creation of practical thought and is presupposed in all action. The postulate or presupposition of the self is self-determination, which entails freedom that itself requires no demonstration, because it, by definition, belongs to the practical self. To reject the principle of self-determination, and the implication of freedom is to deny the world of practice, and its foundational postulate, namely, the 'separateness and uniqueness' of the individual. The individual in practical life is just as much an abstraction, an arrest or modification of experience, as the individual, or thing, presupposed in all the other modes.[26]

Andrew Seth was the first of the British Idealists to voice concerns about the implications for the individual of Absolutism. These concerns were developed by Seth and the Personal Idealists.[27] In 1888, Seth indicated his central concerns. The defect in Hegel, Seth contends, is that he treats the individual simply as a universal or perceptive consciousness, a spectator of things and merged into the universal, occupying a universal standpoint, indifferent to the issue as to whether it is my Ego, or another, that comprehends the world. Seth complained: 'a philosophy which goes no further than this in its treatment of the individual, leaves untouched what we may call the individual in the individual – those subjective memories, thoughts, and plans which make each of us a separate soul.'[28] Personal Idealism, as such, thus begins dissatisfied with the place of individual personality in the post-Kantian Hegelian programme.

Seth's *Hegelianism and Personality* launched a sustained attack on the Hegelian system and its assumptions, inaugurating the beginnings of Personalism, or Personal Idealism, in Britain. Seth is important because it was only 4 years after he edited the manifesto of British Idealism, *Essays in Philosophical Criticism*, with R. B. Haldane, that he now questioned the metaphysical conclusions of Absolute Idealists, leading the revolt against them in the name of Personalism. Seth was particularly perturbed by the tendency within Absolute Idealism to identify the human and divine self-consciousness. He maintained that: 'The radical error both of Hegelianism and of the allied English doctrine I take to be the identification of the human and the divine self-consciousness, or, to put it more broadly, the unification of consciousness in a single Self.'[29]

We should however exercise caution. There was still much in Absolute Idealism with which he agreed. He subscribed, for example, to the coherence theory of truth.[30] He was also committed to the idea of modality in experience, with an underlying unity and connectedness. The truth of anything, in his view, required knowledge of both the process of its becoming and the end to be realized. There were various names for this whole. Some call it Nature, or the Higher Nature, including within itself humanity and human values. Others might call it the Absolute or God. In addition, the finite individual, for him, was not an isolated or atomized entity. It still depended for its content on an objective system of reason. The individual was thus inconceivable without society; philosophically, the individual was organic, that is integral to a universal life. Seth's argument is therefore that the individual 'cannot possibly be regarded as self-contained in relation to that life, for such self-containedness would mean sheer emptiness'.[31] The individual therefore has a universal nature within the whole or universe in which souls are made. Andrew Seth Pringle-Pattison's position is in these respects is almost indistinguishable from Absolute Idealism. It would be unwise to exaggerate the differences between the Personalists and the Absolutists. Indeed, Personalists insisted on the continuity, rather than a complete break with Absolutism. Sturt, for example, contended: 'Personal Idealism is a development of the mode of thought which has dominated Oxford for the last thirty years; it is not a renunciation of it'.[32]

Seth also differentiated himself in the emphasis he gave to selfhood and the uniqueness of the finite individual. The individual could not be regarded as a mere appearance of reality. The individual person is an experienced certainty, foundational to all action and thought, and cannot be explained away. The Absolute therefore cannot negate the finite individual. To deny the reality of finite centres was to deprive the entire superstructure of our experience of its foundation.[33] Seth went to great pains to reinforce, in the minds of Idealists, the importance of the self in accounting for the nature of experience. In discussing Kant, for example, Seth argues that the self exists only through the world, and the world only through the self. Self and the world are the same reality looked at from different points of view. The basic unity, or identity, of reality can only be grasped, however, from the point of view of the subject, or person.[34] In Seth's view, Absolute Idealism was therefore in danger of consigning the individual to insignificance.[35]

In general terms, the Personal Idealists identified Bradley and Bosanquet as the greatest danger to the integrity of the self. Bradley was criticized for casting doubt on the usefulness of the idea of a person in comprehending or understanding experience as a unity in diversity. The Personalists also believed that Bradley was mistaken in characterizing the absolute as unknowable, something beyond human experience, which he refers to as "mere" appearance. Yet, nonetheless, Bradley had done a great service to British Idealism, in Seth's view, in freeing it from its slavish imitation of Hegel. Bradley was, however, still less than convincing in his explanations of how contradictions would be resolved in the Absolute. All Bradley could offer was the vague promise that differences were to be fused and overcome. The question of how the multiplicity of selves and diversity of experience became a unity was avoided in the admission that we do not know how, only that somehow they will.[36]

Personal Idealists still acknowledged that some exponents of Absolute Idealism were closer to them than others. For example, Henry Jones and Josiah Royce, in the view of Henry Sturt, were not as guilty as Bradley and Bosanquet in consigning the individual to oblivion. Both Sturt and Boyce Gibson contended that Personal Idealism, of which they were proud to be exponents, was a development of, rather than a departure from, the Idealism of Green, Bosanquet and Bradley. Boyce Gibson, following Rudolph Eucken, contends the idea that 'the real is the rational' is a central idea of both Absolute and Personal Idealism. Personal Idealists, however, view it 'from the point of view of the personal experiment'.[37] Absolute and Personal Idealism had a common enemy in naturalism, but the Personalists thought the Absolutists were deficient in two main respects. First, the Absolutists criticized human experience, not from the vantage point of human experience itself, 'but from the visionary and impractical standpoint of human nature'.[38] Secondly, the Absolutists refused to give adequate recognition to volition in human nature.

J. M. E. McTaggart, a towering figure among Cambridge philosophers, was also a Personal Idealist and a critic of Absolute Idealism. He immersed himself in metaphysical problems. McTaggart believed that the individual had to be placed at the centre of philosophical enquiry. The whole has to be understood from the standpoint of the experiencing individual. He declared himself an ontological Idealist because he believed that everything that exists is spiritual, but qualified this commitment by declaring that the content of spirit must fall within a self, with no part falling within more than one self.[39] Judgements about whether something is good, bad or worthy have meaning ultimately only for the individual consciousness. Value neither consists in relations among individuals, nor in the whole that they comprise. It is only by being one of the terms of the relation that value has meaning. A person, who loves another, does not find value or goodness residing in the relation, but in being one of those related.[40]

Like Seth, McTaggart was inclined to the meticulous study and criticism of Hegel. Hegel, in McTaggart's view, had better than any philosopher before or after penetrated more deeply into the nature of reality. Hegel's mistake was to conceive the Absolute as the highest expression of philosophy. Philosophy may be the highest level of human knowledge, McTaggart conceded, but not of reality. Reality for him is a community of finite spirits and not one undifferentiated whole. Individual minds and their contents comprise the ultimate spiritual reality.

THE IDEALIST CONCEPTION OF PHILOSOPHY

Starting from the Hegelian principle of unity, the Absolute Idealists take the purpose of philosophy to be the reconciliation of what the modern age has divided and dispersed. They acknowledge all aspects of human experience in the face of the dissolving tendency of the times to separate and sever them from each other, rendering each a mere abstraction. Edward Caird believed that the two pernicious tendencies facilitating such fragmentation were Subjective Idealism that had 'infected' British philosophy since the time of Berkeley, and the philosophy that rejected this subjectivity, namely Realism and Naturalism, which conceived everything as a mechanical system.[41] The common belief among Absolute Idealists was that there is a unity beneath all oppositions, which is capable of bringing about reconciliation.

Contrary to naïve caricatures of Idealism, it has no objection to any of the distinctions and oppositions that enter into the theoretical and practical consciousness of mankind, including distinguishing between mind and matter. It denies, however, that there can be absolute differences or antagonism without rending the distinctions unintelligible. All distinctions imply relations, and ultimately a unity in all things distinguished. Idealism refuses 'to admit that there is an unintelligible world, a world that cannot be brought in relation to the intelligible.'[42] Because this unity is such a fundamental presupposition of all consciousness, we rarely bring it to the surface of ordinary consciousness.[43] It is a fundamental postulate, a colligating hypothesis of understanding, or what R. G. Collingwood later called an Absolute Presupposition of rational thinking.[44]

Caird argues that when thinking is understood as the process by which Spirit or God realizes itself, the subjective and objective are not separated by ideas, but instead are the differentiations of the one comprehensive unity. Philosophy facilitates a reconciliation of ourselves to ourselves and to the world, which entails the aspiration of placing human life in the context of the universe.[45] The whole of experience is the reference point in terms of which to understand each and any of its aspects. Caird sums up Hegel's position thus: the highest aim of philosophy 'is to reinterpret experience, in the light of a unity which is presupposed in it, but which cannot be made conscious or explicit until the relation of experience to the thinking self is seen'.[46]

Implicit in the arguments of the Absolute Idealists (with some notable exceptions) is a philosophy of history in which there is pattern and meaning to human history, exhibited in an observable tendency towards greater unity and organization. They acknowledge that thoughts in all their forms and categories are inextricably linked to each other, and to invoke one or other exclusively for the explanation of experience is inevitably to commit an error.[47] The early Andrew Seth contended that Absolute Idealism deprives the parts of their purported independence and substantiality. Justifiably so, however, in that each member of the system is real, and holds its reality as part of that system, as a part of the whole, which exists absolutely and in its own right.[48]

The implication for philosophy of starting with the principle of unity is that all dualisms are abstractions and must be transcended in a synthesis. When the British Idealists address a substantive problem they present two sides, a subjective and objective, the contradiction between which is resolved in a synthesis.[49] Oakeshott provides us with an interesting exemplification of how the totality brings about a synthesis. In discussing, for example, Hobbes he identifies three traditions in political philosophy, which are dialectically related to each other. They are the antithetical traditions of 'Reason and Nature', and 'Will and Artifice', the deficiencies of which are transcended in the synthesis of 'Rational Will'.[50] Hobbes's significance, in Oakeshott's view, is that he began his enquiries with the human will rather than law. It was an innovation followed by almost every political philosopher since. However, the whole Epicurean tradition to which Hobbes belonged lacked an adequate theory of volition. The solution to the problem consisted in the union of a reconfigured theory of natural law with the Epicurean theory of Hobbes. The union is exemplified in such phrases as Rousseau's 'General Will', or Hegel's 'Rational Will', or Bosanquet's 'Real Will'.[51]

IDEALISM VERSUS REALISM

Idealists and neo-Idealists understand philosophy to be experience self-critical of itself. We do not begin with a *tabula rasa*. The philosopher's job is to analyse the given in experience. For Henry Jones, for example, philosophy does not start from sentient or immediate experience, intuition or sceptical *cogito*. Philosophy begins with ordinary experience reflective of itself. It starts with reality and reflects upon it: philosophy is thus 'the reflective interpretation of human experience, it must accept the laws of experience as its own. Experience is its starting point and whole datum.'[52] The starting point is not ignorance from which we progress to knowledge, but an understanding of something that to some extent we already know. Philosophy is the getting to understand better something that is already understood. Or as Dilthey puts it: 'in order to understand, one must have already understood'.[53] Getting to understand something better does not mean getting to know more about it, but coming to understand it differently and better.[54] Bosanquet elaborates and suggests that philosophy cannot tell you anything that you do not already know. Instead, it tells you the significance of what you know.[55] Oakeshott formulates this philosophical principle in the following terms: 'there is no such thing as a transition from mere ignorance to complete knowledge: the process is always one of coming to know more fully and more clearly what is in some sense already known'.[56]

Realists ostensibly portray philosophical analysis in the same terms. The similarity is, however, deceptive. L. Susan Stebbing, a follower of the Cambridge School and an exponent of its method, contended in 1932 that metaphysical analysis is 'discovering *what it is precisely* which we already in some sense knew'.[57] The method of British Idealists and Cambridge Realists were nevertheless quite different. The former employ the 'regressive', while the latter the 'decompositional' method.

Regressive analysis is concerned more with the postulates, principles and presuppositions upon which, or from which, conclusions are generated. It is a method whose roots reach back to ancient Greek geometry. Philosophy for the Idealists, because they begin with the principle of unity, necessarily entails being aware of the assumptions that underpin the differentiations into which this unity has fragmented.[58]

The Cambridge Realists take what is given and break it down into its structure and components. G. E. Moore's Common Sense philosophy is an example of this method. Moore argues that there is a common stock of propositions, which most rational people know and which provide the background to our reflections, both ordinary and philosophical. Examples include, at some time in the past I was born; I have occupied different locations on this earth at different times relative to other humans; and, there are many live humans populating the earth. Such propositions, Moore contends, are indisputable.[59] His method consisted in defending philosophical claims with reference to our conceptual intuitions. In epistemology, he famously attempted to refute scepticism by claiming that we *do* have knowledge of the external world. His 'proof' consisted in suggesting, here is one hand, and here is another, thus demonstrating knowledge and certainty of the external world.[60]

The Cambridge of Bertrand Russell, G. E. Moore and Ludwig Wittgenstein transformed philosophical thinking. The modality espoused by the Idealists was rejected in favour of the mathematical and scientific certainty of empirical and analytical thinking. Wittgenstein was regarded as equal to Einstein – a genius, even a messiah. John Maynard Keynes likened him to God. It was the Wittgenstein of the *Tractatus* whom the Vienna Circle virtually deified. Its semi-official manifesto, *Viewing the World Scientifically: The Vienna Circle*, identified Albert Einstein, Ludwig Wittgenstein and Bertrand Russell for being the intellectual inspiration of the movement. It was, as far as Wittgenstein was concerned, faint praise and he rejected the accolade.

Einstein was important because he denied that the laws of physics could be deduced from first principles independent of observation. Russell's importance was that he was an uncompromising empiricist, arguing that all our knowledge comes from experience. Rudolph Carnap and Hans Hahn, of the Vienna Circle, were attracted to Russell because of his application of logic to both mathematics and language. Russell contended that the results of the sciences could not in general be imported into philosophy. The methods of the sciences, however, most certainly could.

Russell, however, was John the Baptist in comparison with the messiah Wittgenstein. Russell was the prophet who foretold the coming of Wittgenstein. Wittgenstein's *Tractatus Logico-Philosophicus* was published in German in 1921. Moritz Schlick immediately appreciated its originality, and in the mid 1920s, over the course of almost a year, it was twice read out line by line and meticulously scrutinized by the Vienna Circle.

The Vienna Circle derived its cohesiveness and strength of purpose from the unrelenting belief in the veracity of the idea of the application of scientific method to philosophy. They contended that philosophy, as well as every other discipline, had everything to gain from logical rigour. In this, the Logical Positivists were rather more strident than their Cambridge counterparts. The powerful appeal of the Vienna Circle to such young philosophers as A. J. Ayer was its simple and basic creed that there were only two types of valid statement. One type is analytic statements, which were true by definition, for example, the deductive reasoning of syllogisms or the propositions of geometry. The other type of valid statement is empirical, derived from observation, inductive and open to verification. The famous verification principle determined the truth or falsity of a statement. A statement such as the sun rises in the west, although false, is meaningful because it is open to verification. All other statements are meaningless because they are matters of opinion. Thus, theology, ethics, metaphysics and all other normative statements were excluded from philosophy, giving philosophy the important task of sharpening and clarifying the concepts of scientists. The Vienna Circle understood Wittgenstein to be saying something similar about verification in the *Tractatus*. His point, however, was more subtle. His differentiation of propositions that could be said, such as those of the scientist, and those that should be unsaid, such as those of ethics, was not to conclude that statements of the latter kind were nonsense. Indeed, for Wittgenstein the more interesting and important category was propositions about which nothing could be said.

Such differences between Vienna and Cambridge paled into insignificance when confronted with philosophical Idealism, with its roots in Kant and Fichte, finding its definitive statement in Hegel. Idealism's emphasis upon mind and spirit, instead of science and symbolic logic, was anathema to the members of the Vienna Circle who denounced it as 'unscientific', muddled, mystical and deliberately obtuse.

Furthermore, Realism and Logical Positivism rejected Idealist logic. When H. H. Joachim attacked the Realist correspondence theory of truth in 1906, he referred to "current logic". There was no mistaking to what he was referring. It was the philosophical study of thought and knowledge associated with Bradley and Bosanquet, the legacy of Hegel inherited by Lotze and Sigwart, and passed on to modern-day Idealists. By 1939, when he published the second edition of *The Nature of Truth*, the idea of 'current logic' had become much more ambiguous. It was then seen not so much as a branch of philosophy, but more as a science of symbols and forms severed from what was symbolized or formed. This was evident in symbolic or formalistic logic and those aspects of Logical Positivism that went under the name of the theory of logical analysis.[61]

In this context, both R. G. Collingwood's *Speculum Mentis* and Michael Oakeshott's *Experience and its Modes* constituted direct challenges to Realism and Logical Positivism. Collingwood and Oakeshott, like Bradley, Bosanquet and Joachim, took logic to be the philosophical study of thought and knowledge, and this necessarily entailed interrogating the modes, or arrests in what Joachim called the 'timeless and complete actuality'.[62] Collingwood's forms of experience and Oakeshott's modes gave validity to types of knowledge other than scientific, and indeed in Collingwood's case made science subordinate to history and philosophy, and in Oakeshott's case made science co-equal with the other modes, and merely an arrest in experience in comparison with philosophy. In a dismissive allusion to the Logical Positivists, Oakeshott rebuts their reverence for science. He remarked:

> 'it is scarcely to be expected, in these days, that we should not be tempted to take up the idea of philosophy as, in some sense, "the fusion of the sciences", "the synthesis of the sciences" or the *scientia scientiarum*. Yet, what are the sciences that they must be accepted as the datum, and as a datum not to be changed, of valid knowledge? And if we begin with the sciences, can our conclusions be other or more than merely scientific?'.[63]

The many followers of Wittgenstein and analytic philosophy were disdainful of the ascendency of what they regarded the metaphysical nonsense of Idealism, still represented in Cambridge by McTaggart, Sorley and the young Oakeshott. The groups tended to avoid each other. Oakeshott, for example, did not attend the Moral Science Club seminars where Wittgenstein dominated in the early 1930s. The Cambridge Realists had a good deal of respect for what they regarded the more rigorous of the Idealists at Oxford, particularly Bradley and Joachim who proved to be formidable opponents. Bosanquet also defends Idealism against Realist critics such as Russell, Alexander, Whitehead and Moore.[64] R. G. Collingwood developed his own distinctive position by attempting to refute the fundamental claims of the Realists at both Cambridge and Oxford.[65] The charge that Collingwood made against positivism was that it misconceived the nature of metaphysics.[66]

Although some of the Idealists, including Bradley and Oakeshott, did not wish to suggest that theory and practice were intimately connected, others did and objected most ferociously to what they regarded as the moral abdication of Realists from social responsibility. For many of the British Idealists, as we will see in Chapter 4, philosophy was a weapon in the social and political debates of late Victorian and early Edwardian Britain. The social responsibility of the philosopher was to provide a practical guide to life. Both Absolute and Personal Idealists could agree on this. In 1907, W. R. Boyce Gibson, who later took up a chair in Melbourne University, argued that philosophy had demonstrated its value in economics, sociology and education, and was in the process of enlightening religion on the philosophic power of the categories of love, communion and redemption, which it was rescuing from the interpretations of theology.[67]

In addition, Idealists objected to the privileging by Realists of natural science as the authentic route to knowledge. McTaggart denied Russell's contention that the results and methods of the sciences could be usefully employed by philosophy. McTaggart agreed that metaphysics can offer us no practical guidance, but for quite different reasons from the Realists. For the Realists, metaphysical statements were simply not verifiable. McTaggart contended that a person's views on practical matters are largely unaffected by his or her metaphysical beliefs. People who believe in God, immortality or optimism, seem to act no differently in moral terms from those who do not believe in them.[68] However, McTaggart, unlike Russell, did not dismiss the practical relevance of metaphysics altogether. In *Our*

Knowledge of the External World, for example, Russell argued we will be disappointed if we think that philosophy can satisfy our mundane desires. While it renounces practical contamination, philosophy can nevertheless help us understand 'general aspects of the world and the logical analysis of familiar but complex things'.[69] McTaggart, however, contends that Metaphysics has a great deal of practical value, but not as a guide to conduct. Its value is in providing the reasons for why we hold some of our theories to be true metaphysics may give us considerable comfort. A belief in the truth of certain theories may profoundly affect our happiness. It is much more likely that a belief that all is well with the world leads to happiness, while a belief in the opposite brings misery. This is manifestly obvious when we witness 'the intense practical importance of our beliefs on the problems of religion'.[70]

The sorts of questions that McTaggart and other Idealists asked would for Realists simply be inadmissible, because the answers were not verifiable. In McTaggart's case, the questions included whether God exists; whether the self survives physical death, and if so for what reasons; whether good predominates over evil in the universe, and if over time the ratio changes; and, whether what exists, particularly ourselves, have any purpose and value?

Both Bradley and Oakeshott could accept Russell's denial of the practical value of philosophy, and the irrelevance of the results of the natural sciences to philosophy, but in sympathy with McTaggart, they denied that the method of the sciences had any relevance to philosophy. In addition, for Oakeshott, philosophy has no positive contribution to make to science, or indeed to any of the modes of experience, including practical life. It is the business of philosophy, both Bradley and Oakeshott argued, to understand what is. Moral philosophy has to understand morals, not make them or provide a blueprint for making them.[71]

CONCLUSION

This chapter has provided an indication of the main philosophical and metaphysical elements within British Idealism. In so doing, it has examined certain internal debates within Idealism itself, particularly that between Absolute and Personal Idealisms. It then moved to elaborate on certain elements characterizing the Idealist conception of philosophy. Finally, it turned to a brief critical overview of the debates between the Idealists and various forms of Realism and Naturalism to a much lesser extent. In the next chapter, we move the discussion to a cognate issue, which is the role and place of modality in British Idealist philosophical argument.

CHAPTER THREE

MONISM AND MODALITY

INTRODUCTION

We saw in the previous chapter how Absolutism, the dominant form of Idealism, viewed experience holistically. The concrete totality of experience as a consequence posed for them not an epistemological question, such as how mind attaches itself to an external world, but the ontological question of the conditions of our understanding, that is, how the undifferentiated whole became differentiated into all of the worlds of ideas, through which we come to know the world. In other words, Idealism recognizes the conditionality of our understanding, and much of the philosophical enterprise is concerned with the identification and interrogation of those conditions. It is this feature of Idealism – the right to use whatever ideas work best – that was to prove attractive to Pragmatism, which is, in some ways, a development of aspects of Idealist arguments.

In this chapter, we explore the implications of this philosophical commitment in Idealism in general, and illustrate what is entailed by examining the two principal views of how the modes are related to each other and how they are related to the whole. Idealists such as Hegel, Bosanquet, Bradley, Jones, Gentile and Collingwood viewed the relationship of the modes in logical progression, each transcending the inadequacies of those that precede them, culminating in philosophy, or absolute experience, which has overcome all of the contradictions in the modes or forms of experience. The argument was elaborated into a full-blown theory by Michael Oakeshott, namely, that the modes were all similar modifications or arrests in experience, none of which was superior to the others, and all sovereign in their own domain. They were autonomous in relation to each other, but related in falling short of the Absolute, which is the whole of experience.

IDEALISM AND MODALITY

There is a common core of ideas concerning modality shared by Idealists. All agree that there are different worlds of experience and that each, in some way, falls short of reality and self-consistency, in that each rests upon metaphysical postulates or presuppositions, or assumptions, from which "facts" may be derived or inferred. Thus, F. H. Bradley's first publication, *The Presuppositions of Critical History* (1874), is an exploration of how in history "facts" are not merely given in experience, but are conclusions or theories. Historical facts are a matter of inference, and all inferences rest on presuppositions grounded in 'absolute presuppositions'.[1] Bradley's concern is not to explain what makes any fact, but what specifically constitutes a historical fact. Without such constitutive principles, nothing could achieve the status of historical fact.[2] These presuppositions, Bradley argues, are formed by present experience. Something that is simply inconceivable, and beyond our experience, cannot be the ground of our assumptions from which historical facts are inferred. It is beyond our experience, for example, that a person can be in two places at once, or can be both dead and alive simultaneously. Inferences drawn from such assumptions would jar against the experience of the world as we know it.[3]

Bosanquet shares the same conception of philosophy. He asks himself what a philosophical enquiry implies. He contends that an object understood through different conceptual frameworks is not in any real sense the same thing. A flower is a different thing when understood by the botanist, chemist, or artist. Philosophy cannot hope to compete with these specialists in their own terms. Instead, the philosopher takes the flower, reveals its conditionality and determines its place and significance in the totality of experience: 'And this we call studying it, as it is, and for its own sake, without reservation or presupposition'.[4] These were the terms that Oakeshott was later to employ: 'Philosophical experience, I take to be experience without presupposition, reservation, arrest or modification'.[5]

Henry Jones developed similar ideas into a systematic theory, elements of which may be detected, often unacknowledged, in the new generation of Idealists, Collingwood and Oakeshott, who exemplify the two principal versions of modality. Both writers were though thoroughly familiar with Jones's work. Jones contends that our metaphysical assumptions are not a matter of choice, but we can be conscious or unconscious of those we employ. All our judgements, Jones maintains, rely upon assumptions. Each judgement is related and integrated with a diversity of other judgements together comprising some form of systematic unity. Each judgement resting upon a supposition is ultimately traceable to more fundamental and deep-rooted assumptions. In practical life, for example, these assumptions will add up to a "general theory" of life. For Jones, all of the modes by which we conceive the world and its objects, including ethics, psychology, natural science, and even poetry, necessarily rest upon metaphysical assumptions. Metaphysical study is the exploration of such assumptions.

The absolute presuppositions or postulates, that is, our most fundamental assumptions, serve to hold "facts" together. They are, for him, "colligating hypotheses", or ideas without which no system of thought could get off the ground. They are not confined solely to great systems of thought, such as those of Copernicus, Newton and Darwin, but are employed 'whenever the puzzled mind extricates itself from a difficulty …'[6] Every judgement we make is related to a colligating hypothesis. In Jones' view a presupposition is 'as natural as our skin and as difficult to escape'.[7] Indeed, except for hypotheses, facts and events would seem to us to be 'in no relation of any kind to one another'.[8] These colligating hypotheses are not arbitrary. They are suggested to the intellect by the world whose intelligibility we seek. They are entertained only so long as the world of reality seems to support them.

Jones distinguishes between relative hypotheses which seem to shed light on certain occurrences, but which are clearly conditional and open to question, and those which are fundamental and without which the world as we know it would be a completely different place. The latter, for Jones, are thus "absolute hypotheses" which we take to be ontologically true, and like relative hypotheses are nevertheless open to scrutiny, but their collapse has consequences much more far-reaching. In relation to the moral life, for example, we assume that human agents act purposively and are responsible for their actions, therefore may be held to account for their wrongdoings. If we assume, however, that all actions are fundamentally genetically determined, our view of morality and human agency and responsibility would be radically different. Absolute hypotheses are conjectures or critical guesses which are open to scrutiny, never ultimately provable, but always on trial and liable to be rebutted or undermined. The more "facts" a colligating hypothesis is unable to accommodate, the more likely it is to be abandoned.

Clearly then Jones anticipates Karl Popper's criticism of induction and his rejection of the verification principle associated with logical positivism.[9] Jones contends that a 'hypothesis is a conjecture on trial. Its existence is threatened by every relevant fact which it cannot explain'[10] and which finally, like R. G. Collingwood's constellations of absolute presuppositions or Thomas Kuhn's paradigms, become supplanted and superseded by new hypotheses or paradigms. This 'revolutionary kind of advance' is illustrated most starkly in scientific endeavour when 'one hypothesis is substituted for another'.[11] But such changes are not confined to the world of science. As Bosanquet argues: 'the history of thought shows certain leaps or breaks in culture; when the human mind seems to open its eyes afresh on a new platform, from which new point of view all its adjustments have to be remade and its perceptions reanalysed'.[12]

Jones' teacher and mentor, Edward Caird, thus understood the problem of philosophy as the examination of the conditional fragments of reality and the restoration of unity, that is, reconciling them with the whole. We should not view the differentiated elements at war with each other, nor suppose that the truth and solidarity of the principles of one may be extended beyond its boundaries to compose universal principles. If we extend the principles of natural science beyond the material world and posit them as universal, we inevitably reduce consciousness – thought and will – to the condition of physical phenomena, rendering their very existence an insoluble problem.[13]

For McTaggart also metaphysics is the 'systematic study of the ultimate nature of Reality'.[14] This enterprise entailed being critical of its own assumptions. In addition, it would be critical of the validity of scientific conceptions of reality, without denying that, despite their conditionality, they may nevertheless be compelling.[15] Further, Bradley in *Appearance and Reality* understands metaphysics in exactly the same way. However, Collingwood sees more of a sense of urgency in the problem of philosophy in his own day, attributing the crisis of civilization to the detachment of the forms of experience from one another and from the whole. He contends that 'our cure can only be their reunion in a complete and undivided life. Our task is to seek for that life, to build up the conception of an activity which is at once art, and religion, and science, and the rest'.[16] What therefore informs Collingwood's purpose is a belief that: 'All thought exists for the sake of action' and the enhancement of self-knowledge resulting in a more free and 'vigorous practical life'.[17] In contrast, the philosophical endeavour for Oakeshott is motivated by curiosity, and the knowledge gained is for its own sake. Philosophy makes no contribution to the better conduct of practical life.

For Collingwood, the ultimate purpose of philosophy is self-knowledge of the mind, a role that in his later work he increasingly assigned to history. Self-knowledge is ultimately achievable by transcending the false dichotomies that each form of experience constructs for itself between the mind and external objects. The mind is incapable of having immediate knowledge of itself. It knows itself only by seeing its reflection in an external world. To accomplish this, the mind creates or constructs external worlds. These worlds are abstractions until the mind realizes that they are of its own creation. In interrogating the claims of the different forms of experience, that is, art, religion, science and history, the philosophical mind realizes it has not been 'exploring an external world but tracing its own lineaments in a mirror'.[18]

Despite the radically different conceptions of the relationship between theory and practice, both Oakeshott and Collingwood examine the conditionality of the modes, explore their relation to each other and establish their place in reality as a whole. For both Bosanquet and Oakeshott understanding something for its own sake did not mean understanding it in isolation. Philosophy had to 'reveal its true position and relations with reference to all else that man can do and can know'.[19] If we take politics as the focus of our understanding, for example, the task of philosophy, in Oakeshott's words, is to 'establish the connections, in principle and in detail, directly or mediately, between politics and eternity'.[20]

In summary, one may say that the problem of philosophy in Idealism is to identify and interrogate the different forms or modes of experience; account for how they emerge out of the undifferentiated whole of experience; and, reconcile their differences into a unity. This entails exploring the internal relations of the forms; the relations between each of the forms; and that between the forms and the whole.

THE LINKED HIERARCHY OF MODES

One of the principal ways of conceiving the relations between the modes to each other and to the whole of experience is to place them in a hierarchy in which each of the higher modes embodies a greater degree of reality, or the generic essence of the whole, taking up into themselves the positive in what the lower has to offer.

The background for this general Idealist interest lay within the structures of Hegel's general philosophy. For Hegel mind is 'in its very act only apprehending itself, and the aim of all genuine science is just this, that Mind shall recognise itself in everything in heaven and earth. An out-and-out Other does not exist for Mind'.[21] Reality is therefore understood as the gradual development of Mind, in terms of its self-grasp. Speculative Idealism, as a philosophy, is thus understood by Hegel as the gradual effort of working progressively through levels and categories, to intellectually and practically attain a more adequate conceptual grasp of the whole of reality. Consciousness always appears differently modified according its object. All rational beings are moving gradually along this path of discovery. The role of philosophy becomes a painstaking systematic exposition of categories and forms of consciousness. Each category is examined as an existential possibility in the process of the gradual evolution of consciousness. The overall structure of Hegel's system is outlined in full in his *Encyclopaedia of the Philosophical Sciences*. Reality is there revealed gradually in the rich content of the sciences. The largest sequence of development here is through logic, nature and spirit. The final moment of Hegel's system, in Absolute Mind, is when consciousness grasps itself, or Mind makes itself fully known to itself, as mediated through art, religion and philosophy.

In Bosanquet's view, philosophical understanding entails revealing the 'rank and significance' of its objects in 'the totality of experience as a whole'.[22] Examples of this type of philosophical activity range from Hegel to Gentile and Croce and beyond to Collingwood's linked hierarchy of overlapping forms of experience. Such a conception of the philosopher's calling required demonstrating how each mode attempts unsuccessfully to achieve complete coherence, because it embodies internal contradictions. In overcoming these contradictions, each mode or form of experience brings into being a higher form of experience that transcends and transforms the defective mode, taking it up into itself, while at the same time generating new contradictions, which themselves call into being a higher mode in which they become resolved. The modes or forms are logically, if not temporally, related.

British Idealists, especially Bernard Bosanquet and J. A. Smith, were familiar with developments in Idealism on the continent. Gentile was a significant force at the turn of the twentieth century, and the foremost exponent of "actualism". The Idealism of Gentile was appealing to R. G. Collingwood because of his denial of anything outside of experience and because of his belief in the self-creating capacity of the mind. Gentile had attempted to overcome the mind/object dualism by relying, to some extent, upon Berkeley's radically subjective view of experience. Gentile denied though Bradley's claim that we come into contact with the Absolute, in its undifferentiated form, at the level of sentient experience, prior to its mutilation by thought. Gentile rejected the very idea that the mind apprehended something external to itself. He contended that: 'there is no *theory*, no contemplation of reality, which is not at the same time action and therefore a creation of reality'.[23]

Like all the Absolute Idealists, Gentile begins with the principle of unity, contending that the mind differentiates itself into the multiplicity of the things with which we are familiar. Mind thus begins with a subjective moment in the process of self-realization by asserting itself through art. Through religion, Mind asserts its objective moment. Self-knowledge of the mind, which is knowledge itself, entails the mind asserting itself in a synthesis of the subjective and objective modes. Knowledge itself is expressed triadically. Scientific activity is the objective or questioning moment of the mind; history is the subjective or answering moment.[24] Each of the modes – art, religion, science, and history – in itself is unsatisfactory, because each is one-sided and requires insights from the others to augment its vision. The Absolute synthesis is achieved only in philosophy. The unsatisfactory assertions of reality are interpreted by philosophy and assigned places in the unity of the whole. In conceiving history, not as an object which stands outside the subject, but as a unity created in the act of thinking, philosophy and the history of philosophy become one.[25]

A similar intellectual exercise was undertaken in 1924 by an admirer of Gentile, who attempted to reconcile his views with those of Vico, Croce and de Ruggiero, namely, R. G. Collingwood. Collingwood was drawn to the actualism of the early Gentile, whose work was subsequently tainted because of his association with fascism. Collingwood, however, was critical of Gentile's position from the start. In an unpublished manuscript of 1920, the *'Libellus de Generatione'*, Collingwood refers to Gentile's dialectic of *pensante* (the act of thinking) and *pensato* (the content of thought). For Gentile the *pensante* is outside time in that it creates *pensato*. *Pensato* is the content of thought and the product of *pensante*, but always happens in time. Collingwood thought that Gentile's philosophy suffered from the same defect as Spinoza's, namely that of identifying *pensante* with the pure act of thought, reducing all experience to thought, and in particular philosophical thought. In 1923, however, Collingwood was more favourably disposed. The mind that originates change, Collingwood contended, is at once inside and outside of time. Collingwood argues: 'as the source and ground of change, it will not be subject to change; while on the other hand, as undergoing change through its own free act, it will exhibit change'.[26]

Collingwood gave even greater emphasis to history than Gentile. He maintained that reality is history, and that history is the knowing mind conscious of itself. It is because mind is self-conscious of this history that it has a history at all. The importance of Gentile's philosophy in this respect was his formulation of a 'metaphysic of knowledge', which never lost sight of the question: How we come to know what we know?[27]

As Collingwood's thought developed, he came to view Gentile as little more than a 'fossilized or arthritic version' of Croce.[28] Collingwood objects to the implication in Gentile's thought of an eternal present that creates its own past. This, for Collingwood, was nothing more than an abstraction, which fails to take the past up into itself, and instead produces a desiccated past of itself. Collingwood was concerned that in concentrating his attention on the epistemological problems of the historian in creating the past and forming a perspective on it, Gentile neglected to address the relation of the perspectives to each other. This rendered Gentile's thought for Collingwood, a form of subjective Idealism that wholly overlooked the problem of development, 'with the result that Fascist thought, egocentric and subjective, can rightly be called by Croce *antistoricismo.*'[29]

Even though he owed a considerable debt to Gentile, for example, in the formulation of his logic of question and answer, Collingwood could not condone the fascist conclusions that Gentile drew from his philosophical theory of the will which saw wills in conflict with each other and compelled to dominate those of others. Collingwood's theory of the will necessarily implied mutual respect, acknowledging the same freedom of the will in others as a precondition of society and civilisation.

In his formulation of a scale of forms of experience, Hegel's philosophy for Collingwood was mediated through Croce. Croce had in fact rejected Hegel's dialectic of opposites because of its misunderstanding of the relation between concepts. Hegel viewed the relation as distinct contraries in an opposition that is resolved in a higher form or specification. Hegel made a real contribution to philosophy in recognizing that experience may be understood as a series of degrees of reality, and that opposites were not in opposition to unity. His success was marred by his failure to distinguish between opposites and distincts. By definition, the philosophical concept, in the view of Croce and Collingwood, is a unity that is composed of distinctions, each of which is itself a concept. Each concept is distinct in that it is a different specification, or characterisation of the whole. Croce contends that Spirit takes theoretical and practical forms. Intuition and thought are the theoretical forms, while the utilitarian and ethical wills are the Practical. The four specifications of Spirit are distinct, but not separate. Each is logically dependent upon the lower, and potentially, but not actually, dependent upon, the higher. The concepts are distinct but related to each other in a necessary logical sequence of degrees of reality, which constitute the concept of Spirit. The contraries, or opposites, are included in the concepts themselves. Take the concept of beauty as an example. Beauty is associated with intuition and art, and is what it is because of its denial of the ugly. The idea of ugliness as the negative, or contrary, is not in opposition to the concept, but part of the concept of beauty itself.[30]

Deriving its inspiration directly from Croce, Collingwood's theory of the philosophical concept posits a series of overlapping forms, differing at once in degree and kind, and comprises a unity of opposites and distincts. The philosophical concept differs from the scientific. The philosophical concept, *pace* the scientific, defies being distinguished into distinct coordinate species of a genus. If we try to classify actions in respect of their motives, for example, we discover that some are not confined to one or another type but exhibit mixed motives such as doing what one thinks useful, right and obligatory. If we ignore the overlap by identifying the margins at which the pure essence of the concept becomes apparent, excluding any other species of the genus, is to commit the fallacy of "precarious margins". To acknowledge overlap, and then to ignore it by focussing on the margins, gives us no grounds for asserting that the overlap will not become more pervasive. To suggest that the overlap is limitless puts us in danger of succumbing to the 'fallacy of identified coincidents'. This simply ignores the differences in the kind of generic specification altogether, and renders us incapable of seeing the differences between what is useful, right and dutiful. For example, a utilitarian who claims that performing one's duties contributes to an increase in the general happiness is unable to distinguish between the concept of promoting the general happiness and the concept of duty. To collapse the different specifications in this manner renders us incapable of seeing that they embody the generic essence in different degrees, each of which is a different kind of specification.

The reason why there are different forms is because within each there is a discrepancy between what it is and what it aspires to be, and in the course of self-modification each becomes transformed into something else and embodies the generic essence to a more adequate degree.[31] Art, for example, purports to be pure imagination, but nowhere does pure imagination exist because all imagination builds on fact and returns to fact. There is not an autonomous self-contained world of art, aesthetic experience, in which every trace of fact is absent. The error of art is the belief in the separateness and independence of imagination.[32]

Collingwood argues that the lower form of experience, from the point of view of the higher, is an inadequate embodiment of the generic essence and must be negated. The lower, however, is affirmed by the higher in having its positive content taken up by the superordinate form. The lower is the experience, which the higher modifies and transforms by constructing a theory to explain it.[33] At each of the stages, or specifications, the whole of the scale is summed up to that point 'because the specific form at which we stand is the generic concept itself, so far as our thought yet conceives it.'[34]

Art, religion, science, history and philosophy succeed each other logically. With the exception of philosophy, each transforms itself by aspiring to be what it is not, and each is a more adequate specification of the general essence of spirit, namely, self-consciousness. The forms presuppose, and take into themselves, those that they supersede. In order to be absorbed in this way by the higher, each must have the potential of their successor within them. The forms of experience are not separate faculties, but the whole self from a different point of view, related to each other, not as coordinate species of a genus, but in a logically ascending scale of overlapping forms.

Collingwood argues that 'in every field of activity there is a theoretical element, in virtue of which the mind is aware of something; there is a practical element in virtue of which the mind is bringing about a change in itself and in its world'.[35] The different forms of experience, or spirit, all have an associated form of practical reason, or action. Play becomes manifest in art, convention in religion; abstract, or utilitarian, ethics in science; duty, or concrete ethics in history; and absolute ethics in philosophy.[36]

The relationship which holds among the forms, and between the forms and the whole is characterized concisely in Collingwood's *Outlines of a Philosophy of Art*, where he contends that they are not:

'... species of a common genus. They are activities each of which presupposes and includes within itself those that logically precede it; thus religion is inclusively art, science inclusively religion and therefore art, and so on. And on the other hand each is in a sense all that follows it; for instance, in possessing religion we already possess philosophy of a sort, but we possess it only in the form in which it is present in, and indeed constitutes, religion.'[37]

THE AUTONOMOUS MODES

Bradley, at first glance, appears to subscribe to the role that both Gentile and Collingwood ascribed to philosophy. Bradley contends that a complete philosophy would take each aspect of the world of appearance, measure it by the absolute standard of reality as a whole, Absolute experience, and assign it a rank according to its relative merits and defects. On this scale, Nature and Spirit stand at opposite ends, and each degree further up the scale would exhibit more of the character of Spirit than that of Nature.[38] Bradley here accepts the legitimacy of the task of determining, with reference to the criterion of coherence, the exact degree to which each mode falls short of reality as a whole. Unlike Collingwood, however, Bradley does not see the modes in an ascending scale of forms, in which the deficiencies of their predecessors are transformed.

In relation to each other, none of the modes may claim logical priority, nor claim that it is higher in rank, and qualitatively superior. Furthermore, none may claim to explain the other modes, let alone experience as a whole. Each must be left to pursue its own methods and infer its own conclusions. That natural science rejects all forms of explanation that are not mechanical is its own business, and within its own boundaries it remains sovereign.[39]

Bradley does, nevertheless, suggest that each in attempting to remedy its defects implicates something outside itself.[40] Because Bradley subscribes to the view that there are degrees of reality, he maintains that the watertight distinctions we attempt to make between the different worlds in which we find a home break down the barriers between them.[41] Let us take metaphysics as an example. Metaphysics contributes something to the philosophy of Nature, not by purporting to direct scientific enquiry, but in evaluating the results of science on the principle of perfect individuality, and assigning them a place on 'the scale of being'. On such a scale, the lower, insofar as they make good their defects, pass beyond themselves into the higher.[42] So far this sounds very like Collingwood's scale of forms. Bradley goes on to suggest, however, that all of these 'main aspects of the universe' are irresolvable into the rest, and from this standpoint 'none is higher in rank or better than another'.[43] Indeed, not even philosophy may claim superiority without betraying 'a most deplorable error', that the intellect exhibits the highest aspect of our nature, and that in the world of intellect work done on the highest subjects is for that reason the highest work.[44]

Michael Oakeshott gave serious consideration to ranking the modes of experiences in terms of the degree of coherence attained. He concluded that such an exercise is a difficult task to accomplish, but that is not an adequate reason for rejecting it. Instead, Oakeshott argued that such an undertaking rests on a misconception of the legitimate aims of philosophy. He admitted that each mode may exhibit a different degree of abstraction. From the point of view of philosophy, however, it is an irrelevance. The important point is not the degree of abstraction, but the fact of abstraction, defect and shortcoming. Measuring the extent of the defect is not necessary: 'it is necessary only to recognise abstraction and to overcome it'. In recognizing and investigating the conditional intelligibility of history, for example, it is not necessary to attempt to place it in a logical or genetic hierarchy.[45]

Hegel and those who place the modes on a scale of forms do so in order to demonstrate a certain logical necessity for the emergence of each. In essence, a hierarchy of forms gives an account of why each has arisen. Oakeshott does not wish to address this question. For him, there is no logical necessity for their appearance, other than to suggest that the philosophical disposition cannot be sustained indefinitely. For Oakeshott, the modes emerge like the games that children play: 'Each appears, first, not in response to a premeditated achievement, but as a direction of attention pursued without premonition of what it will lead to'.[46] He concurs with Collingwood, however, that the modes are not products of separate faculties of the mind.

For Oakeshott, there is no limit in principle to the number of determinate modes that may arise, but in *Experience and its Modes* he identified only three that had achieved levels of coherence capable of maintaining what they asserted. The modes were the practical, history and science. Each rests upon unquestioned postulates capable of generating relatively sophisticated conclusions, but all ultimately fall short of experience as a whole because of their conditionality. History, for instance, maintains that there is a past that "really" happened of which it purports to give an account. The past in history, however, is a postulate and is logically specific to history and categorically distinct from the practical past. All experience is present experience, and history organizes its evidence in the present in terms of the category of the past. It does not and cannot "correspond" to a dead past that is no longer retrievable as the criterion for judging the truthfulness of an account. History is created by historians on the basis of what the evidence obliges them to believe.[47]

The modes are conditional arrests, which differ from philosophy, or experience as a whole. They build worlds of ideas upon unquestioned assumptions or postulates. Criteria of appropriateness are formulated in each; and "legitimate" manners of enquiry, procedures and practices are developed. What they provide, however, is conditional intelligibility. Philosophy is unlike the modes in being the concrete totality of experience. It is experience without reservation, presupposition or arrest. Its purpose and role is to interrogate the postulates of each mode, and expose the contradictions inherent in their partial view of experience. Philosophy reveals the contradictory character of the arrests in experience, and it does not make a substantive contribution to how they should conduct their affairs. Philosophers who mistake their calling for that of the preacher abandon at the point of recommendation the philosophical endeavour. Those who persistently intrude their views on the better conduct of the practices of the modes are little more than *philosophes* or theoreticians. Oakeshott would include among them Bentham and Marx.

The philosophical endeavour is difficult to sustain unrelentingly, and even the most sophisticated of philosophers from time to time take respite in the practical mode, voicing their opinions or concerns about this or that matter. Thomas Hobbes, the greatest of English philosophers, was not himself immune, but at those points where he lapses into recommendation he ceases to philosophize.

In this view of the relationship between the modes, they are completely autonomous. It is not their subject matter that distinguishes them from each other. The subject matter is in fact "created" by the modes and is therefore not given as such, but as a conclusion. Oakeshott argues that our understanding of something 'is necessarily the creature of the ideal character in terms of which it is being understood'.[48] The interpretative practices of the modes in so far as evidence is recognized as evidence, are the creation of the mode itself. There is no independent given in experience independent of the mode in terms of which it is interpreted.[49] The implication is 'text and interpretation are one and inseparable'.[50]

The modes are protected by their own exclusivity from the irrelevant intrusions of the others and from the concrete totality of experience. Each is true for itself. None may confirm or deny the conclusions of the others. None of them can claim to be foundational or prior to the rest. The modes are, then, in relation to each other, independent, but in respect to the whole their relation is one of dependence in that they exist only as abstractions of the concrete totality of experience.[51]

There is no essence, or epistemological foundation, to which they can all be reduced. In Oakeshott's famous imagery, they are 'voices in the conversation of mankind', incapable of refuting each other. They are not adversaries, but companions and acquaintances engaged in polite discourse. From time to time one voice may try to dominate the conversation in the mistaken belief that its conclusions are those to which all the others must defer.[52] The image of philosophical discourse as a conversation is one that Richard Rorty was to adopt later.[53]

Whereas Collingwood, Croce and Gentile had all acknowledged the modal character of art or aesthetics, Oakeshott initially believed that it was simply an aspect of practical life, and like all practical judgement art asserts reality and attributes to it a certain character.[54] In other words, it makes propositions about the world, which may be deemed right or wrong according to the criteria of practical life. He later came to modify his view because he concluded that the utterances of poetry, which encompass all forms of artistic practice, have distinctive postulates, which serve as their *differentiae*.

Poetry, for Oakeshott, is a distinct way of imagining, differing from the practical, scientific or historical ways of imagining.[55] The voice of poetry is distinguished from the other voices by the manner of its activity. It contemplates or delights in the making of images. As opposed to the images in other idioms of discourse they are "mere" images. They are not facts about the world because they are not propositions. It is inappropriate then to appreciate them in terms of truth and falsity.

It is not appropriate to ask of the images whether what is depicted really happened, or whether it is just possible, probable, or illusion and make-believe. To ask such questions assumes the distinction between fact and not fact, which has no place in poetic contemplative imagining. The images themselves have no past or future, they are merely present and delighted in for what they are, and not for what they are related to, such as the event, occasion or emotion that may have given rise to them. A poetic image cannot lie because it affirms nothing. That a work of art does not faithfully represent its subject is irrelevant. Monet's 'Water lilies' is a composition of shapes, light and colour comprising an image whose aesthetic quality has nothing to do with whether it looks like the lily pond in Monet's garden, and the appeal of Salvadore Dali's 'Clock' is not diminished by the fact that it is unlikely to keep time in its distorted condition. The stars in Vincent van Gogh's 'Starry Night' are of no practical use to the traveller who needs to get from one place to another, but that makes no difference to its character as art. Monet's 'Water Lilies', Dali's 'Clock' and van Gogh's 'Starry Night' exist only in the poetic image that they have created. One poet is distinguished from another in the arrangement and diction of the contemplative images imagined. The symbols are not interchangeable; to substitute one synonym for another destroys the image.

Poetic images are mere images because the relationship between symbol (language) and meaning (thought) differs in poetry from the relation in other modes of experience. This is a view Michael

Oakeshott shares with Collingwood who, in *Speculum Mentis* (1924), distinguishes art, religion, science, history and philosophy with reference to their different relationships between symbol and meaning. In our everyday practical lives, for example, each symbol or word has a determinate referent or signification. The more determinate, the better the communication. If I ask for a loaf of bread, I am using a symbol to evoke an image, not to create one. I am not trying to give a novel nuance to the symbol, merely to be understood in a settled language. In other words, meaning and symbol are distinct, but not radically separable because in this mode 'every word has its proper reference or signification'.[56] The symbol is separable from that which conveys meaning. In art or poetry, there is no separation of symbol and meaning: a poetic image is its meaning: it symbolizes nothing outside of itself.[57]

As we saw, in *Speculum Mentis* Collingwood characterized art as pure imagination. In *The Principles of Art* he was to elaborate a theory at the centre of which was the expression of emotion.[58] Oakeshott denies that poetry, or art, is the expression of emotion designed to evoke the same emotion in the recipient. The ability to evoke that same emotion in others is the criterion of good art. Collingwood does not, in fact, think about art in this way. He rejects a means-ends relationship in art, which the language of design and execution requires. Emotion is discovered only in its expression. It is not a premeditated design.

Oakeshott's critique does, nevertheless, apply in part to Collingwood's theory. The idea that art is the expression of emotion rests on the mistaken view that poetry must be in some way informative and instructive. The poet must have experienced the emotion that generated the poetic image. This, Oakeshott argues, 'makes a necessity of what is no more than an unlikely possibility'.[59]

It is no criticism of Oakeshott to argue that artists, historians, scientists or philosophers engage in much more than he attributes to them. The point is that he is trying to establish what makes the utterances unique; he is not suggesting, for example, that poets only contemplate or delight in images, but that what they do in addition to this is not poetry.

Unlike Collingwood, then, Oakeshott affirms a clear distinction between practical and theoretical activities, or between conduct and theorizing. Collingwood's understanding of the specifications of the philosophical concept as a linked hierarchical series of overlapping forms, and Oakeshott's conception of the relationship between each of the modes of experience as one of complete autonomy and categorical integrity, serve to explain their opposed views of the relation between theory and practice, and of history's relation to practical life.

In Collingwood's view, it is history that negates 'the traditional distinction between theory and practice' because 'in history the object is enacted and is therefore not an object at all'.[60] The significance of the idea of re-enactment in Collingwood's thought, although subject to considerable criticism,[61] with its emphasis upon the purposes and intentions of the historical actors, is that it requires the historian to re-live past-events in the contemporaneous practical injunctive moods of the participants. Collingwood continuously emphasized that history is eminently practical in enhancing one's own self-knowledge and preparing oneself for action. In this respect, history has a crucial role to play because historical problems ultimately arise out of the plane of real or practical life, and it is to history that practical problems are referred for their solution. History, therefore, stands 'in the closest possible relation to practical life'.[62] For Oakeshott, on the other hand, the practical mode, or conduct, is 'categorically irrelevant' to historical inquiry.[63] History, in Oakeshott's view, is a form of theorizing and therefore 'released from considerations of conduct'.[64] Contrary to popular opinion, history is not derived from, nor built upon, practical life, and conversely practical life has nothing to learn from the categorically irrelevant mode of history.[65] The past in history, Oakeshott contends, 'is without the moral, the political or social structure which the practical man transfers from *his* present to *his* past'.[66] Oakeshott denies that history concerns itself with the intentions, purposes, reasons, motives or the 'deliberative calculations' of an agent, and therefore history simply cannot be conceived as the recalling, re-living, or re-enacting of past events.[67]

In addition to the determinate modes, Oakeshott identified indeterminate modes. Each fails to achieve the coherence of the determinate, and because of this lack of homogeneity, they do not have robust defences against experience as a whole. In these indeterminate modifications of experience, philosophy may intrude without irrelevance. The indeterminate modes are pseudo-philosophical. They have the character of philosophy in interrogating experience, but are abstract in falling short of unconditional experience as a whole. Ethical thought provides us with an exemplar. It does not explore morality practically, historically or scientifically. Its world of ideas does not enjoy the conditional intelligibility of the determinate modes, but it is nevertheless attached to the world as a whole. Following Bradley, Oakeshott contends that there can be no free-floating ideas detached from a world, and in consequence the world to which ethics belongs, or attaches itself, is the concrete totality of experience. Philosophical and pseudo-philosophical ideas belong to the same world, but whereas the former are aware of its world, the latter are not.[68]

In *On Human Conduct,* published some 43 years later, Oakeshott introduces difference emphases, but certainly does not abandon his earlier views as some have suggested.[69] The indeterminate modes, for example, such as ethics and political philosophy, he refers to as indeterminate levels of understanding. Each is 'certainly a platform of conditional understanding', but now he claims that they are superior to the determinate modes, or platforms of conditional understanding.[70] Those who occupy this intermediate level distinguish themselves from those who are satisfied with the conditionality of such modes as history or science, in that they investigate the conditions but do not engage in the activities they investigate. They are 'poised between heaven and earth', acknowledging the unconditional nature of theorizing, but temporarily renounce metaphysics and experience as a whole in order to occupy a platform of conditional understanding, such as political philosophy, appropriate to their needs.

CONCLUSION

In this chapter, we have shown how the British Idealists, inspired by both their German and Italian counterparts, conceived of experience in terms of modality, that is, worlds of ideas resting upon conditional postulates capable of sustaining a high degree of coherence, but falling short of the concrete totality of experience. Philosophy has as one of its roles, the investigation of the conditionality of these modes. We demonstrated the two main ways in which the relationship between the modes, and between the modes and the whole, were conceptualized: first, as a linked hierarchy of forms culminating in the absolute, and, secondly as modes autonomous of each other, but related in all being modifications, or arrests, in experience as a whole.

MONISM AND MODALITY

Special attention was given to aesthetics, or poetry, because, like metaphysics in the previous chapter, such modes emphasized the non-propositional character of some of our utterances. These are things in which we take delight without asking such questions as did it really happen, or is it a true likeness. The two conceptions of the relationship among modes (and to the whole), as exemplified by Oakeshott and Collingwood, led to different conceptions of the relationships between theory and practice. We should not, however, assume that it necessarily follows that if one ranks the modes of experience in a hierarchy one will also contend that the philosopher has a duty to inform conduct. Hegel, for example, believed in such a hierarchy but thought philosophy came onto the scene too late to influence events.

CHAPTER FOUR

POLITICAL AND ETHICAL PHILOSOPHY

INTRODUCTION

One of the most well-known dimensions of British Idealist thought is its political and ethical philosophy. Political philosophy is a crucial characteristic of some of the most celebrated works of the British Idealists, that is, books such as T. H. Green's *Lectures on the Principles of Political Obligation*, Bernard Bosanquet's *The Philosophical Theory of the State* or D. G. Ritchie's *Principles of State Interference*. However, not all the British Idealists focused directly on political philosophy. The work, for example, of F. H. Bradley is a case in point. The same holds for the works of most of the Personal Idealists, such as McTaggart, Andrew Seth Pringle-Pattison or Hastings Rashdall, where issues of religion, morality, epistemology and metaphysics figured much more prominently. A second proviso to bear in mind is that the above works on political philosophy were not written in isolation from metaphysical, epistemological or moral concerns; such concerns in fact saturate these works. This point alone makes British Idealist political philosophy unusual in terms of the prevalent anti-metaphysical concerns of the bulk of mid- to late twentieth-century Anglo-American and European political philosophy. A third rider is that in terms of *practical* political allegiance, many of the Idealist school had commitments to a form of radical or social liberalism (which we will explore in a later chapter). Although, again, there were clear exceptions: F. H. Bradley and Michael Oakeshott are cases in point. However, in this chapter, we wish to provide a critical overview of a number of the key concerns of the bulk of British Idealist political philosophy. The main sections will focus on the debates concerning the state, sovereignty, will theory, obligation, the conception of individuality, morality and the common good and citizenship.

THE STATE

British Idealist political philosophy precipitated, in many minds, a gradual reassessment of the idea and practice of the state, predominantly in the period from 1870 to 1914. The idea of the British state that Idealists were seeking to contest was largely focused on what might now be called a classical liberal vision. The broader liberal conception of the state arose from a much older intellectual tradition of European constitutionalism. The principal concerns of this constitutional tradition were to limit the scope of the state, to make it accountable and responsible for its actions and to ensure that it was committed to certain values such as liberty. The arguments of liberals in mid- to late nineteenth-century Britain varied between those who hovered close to libertarianism and anarchism, disliking the growth of the state in any sphere, or seeing it as a deeply unfortunate necessity, as against those who saw a more positive and active role for it in promoting genuine individuality, fairness and civic virtue.[1]

Herbert Spencer was a typical representative of the late nineteenth-century negative liberal response. Spencer, in fact, became a particular target of many British Idealists, such as T. H. Green, Bernard Bosanquet and D. G. Ritchie. Spencer saw the state as a regrettable but necessary 'committee of management'. He had an extensive list of "do nots" for the state. As a result, he viewed the statute book of the British state as an unmitigated disaster, legislation piled on more legislation to cure the defects of previous legislation. Such state growth interfered with genuine social evolution towards (what he termed) the "industrial society", by cultivating dependence in the population and undermining individual self-help and self-reliance. The state, for Spencer, should therefore have no concern whatsoever with aiding the poor, factory legislation, public health, drainage, sewage or even vaccination. Spencer also disapproved of any form of state involvement in education on the same grounds. He objected to state-organized postal networks and lighthouses, and, oddly, took deep exception to the British Nursing Association and National Society for the Prevention of Cruelty to Children, as overtly "collectivist" groups undermining pure individualism. On the other hand, Spencer did suggest the state control of libel laws and the regulation of pollution, noise and smoke. He also toyed with a scheme for land nationalization by the state, land ownership being regarded as an aggression against individual rights. Later in life he also conceded the need for state involvement in the upkeep of roads, pavements and sewerage. All this greatly disappointed his libertarian disciples.

A similar subdued negativity towards the state can be seen in the utilitarian liberals such as Bentham, Mill and Sidgwick. However, despite their overt commitment to a limited state, they were prepared to allow it to perform progressively more tasks, going well beyond Spencer's proposals. The science of social utility thus allowed utilitarians to assess the felicific value of state activity. There were therefore no absolute grounds to oppose state action per se. Furthermore, no continental liberals really rivalled Spencer's brand of libertarian state minimalism. For example, Benjamin Constant and Alexis de Tocqueville were both looking at limitations through balance and separation of powers within the state structure. Their major fear, however, was revolution, the growth of popular state dictatorship and the consequent decline of individual freedoms.

For the British Idealists, state action was too often seen in a negative light. Compulsion (vis-à-vis the state) was still a central feature of their argument, although in Bosanquet's terminology it was conceived as a 'hindrance to hindrances'. However, the idea of the hindrance to hindrances was not conceptualizing compulsion as negative. It was conversely seeing it as contributing to human development. As Green, for example, commented: 'The man who, of his own right feeling, saves his wife from overwork, and sends his children to school, suffers no moral degradation from a law which, if he did not do this for himself, would seek to make him do it'.[2] If a state could – by exercising force or compulsion – guarantee that factory owners did not endanger their workers with unprotected machinery, could make certain that parents sent their children to school, and ensure that unemployment insurance was legally mandatory, then, for the Idealist, none of these measures were a genuine infringement of human liberty. Such measures were, in fact, providing the conditions for a genuine richer exercise of social freedom.

The above argument did not entail that British Idealism was in any way overtly committed to state action for its own sake. As we will see, it was uniformly as uneasy (to greater and lesser degrees) with forms of collectivized organization – as in state socialism – as it with the atomized individualism of the likes of Spencer. The British Idealist philosophy of the state was therefore neither ultra-collective nor ultra-individualistic in its general ethos. There was though (as indicated) a delicate and sometimes shifting balance among different Idealists on the issue of state action. For example, Bosanquet and Green give a great deal of emphasis to individual self-reliance. Improved housing conditions or sanitation, in themselves, do not improve moral character. People have to will their self-improvement. Consequently, whereas Bosanquet took a harder line on poor relief, other Idealists, such as Jones and Muirhead, were much more sympathetic to its extension.[3] It is worth noting here that Collingwood also stood firmly in the social liberal tradition (vis-à-vis Jones and Muirhead) and believed that blatant inequalities of wealth reflected unequal relations of force, which effectively undermined individual development and freedom of choice. The state, for Collingwood, like Jones and Muirhead, thus had a positive role in eliminating force from relations among individuals in the same body politic, and between diverse bodies politic. Alternatively, Oakeshott (more in line with Bosanquet and Green), tended towards a more limited conception of state activity, in which its role was seen as upholding non-instrumental laws that provide conditions for individual initiative or choice. However, the end of the state was always (for all Idealists) the "good life" for all citizens.

Thus, what one finds in Idealism overall is a more positive rendition of the state than one finds in classical liberals, libertarians and indeed much continental liberalism. This conception was neither the result of any sudden social and political transition, nor necessarily a fundamental revision of liberal constitutionalist thought. For British Idealists, it was rather the result of a slow internal movement within certain key liberal ideas, such as liberty. It would still be true to say that this movement towards a more liberal social welfare state in the early twentieth century was accelerated by prominent British Idealist thinkers, such as Green. The Idealist notion of the state was envisaged as having a positive enabling role in society. It was not just an abstracted alien body of institutions, but rather, and quite crucially, seen as an organic outgrowth of the wills, dispositions and aspirations of the citizens comprising it. It was thus viewed as something designed for the realization of the common human purposes, which were (in the Idealist mind) coincidental with a truer conception of social individuality and liberty. The meaning and significance of the state were, in all essentials, therefore focused on the improvement and well-being of its members. This position, in an important sense, was still both individualist and committed to individual liberty. However, such liberty and individuality required the state to provide the necessary conditions for all citizens to develop.

Thus, in sum, the state for the Idealists was considered as a moral agent, with ideals and purposes that it formulated and pursued for the betterment of society as a whole. Thus Ritchie, for example, saw the state as the most adequate representative of the general will in the community.[4] For Bosanquet, it was the sustainer of the rights that underpinned any good life. Without the state the individual was nothing. This did not mean that the individual owed the state blind obedience. Contrary to the views of critics, such as H. Laski, C. E. M. Joad, L.T. Hobhouse and J. A. Hobson, the state for the Idealists was only a moral absolute when acting in conformity with its purpose of promoting and sustaining the common good. States that contravened their purpose and promoted factionalism had to be resisted on moral grounds. Green, for example, imposed no unconditional duty on the citizen to obey the law at all costs, 'since those laws may be inconsistent with the true end of the state, as the sustainer and harmoniser of social relations'.[5]

It must be remembered that Green was a great admirer of the revolutionary impetus and achievements of the English civil war. He recognized that resistance and disobedience, in certain circumstances, was absolutely necessary. Similarly, Ritchie argued that if a law was so at odds with a person's conscience, it must be disobeyed, otherwise one's self-respect and character would be degraded. The state had, however, no duty to find in favour of the individual, and an individual's resistance might, in fact, only be vindicated in the fullness of time.

These ideas, plus more radical uses of utilitarian and evolutionary thought, lay firmly behind the advent of the new liberalism in Britain. For thinkers such as Hobson and Hobhouse, and in America John Dewey, and later in the century John Rawls, the state was increasingly viewed as an integral part of the economic and social life of the community. It was not just concerned with freeing individuals from obstacles to their economic activity, but was actively involved in the promotion of a better life for its citizens. Liberals, up to the present day, have never been completely at ease with the state. The two major world wars of the twentieth century and the penetration of the state into many spheres have genuinely unsettled them to the present day. This unease was true of new liberals in Britain during and after the

First World War. However, discontent with the state has never stopped liberals from using it to promote freedom, utilizing distributive justice, establishing a legal framework for economic relations, promoting a mixed economy and providing certain public goods. The state in this sense can be an enabling institution for the good life for all citizens.

The state as such is not primarily for Idealism concerned with simply aggregating human beings, it is not merely about hegemonic power, unchallenged absolute sovereignty, military weaponry, sole jurisdiction, strict boundaries or even territory. The state is conversely an organic state of mind, will and consciousness among a wide range of individuals who have a fairly consistent perception of their social relatedness and accredit each other equally with rights. It is a condition, which has evolved gradually from earlier forms of non-state social relations. It concretizes and institutionalizes a social relatedness, which predates it – a form of profound and rich custom-based social relationship between human beings.

SOVEREIGNTY

The concept of sovereignty is closely related to that of the state in Idealism; however, it was reinterpreted in the light of the Idealists' own unique understanding. Sovereign power can and obviously is often directed at individuals contrary to their perceived interests. This issue has given rise to many hostages to fortune and often leads to arguments focused on the coercive and violent potential of states. For Idealists, the very focus that many place upon the concept of sovereignty (and "coercive power") is actually *the* root of the problem, certainly in the manner in which they are used in discussion of the practice of the state. Thus, for example, T.H. Green suggested that there was a deep "mischief" in using the concept of sovereignty in this manner. If sovereignty was just considered an alien power supervened over individuals, then it involved a radical misunderstanding.

For Idealists, such as Green, the source of this misunderstanding of sovereignty lays particularly in the writings of Thomas Hobbes and John Austin. Hobbes states the general ethos of this problematic sense of sovereignty with admirable, if ironic, clarity:

'For if we could suppose a great Multitude of men to consent in the observation of Justice, and other Lawes of Nature, without a common Power to keep them in awe; we might as well suppose all

Man-kind to do the same; and then there would-be, nor need to be any Civill Government ... because there would be Peace without subjection'.[6]

Peace without awe, terror, overt coercion and subjection is ludicrous for Hobbes. The sovereign thus 'hath the use of so much Power and strength conferred on him, that by terror thereof... he is inabled to form the wills of all ... And in him consisteth the Essence of the Commonwealth'.[7] Sovereignty becomes the crucial cement in this particular statist vernacular.

British Idealists were explicitly critical of Hobbes and Austin on this specific issue. At a very basic level, one could not be "forced" to be "obligated". Awe, force and terror are not the basis of the state. For Idealists, the Hobbesian idea that laws or rights could be pernicious, but still just, is patently unreasonable: in the words of T. H. Green's well-known lecture, 'will, not force, is the basis of the state'.[8] Ultimately, for Green, this is the "good will" embodied in the common good. In effect, the doctrine concerned with the precedence of unregulated sovereignty, leads, in turn, to unregulated reason of state. It is an argument, which therefore facilitates a political irresponsibility. This, in turn, creates the implicit danger of claims to supreme power being eagerly conceded to imprudent or iniquitous politicians, parliaments, monarchs or aristocrats. A world of unconstrained sovereigns would result in a disordered international environment. Thus, the idea of sovereignty articulated in this manner becomes an invitation to both internal tyranny and external irresponsibility. For Idealists, unconstrained abstracted sovereignty – particularly as regards both rights and freedoms – presents us with a profound quandary. Any internal order gained by sovereignty would also be continuously under threat from the potential violence and threat to external order. There was therefore something politically disquieting in the whole notion of abstract unregulated sovereignty marking out the state.

As indicated above, for Idealism therefore it is *not* coercion, power or unregulated sovereignty, as such, which marks out the state. On the contrary, it is coercion and power 'exercised in a certain way and for certain ends, that makes a state'.[9] Sovereignty is ultimately rooted, like any social institutions or social process, in a 'common desire for certain ends ...to which the observance of law or established usage contributes, and in most case implies no conscious reference on the part of those whom it influences to any coercive power at all.[10] Sovereignty needs therefore to be grasped through the idea of a state as a civil or political association. Such an association is *constituted* as a power that guarantees rights. It is a body of citizens habitually obedient to some governmental power, but the power of that governing body is not absolute or unregulated.

The notion of sovereignty embedded in the more absolutist abstracted unregulated reading thus misses the point. It gives sovereignty too much credence and *generative* power. As such it misunderstands some of the fundamental characteristics of what a state actually is. The Idealist perspective aims to establish conceptual and practical links between an account of sovereignty and an account of the social good and by default the epistemic manner in which individuals will such a social good. Sovereignty only exists insofar as it embodies, accredits and recognizes the rights of the individual citizens. The political association of the state refers, approximately, therefore to a 'sense of possessing common interest, a desire for common objects'. If this 'desire for common objects' conflicts with governmental or executive commands, then obedience will simply 'cease to operate'.[11]

WILL, NOT FORCE

One of the central ideas to be derived from the above set of arguments was a sense that the state and sovereignty had to be viewed in a different manner. One of the key concepts to arise in this new discourse was "will". Sovereignty, if it was to be meaningful, was essentially referring to the sovereignty of will, in point of fact, the general will. There are though many possible reading of this argument.

The deeper background for this theory in British Idealism lays in the work of Rousseau, Kant and Hegel. In effect, the moral agent was not seen to be governed by any causal necessity, but conversely (in potentiality) was a self-legislating and self-determining agent. The individual was thus essentially author of the principles she obeys. The Idealist tradition, in the main, adopted this Kantian-inspired theory of the will to show essentially that there was no experience or action apart from that which takes place though the medium of experience and judgement. There could be nothing prior to human experience and judgement. Will is realizing ideas or judgements in action. As F. H. Bradley put it, volition is 'the realization of itself by an idea, an idea ... with which the self here and now is identified'.[12] The background to this claim was Hegel's contention that the will is literally 'thinking translating itself into existence, thinking is the urge to give itself existence'.[13] Hegel calls this notion of will a 'self-determining universality'.

Bosanquet gives a very crisp and precise rendering of this same argument in an essay entitled 'The Reality of the General Will'. For him, the individual human mind should be considered analogous to a machine 'of which the parts are ideas or groups of ideas, all tending to pass into action'. The will can then be said to consist 'of those ideas which are guiding attention and action'.[14] For Bosanquet, though, certain ideas had a logical and systematic power to govern and focus the contents of the individual mind. Such ideas enabled the individual to grasp and solve a range of problems. Success in coping with problems reinforced the credibility and strength of such ideas and the forms of action that flowed from them. Bosanquet thought that such formative ideas reflected the real necessities of human life. He also maintained that such ideas were largely derived from the tried and tested customary institutions of social and political life itself. They formed 'the inside which reflects the material action and real conditions that form the outside'.[15] The good will, for Bosanquet, was one in which reason and will were united within certain dominant fertile ideas. These ideas ultimately formed the substance to the idea and practice of the general will.

The logical sequence of this argument was, in essential, that each individual will was an expression of a dominant, creative and reasoned idea (or colligating idea). This idea "marshalled" and "focused" the contents of the mind and structured both will and thus the actions in specific concrete ways. Such ideas were derived ultimately from pre-existing institutional structures of social existence. The general will, in this sense, was analogous to the individual will (and was in fact organically related to it). The general will thus embodied those generic creative and dominant ideas of the whole society. In the same manner that the individual marshalled the contents of their own consciousness, so the general will represented the marshalling of all the individual wills of civil society as a whole. As Bosanquet put it, the general will was 'the whole working system of dominant ideas which determines the places and functions of its members'.[16] The sovereignty of the general will embodied the sovereignty of certain dominant reasonable ideas. Such dominant ideas also figured as the crucial dimension of the good will of individuals. This, as we will see, also corresponded directly with the Idealist theory of citizenship. Overall, the good state was the organized body within which consciousness and rational will functioned. Sovereignty therefore as such was the sovereignty of the good will and thus the common good.

OBLIGATION

The above accounts of sovereignty and will were also the key to the Idealist understanding of obligation. As indicated above, at the most basic level, for Idealists one could not be "forced" to be "obligated". The structure of the state and its legal processes were present to provide the conditions for moral action. No moral action, as such, could be forced on citizens. Moral duty was distinct, in this sense, from legal and political obligation. What the state does is to restrain the inclinations of individuals – what Bosanquet called 'hindering of hindrances' – to enable and encourage individuals to see that they shared a common life with others. The best account of law would therefore be one that brings individuals to a point where they have the possibility to realize their moral nature. Self-realization is thus largely dependent upon the background conditions of state and legal action. This forms the basis for the principles of political and legal obligation. Law and the state cannot make citizens morally good, but they can restrain certain elements of human action that would undermine the common good of society and prevent humans realizing their potential capacities. Obligations thus refer largely to external acts. The individual is obligated to the state insofar as he or she seeks the common good. If such a state enforces certain responsibilities (premised on the common good), it is no infringement of individual freedom.

The above theory entailed a negative and critical account of the classical liberal individualist vision of obligation, which often focused on devices such as contract theory to explicate obligation. The idea of any hypothetical or historical condition in which individuals made contracts and consented to obey the state struck the majority of Idealists as nonsensical. At most one could say that contract and the related idea of natural right were symbolic devices indicating something important about the character of law and obligation. There were though *qualified* exceptions to this Idealist argument. The later writings of Collingwood, for example, do employ a specific understanding of contract. Yet, even though Collingwood was a social contract theorist of sorts, he did not use the device for the same purposes as either traditional classical liberal thinkers or the modern liberal contractarians of the Rawlsian generation. Freedom of will and choice were nonetheless still crucial to his conception of what it is to be human.

For Collingwood, to exercise free will positively is to choose, and negatively it is to be free from desires in the sense of not being at their mercy.[17] Given this emphasis upon choice, it is not surprising that civil association, for Collingwood, is best characterized as the result of freedom of choice. The capacity for free choice is not, however, itself freely chosen, it is an achievement, but it is not consciously willed.[18] It is attained by an act of self-liberation at a crucial stage in the development of the individual human mind. It is a liberation from one's desires, and liberation to make decisions, to choose between alternatives, rather than merely to express self-interested preferences. To prefer one thing over another is simply to suffer desire for one thing among alternatives. Self-liberation from desire is achieved by naming the desire, it is an act of speech, using the language of the community to which the person belongs. Collingwood is not therefore talking about an isolated atomized individual, contracting via a pre-social state of nature. It is conversely an individual who already *belongs* to a community, but who is not yet fully social. The qualifications for conversion from the non-social community to the social community vary according to the historical circumstances facing bodies politics, and the capacities the ruling class deem the ruled possess.

A body politic, for Collingwood, is thus a community comprised of non-social and social elements, people capable of exercising free will, or choice, and those who are not. The former are self-governing and have freely agreed to associate, the latter are incapable of such choice and are therefore governed by those who comprise the social element. Because the relationship is unequal, the one ruling over the other without their consent, an element of force is invariably involved. This force cannot be totally eradicated, because a body politic can never completely eliminate the non-social element, that is, those who have not yet reached mental maturity. What Collingwood means by force is moral or mental strength exercised by one person over another in order to make him or her perform an act that the mentally stronger wants. Force is relative in that anyone occupying a place at a higher level of consciousness than another is able to make that weaker person comply with his or her will by the exercise of mental strength or superiority.[19]

ETHICS AND THE COMMON GOOD

Ethical themes permeate the bulk of Idealist political philosophy, although the relation between ethics and politics still remains multifaceted. The key treatises on ethics for the British Idealists, between the 1870s and the 1920s, were Bradley's *Ethical Studies* (1876) and Green's *Prolegomena to Ethics* (1883). Others, such as Muirhead, Mackenzie and Bosanquet, also wrote more synoptic works on ethics, but the former works by Green and Bradley retained a certain pre-eminence.

Primarily, Idealistic ethics is premised on the idea of human sociality, although it is a complex and nuanced understanding of this idea. Basically, sociality implies that ethics is a body of directives, to which one is obligated, which are required both by other persons and oneself, within a form of associated life. We might call this a *communal directive* account of ethics. The fundamental aim of this theory is to bring together, on the one hand, the individual's own will and judgements, with, on the other hand, the laws and institutions of an organized life in the state. As a result, in Hegel's terminology, the individual can be seen to be part of an "ethical substance" that consists of "laws and powers", where 'these substantial determinations are *duties* which are binding on the will of the individual'.[20] The relation of the individual to the communal directives is intricate. It is not a relativist argument, such that *any* kinds of communal directives are permissible. Rather, such directives refer to the necessary conditions for creating a moral obligation – as embedded in a rational state – and premised on undergirding the freedom and self-realization of its citizens. There is thus a duty imposed, but the interests and particularity of the individual are lifted above any thin or self-centred concerns. Moral obligations are seen to occur from *within* the associated norms of a civil community of which they are an element.

This idea of a social ethics – outlined above – is premised against the backdrop of an Idealist ontology, namely a form of social individualism. As Bradley comments 'what we call an individual man is what he is because of and by virtue of community, and ...communities are thus not mere names but something real, and can be regarded (if we mean to keep to facts) only as the one in the many'.[21] In short, individuals are intrinsically social. Persons realize themselves as social beings. The rational form of associated social life is usually correlated by British Idealists with a form of civil state.

Certain oddities do though remain within Idealist ethics. One issue concerns whether Idealist ethical theory is simply a form of meta-ethical reasoning and thus has, potentially, no justificatory role. This complex relation between theory and practice is something that we have noted in earlier chapters. For example, Bradley remarks in *Ethical Studies* that: 'All philosophy has to do is "to understand what is", and moral philosophy has to understand morals which exist, not to make them or give directions for making them. Philosophy in general has not to anticipate the discoveries of the particular sciences nor the evolution of history; the philosophy of religion has not to make a new religion... political philosophy has not to play tricks with the state, but to understand it; and ethics has not to make the world moral'.[22] Philosophy looks back at the world cut and dried and reflects critically upon what is.[23] Moral practice is *not* something that flows from the philosopher's premises. Bradley caricatures the alternative view as the "moral almanac" view of the world (a view which he thinks plagues utilitarians).[24]

Green unexpectedly articulates a very similar argument to both Bradley and Hegel.[25] He admits, for example, that most of us suffer moral perplexity, yet philosophical theories of the good are generally 'superfluous' at such points.[26] The concrete lived process is crucial for morality, *not* overt philosophical arguments. As Green notes: 'Any value which a true moral theory may have... depends on its being applied and interpreted by a mind in which the ideal, as a practical principle, already actuates'.[27] Consequently, he contends that moral ideas 'are not abstract conceptions'. Conversely, they 'actuate men independently of the operations of the discursive intellect'.[28] Such ideas are deeply at work in human practices long before they are philosophically understood.[29] They 'not only give rise to institutions and modes of life, but also express themselves in forms of the imagination', that is, in poetry and the arts generally.[30] To get anything from philosophy, one needs to have already *had* moral discipline, a discipline that 'cannot be derived from philosophy'.[31] He therefore suggests that moral philosophy 'is only needed to remedy the evils which it has itself caused'.[32]

This strand of Idealist ethical theorizing can also be observed in the work of Michael Oakeshott, although he gives the argument an extra contingent twist. Like Hegel, Bradley and to a degree Bosanquet, Oakeshott contends that we come into a world 'already illuminated by moral practice'.[33] Moral language is, however, a shifting body of conventions. He notes, vis-à-vis morality, that 'its abstract nouns (right and wrong, proper and improper, obligation, dueness, fairness, respect, justice, etc.), when they appear, are faded metaphors'. He adds here, with no doubt, a weather eye on many contemporaneous Kantian and utilitarian political theorists of the 1970s and 1980s, 'it is only the uneducated who insists that each must have a single unequivocal meaning indifferent to context'. Moral language, embodied in conduct, is never fixed or finished. It has no settled meaning. Echoing a Wittgensteinian argument, he claims that moral language is *only* learned in use. He comments that moral language '*is* its vicissitudes, and its virtue is to be a living, vulgar language'.[34] A language of moral conduct 'has rhythms which remain when the words are forgotten'. Thus, there is a sense in which such language is an embedded substrate of actions. Agents will, in fact, often lose any sense of its genesis and "ideal character", consequently, 'expressions in it harden into clichés and are released again; the ill-educated speak it vulgarly, the purists inflexibly, and each generation invents its own moral slang'.[35]

To focus on moral "rules" – as a large number of contemporary moral philosophers do – is, for Oakeshott, to engage in a distortion of moral conduct. Rules are just "abridgements", passing contingent snapshots of fluid and restless phenomena. Rules suggest a rigid and abstracted expression of such conduct. Thus, rules are *not* the reality of morality or politics. Further, to focus excessive attention on the *justification* of rules is also utterly misplaced, since it again cuts into the living flesh of a moral language. Moral rules 'are not criteria of good conduct, nor are they primarily instruments of judgement; they are prevailing winds which agents should take account of in sailing their several courses'.[36] Thus, morality cannot be just about observed rules or obeying injunctions. It is also not concerned with justification. It is a much more complex contingent process used for both exploring one's own self and also one's interaction with other agents. Rules can be elicited as representations of a moment, but morality is emphatically not the same as that "one moment", nor is it the creation of moralists or grammarians (as Oakeshott phrases it). It is made in and through ordinary conventional usage.

A related idiosyncrasy within Idealist ethics concerns what actually marks out Idealist ethics as distinctive. Has it any specific character, such as the Kantian categorical imperative or the utilitarian maximization of happiness? As indicated above, one popular response to this question has been to emphasize the credo embedded in Bradley's 'station and duties' essay, although this has been occasionally modified into a form of relativistic communitarianism. This latter body of views characterizes many crude and uninformed estimates of Idealist ethics. Henry Sidgwick, for example, in one of the first hostile reviews of Bradley's *Ethical Studies* in *Mind* (1876), complains that his Idealist ethics does not really advance much beyond a crude sociological relativism.[37] Sidgwick was clearly both just wrong and ill-considered in his judgment, but it nonetheless encapsulated a very pervasive cartoon version of Idealist ethics, which figures to the present day. In general, the station and duties essay and the crude sociologically inspired communitarianism both represent caricatured misunderstandings of Idealism.

What is missing in such criticism (above) is another broad dimension of Idealist ethical philosophy; this concerns the principles that ought to govern our moral conduct. A philosophical ethics worth its salt should, in this latter view, be providing rigorous justificatory reasons for specific kinds of conduct. Some critics have argued that this dimension of Idealist ethical theory is hampered by the relativist preoccupations of the former more meta-ethically inclined argument. There is undoubtedly a philosophical problem here but it can be, in part, resolved in terms of the argument laid out earlier linking the individual's will and judgement with a particular type of rational social organization.[38]

The easiest way to look at this latter normative idea is in the context of Green's arguments on the common good. The underpinning for this latter argument can be found in Green's *Prolegomena to Ethics*, which tries to give the philosophical grounds for what, in a sense, we know already and indeed practice. This sense of "already known" reflects what Green, Bradley and Bosanquet think of as the *concrete lived process*, which precedes explicit philosophical argument. It is the extant institutions of civil society, the laws, conventions, religion and literature, which both embody and suggest such moral ideas. Morality is not invented, but articulated from within existing practices.

Green's philosophical arguments here involve an extended refutation of the idea of naturalistic explanation of human action. Further, for Green there can be no naturalistic account of morals. Green, like Kant, counters naturalism by arguing that experience is not a chaotic manifold, but is rather the awareness of an enduring unified subject. He differs from Kant insofar as the experiential manifold *cannot* be accounted for independently of the activity of the human mind. This is because it is only minds or consciousness that can make intellectual relationships. The self is the author of the world it knows. Mind is its own act. Without the conscious subject – presupposed in experience – any experience would be impossible. Thus, knowledge of the experiential world (and nature) could *not* explain the nature of knowledge.

Green has a specific moral purpose in refuting naturalism. A human driven solely by natural instincts makes little sense of morality. It is in the individual mind's activity that morality can be found. In each individual there is a spiritual possibility, which stands above the naturalistic claim. Humans are thus distinguished from animals by the ability to self-consciously think about their desires. The fact that a desire is conceived implies that the self is distinguished from the desire. The conceived desire is a motive. A motive is therefore not physiologically caused, but is rather an end which a conscious subject presents to itself and which it strives to realize in actions. The self posits an object that will satisfy the conceived desire. A desire might thus be seen as a tendency to realize an object. In all actions, an individual is positing an object that will satisfy the conceived desire, a state that he or she takes to be good. A conscious human mind thus pursues ends that are not caused, but rather self-posited.

However, for Idealists such as Green, the good is the object that truly satisfies the self, something that constitutes a more complete realization of the self. Pleasure and happiness are possible by-products of moral action. However, the self could not be identified with such by-products. The good could not be a discrete passing sensation. Epistemologically, Idealists associated this idea of discrete passing sensations with atomistic and extreme individualist theory. In this sense, knowledge was derived from sensations, perceptions and experiences, via an engagement with an external world. Truth claims therefore entailed correspondence with this external world. For Idealists, in very general terms (as we have already seen), the self could not be identified with any series of discrete perceptions, experiences or sensations, since the self, as such, was seen as the presupposition to there being any sensations, perceptions of experiences, particularly sensations or experiences that were identified in terms of a series. For Idealism therefore knowledge of the world exists only in the context of the self-conscious subject. There could be no experience of things antecedent to the conscious subject. Thus, a consistent empiricist account of knowledge (characteristic of utilitarian thought) would literally be speechless unless it presupposed a conscious subject as the ground for such a series.

Morally, utilitarianism was therefore seen as a seriously problematic doctrine insofar as it was linked in the minds of most Idealists to an unsubstantiated abstract atomism. Utilitarianism was seen to treat human individuals as, more or less, self-enclosed homogeneous moral atoms, with similar feelings that could be mechanically quantified, and among whom a quantity of pleasures could be distributed. Its demand on institutions was that they justified themselves in terms of their conduciveness to the general happiness. Utilitarianism consequently assumed a narrow uniformity of human nature over time and place. It combined the abstract individualism of treating every person as a discrete unit, with the abstract universalism concerning its view of happiness, which is taken to have an existence divorced from the concrete individuals who are singularly capable of experiencing it.

Green, in rejecting utilitarianism, argued that certain objects of will are more conducive to self-realization. Moral activity is the pursuit of an ideal set by ourselves and to which we aspire; it constitutes a possible self that we could become. In the moral sphere, this entails constant endeavours. Freedom is understood as motivated action that *transforms* impulses and instincts to serve ends and purposes with which one has identified one's self. Freedom is thus self-realization and actualization of the possible self. The moral ideal, which is the object of free endeavour, is the realization of the good will, that is to say, the will that transforms and transfigures the passions and instincts. If one specified this ideal in more detail, there is then no hard and fast distinction between an individual and a public good; an individual's possible self has an intrinsic social dimension. Another way of describing this whole social dimension is the "common good".

The common good is, for Green, the complete realization of the potential of the human being.[39] This entails a maturity of a character, which wills the good, because it is good. Individuals only turn out to be good if they take the perfection of their character in themselves and others as their endeavour. The good is common in being the same good for all. It is therefore non-competitive.[40] Further, the common good cannot be any material object, which could be contended for, although there could be a conflict between a moral and material interest. Putting material goods first is, by definition, selfishness. The common good is the moral ideal, which should organize and guide a person's action. It presents a motive for action and a standard to evaluate actions. Many pre-1914 Idealists followed Green on this particular line of argument.

Green also suggests that there are criteria that allow one to ascertain whether a particular law or policy reflects the common good. Thus it should be good for all, no one should gain by another's loss, and everyone should be considered equally in terms of loss and gain. This common good is, in fact, crucial to Green's theory; it provides the basis for his whole discussion of politics. Laws, institutions and states only have significance insofar as they contribute to the common good. These structures do not make men moral in themselves, that requires motives and reasons, but they can provide a crucial enabling function.

One critical point to note here is that Green himself indicates, at points, that the common good is not an overtly distributive principle. The common good was not concerned with the equal ownership of resources or equal distribution. Material equalities alone will not achieve a common good. Material goods are mutable, finite and scarce. Mutual respect and citizenship did not for Green require therefore a radical revision of inequalities of property. However, unquestionably this argument gave rise to a number of hostages to fortune in Idealist argument. On one count (as indicated earlier in this chapter), it is clear that Bosanquet derived his theory of citizenship, and containment of state action with regard to poverty, from the principles outlined in one reading of Green's account of the common good. Problematically, though, the common good can be seen to be explicitly identified with particular capacities, and in an environment with scare resources, this could lead to potential competition. Green is clearly hesitant on this issue. He comments, for example, in comparing Greek slavery to modern industrial work, that all humans have the exact same "undeveloped possibility". There is thus an underlying expectation of formal equality in civil states. He continues that no one in a civilized state can enjoy their condition when 'the mass of men whom we call our brethren, and whom we declare to be meant with us for eternal destinies, are left without the chance ...of making themselves in act what in possibility we believe them to be'.[41] The implication of Green's argument, both here and in his writings on liberalism and positive liberty, indicates that materially some citizens might have to forgo some of their property interests for the sake of others' development. In this sense, as other Idealists such as Ritchie and Jones clearly read him, the common good argument entailed an impetus towards social justice and distribution, if only to enable and provide equal opportunities for citizens. It is here that we find the intellectual grounds for Green's ethical socialist legacy.[42]

RIGHTS

Idealists developed a distinctive theory of rights, which rejected conceptions of natural rights both in their normative and naturalistic forms. The natural right legacy, which posited universal laws independent of the individuals who were subject to them and either written in men's hearts, or apprehended by the exercise of pure reason, did not, for them, pay adequate attention to the interests and motivations of individuals. They were abstract laws capable of many interpretations when translated into concrete situations. Such laws were exemplified by Locke in his *Second Treatise*. The rights we have are derivative from the laws and generally have correlative obligations. If I have a right to private property, and I own a piece of land, you have a duty to respect my right to the use of that land unhindered. The foundation upon which these rights were based usually and ultimately rested upon a belief in a Divine power, which provided justification for why I may be obligated to perform such a duty. Even Grotius, who is often said to have secularized the natural rights tradition, always resorted to arguments that brought God back into the equation as the ultimate source of obligation. Reason facilitates our comprehension of natural laws, both *a priori* and *a posteriori*, but no amount of reason can create an obligation to discharge the duties associated with these rights. The obligation ultimately rests on God's will.

On the other hand, the Idealists were also critical of naturalistic, or descriptive, conceptions of natural rights. These are the natural rights about which Hobbes wrote. They relate more to our appetites and desires than to reason. They are rights without obligations, and when everyone has a right to everything, no one has a right to anything. If I take an apple off a tree, I have a right to it because I want it, but if you also want it you too have a right, what decides the matter will be the superior strength or force of one of the disputants. If a wild beast cannot live without meat, then it has a right to kill and eat its prey. If I happen to be the object of the animal's appetite, I have no correlative obligation to submit to its will. In other words, they are not moral rights. The foundation of these rights is basic human nature, or appetite and instinct. We have seen already that nature cannot for the Idealists be the basis of morality, and the isolated unencumbered self upon which these rights are posited is a fiction.

The British Idealists formulated the rights recognition thesis in reaction to natural rights theories. Philosophically traditional natural rights theories had been discredited, but the rhetoric of natural rights was still very much alive in political debate across the range of ideological persuasions. While rejecting the traditional formulations of natural rights, they did not want to deny that some rights are so fundamental that without them we would cease to be what we are, and in this sense they are fundamental, and therefore just as well be regarded as natural.

T. H. Green sets the tone for the Idealist theory. For Green rights exist independently of political society. They are manifest in the family, even among a group of slaves in their relations with each other, and within the broader community to which they are related. In Green's view, a person develops through the development of society, and this was something that natural rights theorists such as Spinoza, Hobbes and Locke were unable to appreciate. They were mistaken in thinking that the higher essence of the person could be separated from the social norms of society. The question for Green was why in their relations with others certain powers are recognized by people as those that ought to be exercised or secured for possible exercise.

Rights are, for Green, those powers possessed by an individual that others recognize as necessary for the achievement of a shared good.[43] There are three elements to this claim. First, a right is a power; secondly, it is recognized by society, or by other persons; and thirdly, it is a contribution to a common good. Recognition makes rights, and therefore recognition is a necessary condition, along with the fact that they must also be powers and contribute to the common good. Society is able to justify the possession of powers, or capabilities, by individuals and those that it exercises over them because they are a necessary prerequisite to fulfilling 'man's vocation as a moral being'.[44] We understand rights in this way, not because they are natural, but because the individual has the capacity to imagine a good that is common, which is the same for others as for himself, or herself, and is inspired to act on that conception. Rights are what enable our capacities to be realized, and serve to define the moral person.[45] Despite the fact that a person is not born with the rights or powers necessary for fulfilling such a conception of the moral person, and does not possess them outside of society, they[rights] are not arbitrary creations of law or custom. They are natural in a different sense from that required in the natural law and natural rights traditions because 'they arise out of, and are necessary for the fulfilment of, a moral capacity without which a man would not be a man'.[46] David Ritchie understood such rights to be natural only in the sense that they are those 'legal or customary rights we have come to believe most advantageous to recognise'.[47] Rights are an appeal to what is socially useful for both the present and future generations, and where possible for humanity as a whole.[48]

While there are variations among the Idealists on matters of detail, the recognition theory of rights as articulated by each has certain common features in addition to the rejection of the descriptive and prescriptive versions of natural rights. The Idealists believe that the definition of a right is inextricably tied to social recognition, by society or the state, or both. Rights do not exist without recognition. In Green, there are two senses to the term, which are not always clearly distinguished. Recognition as the creation of a right, and recognition as acknowledging that a rule or practice is a right. Justification is separate from definition. A right is justified by its contribution to the common good, understood by each to be common to all. This is what is typically known as the general will, which must be distinguished from the particular wills of sectional interests. Both the definition and justification of a right are designed to refute the charge that on the descriptive model they are capricious and arbitrary based on individual self-interest and human desires, and on the intuitionist model they are abstract and incapable of being translated into moral imperatives. In summary, rights are firmly embedded in and are dependent on moral communities. We will see in Chapter 6 how these communities may even extend beyond state borders.

INDIVIDUALITY AND CITIZENSHIP

As suggested earlier, the idea of society based on mutual individual limitation and contract was a prevalent theme underpinning nineteenth-century classical liberal political theory and practice. For Henry Sidgwick, for example, in his *Elements of Politics* (1897), contract was seen to be of fundamental importance for the whole individualistic structure. The contract was essential to unite the individual atoms of society. The concept of the citizen deployed in such classical liberal thinking might loosely be described as *negative* in character. The citizen was viewed as an independent agent with partially preformed desires and interests. The function of any public order was to protect and uphold these fundamental atomized human interests. These interests were often spoken of in terms of rights – natural or civil. Citizenship was thus conceived negatively in terms of the legal protection of pre-existing rights to, for example, life, liberty and property. The actual private concerns and interests of individuals were though distinct from the formal but minimal public ethos of citizenship – although at the same time the notion of the citizen still implied an internal private autonomy of the individual. For classical liberal theorists, throughout the nineteenth and twentieth century, although individuals may have lost some of the "civic" benefits of close communal life, nonetheless, they had gained from the privacy, modern liberty and new found prosperity of commercial liberal society. Classical liberal views on citizenship generally excluded any positive rights or entitlements to economic and social resources, as parts of any programme of collective good or social justice. Unencumbered economic markets, within this perspective, were the preferred mode of resource allocation. Essentially, this was a procedural, minimal, constitutional and rule of law governed understanding of politics.

The Idealist response to this latter vision of liberal individuality drew upon a distinction between two important senses of individualism, that is, an older and newer variant or alternatively a passive and active variant. These terms also correspond with distinct understandings of citizenship. The older individualism (of classical liberalism), which envisaged society as an aggregation of atomized particulars, gave a thin and inaccurate reading of social life for most Idealists. The units of analysis were empty asocial individuals.[49] Thin individualism, which was seen as both abstractly conceived and socially false (whether it appeared in Jacobin revolutionaries or abstract liberal political economy), was the root to passive or negative citizenship, as found in the classical liberal views of Sidgwick, Bentham and Spencer. Conversely, for British Idealists, the thicker or richer understanding of "social individualism" or "positive individualism" recognized the deep social nature of humans, rooted in the idea of citizens having a common social identity and substance and actually recognizing a sense of the *common good*. The older individualism's appeal to the importance of self-help and character cut little ice for Idealists. Self-help and character were not something that flourished in glorious social isolation; rather, as Henry Jones put it succinctly, 'The interpreter of *character* can no longer rely on the old individualism: he must study it in relation to the social life, of which it is both cause and effect, both expression and product.'[50]

Civil association and the state were, for the Idealists, viewed as rooted in the social nature of human beings (as indicated in previous sections). They were the means for individual self-realization and character development. They existed to draw forth the potentialities of the individual. The possibility for such development depended upon the existence of articulate and ethically rooted social institutions. Each human individual was thus seen as a spiritual possibility, which could be realized through civil association. Human good was identified with practices that provided an enduring contribution to the common good of fellow citizens. It was this common good (as embodied in the state) that provided true satisfaction for a more permanent understanding of the human self.[51] The permanent self was thus at one with the common good.

Civic institutions were the outward form or expression of these moral ideals. Therefore the only justification for civic institutions was their contribution towards the moral development of individuals. The communal good could not therefore be divorced from the individual good. Individuals only had rights and duties as members of the civic community – a community that should enable individuals to develop. Green, Bosanquet, Caird, Jones, Ritchie, among others, all shared similar concerns here. They all wished to transcend what they believed to be the false opposition between individualism and collectivism. There were though some exceptions to this thesis in the Idealist ranks. For example, Michael Oakeshott, particularly in works such *Rationalism in Politics* (1962) and *On Human Conduct* (1975), moved away from the above Idealist arguments towards a more limited conception of the state's role as a civil association (as distinct from an enterprise association). Oakeshott, together with F. H. Bradley, thus tended to be more sceptical in his Idealism and indeed his political ideas. The crucial distinction, for Oakeshott, was between instrumental rules appropriate for achieving substantive purposes, and appropriate to joint enterprises with specific goals, such as the maximization of production and profit, and non-instrumental rules. These are rules that are adjectival, and are taken into account when making our own decisions about substantive ends. These latter rules are more appropriate to civil association, and therefore limit the extent to which the state may formulate and implement "five-year" plans or substantive common goals. Every state is the embodiment of the two ideal characters he articulates, but in the modern era, he regrets, enterprise association has tended to dominate. Oakeshott's concern reflects the reservations that earlier Idealists had that any increase in state activity must be justified in terms of enhancing individual responsibility and increasing their capacities for choice.

In terms of the earlier main elements of the Idealist school – Green, Bosanquet, Caird and Jones – the central category of political philosophy was and remained "citizenship". This had intrinsic connections to concepts such as positive liberty, morality, the common good and character. Citizenship implied a consciousness of the ethical ends of human life as embodied within the institutional structures of the state, in other words, a consciousness of the common good. Citizenship was not just a political or legal category. It was a state of mind and social being. It carried theological, epistemological and ontological implications. The citizen assimilated ethical norms by participating in social life. Citizenship thus denoted a high level of civic awareness, moral character, rationality and a strong sense of duty. In terms of this strong sense of citizenship, the state was consequently seen as the organized body within which this citizen consciousness functions. For Idealists, society and its institutional structures were the means to individual self-realization. Social institutions were justified only to the extent that they furthered the self-realization of individuals.

Idealists tended to view all political concepts from this general standpoint. Rights, duties, property and freedom were conditional devices to allow individuals to realize their (ethical) powers and abilities and thus the common good. It was only by willing the common good that the citizens became truly free. The nub of the Idealist vision of politics was therefore that of providing an ethical "enabling state". If there was one important intellectual bequest from Idealism, it was an ethical theory of citizenship combined with the enabling state. This also provided one important undergirding for the early-twentieth-century vision of the welfare state.

The above argument did leave a problematic legacy to the twentieth century. It underpinned to a degree the new liberal understandings of state, welfare and citizenship in the 1900s. The Idealist legacy on this issue was ambivalent for two reasons. First, Idealism was essentially trying to adapt active civic citizenship ideas to British liberalism. Secondly, the more antique Greek side of the Idealist civic legacy was strongly present in many Idealist writers. Bernard Bosanquet provides one example of this tendency. In his article 'The Duties of Citizenship' (1895), Bosanquet commented ruefully that 'The commonest Greek citizen could never altogether forget that his actual existence was bound up with the discharge of civic duty'. Bosanquet goes on to complain that even the most educated citizen in Britain in the 1890s, of his time, did not appear to grasp the need for civic duties. Individual acquisitive self-interest was uppermost.[52] Bosanquet's, like T. H. Green's, interest in citizenship was therefore duty-orientated. Both lamented the growth of liberal individualist self-interest and conversely stressed the need for strong civic duties correlative with rights. The citizen was not simply the passive recipient of rights, but an active self-realizing being with recognized civic duties to fellow citizens.

The new liberal conception of citizenship, which reacted to the classical liberal perspective from the 1880s, was initially theorized in terms of civic duties, as well as a more expansive vision of rights. The civic duty component was crucial to the initial justification of the welfare state in the pre-1914 period. Yet, the stress on liberal rights also maintained an underlying self-conscious continuity with classical liberalism. This continuity had an unexpected cost. The emphasis on rights slowly weakened the idea of public-spirited civic duties as correlative to such rights. By deploying such negative rights language new liberals, unintentionally, set the stage for the gradual decline, during the twentieth century, of solidaristic notions of public-spirited civic duty. From its inception, the new liberalism therefore embodied a complex tension, which has carried through to the present day in Britain. This tension focused on the conflict between civism and civility, between an essentially "rights-orientated" passive recipience vision (which tended to affect the way individuals viewed welfare and distributive justice) and a civic activist vision of duties to the common good. This tension highlights part of the late-twentieth-century sense of crisis within the welfare state – a crisis centred on the conflict between passive rights entitlements and active civic duties. Paradoxically, this complex tension was introduced by the new liberalism, via some of the important writings of British Idealism.

CONCLUSION

In politics and morality, particularly before 1914, British Idealist philosophy precipitated, in many minds, a fundamental reassessment of some of the key values of liberalism, the state and the purpose of political life. T.H. Green, as indicated, was a particularly important figure. The Idealists did not suggest a wholesale revision of civil and moral existence, more a bringing to fruition of some of its latent tendencies for social reform, implicit in the liberal state. In certain cases, the Idealist ethical and political philosophy, with some notable exceptions, provided a cogent rationale for a more welfare-orientated social liberalism, enabling it to meet, more humanely, the problems of an increasingly complex industrial society. This latter Idealist vision of the state largely prevailed as a background thematic in Britain until the 1980s, when we see, ironically, the rebirth of its old adversary, that is, classical liberal market-orientated theory.

CHAPTER FIVE

IDEALISM AS A PRACTICAL CREED

INTRODUCTION

Having outlined some of the central components of Idealist metaphysics, epistemology, political and moral philosophy, the focus now shifts to some of the more specific practical applications of British Idealist thought. Idealism saw itself, particularly in many of its pre-1914 exponents, as an immensely practical philosophy. As should be obvious by now, there were other Idealists who were deeply sceptical of this impetus. However, certainly in terms of the earlier group, the sceptics were largely in a minority on this practical issue. The present discussion will centre on the political and ideological context of British Idealist thought, particularly the interplay with doctrines such as Liberalism and socialism. This will then lead to a consideration of the issues of education, poverty, social work, property, temperance and liberty.

POLITICAL CONTEXT

We should not lose sight of the fact that during the early years of the twentieth century, mainstream intellectual debate was less compartmentalized and more obviously elitist than it is today. There was a great deal of personal and intellectual contact between people, who described themselves as belonging to different political persuasions, but who nevertheless moved in relatively fluid social circles. Liberals and democratic socialist thinkers largely inhabited the same intellectual milieu, often together with the more intellectual conservatives and libertarians. They belonged to the same organizations and discussion groups and often became related to one another through marriage. The Idealist and Liberal politician R. B. Haldane was a close personal friend of the Fabian socialist Webbs, and Henry Jones was an acquaintance of the socialist writer Sidney Ball. L.T. Hobhouse, despite his deep criticism of Bosanquet, remained a lifelong admirer of T. H. Green as well as an acute and sympathetic observer of the labour movement. D. G. Ritchie was also a member of the Fabian society for a number of years. It was Edward Caird who persuaded R. H. Tawney and William Beveridge to visit the Idealist-inspired Toynbee Hall University Settlement. Beveridge later became Tawney's brother-in-law. Tawney became a member of the Fabian Society only in 1906 and the Independent Labour Party in 1909, but nevertheless remained close to New Liberals and was intellectually indebted to Idealism. What united many of the Idealists, New Liberals, Liberal Socialists and Social Democrats at this time was a fundamental agreement that classical Liberalism had produced social and economic conditions of such deplorable dimensions, that the deliverance of many working people from their wretched predicament was seen as a deep humanistic duty. It was thus common among progressives to acknowledge the considerable overlaps between the New Liberalism and Democratic Socialism.

ARE RADICALS SOCIALIST?

British Idealists had a fluid relation with contemporaneous ideologies, particularly Socialism and Liberalism. Many retained a close sympathy and in some cases, such as Green, Jones, Bosanquet and Haldane, a direct association with the Liberal Party. Despite this association with Liberalism, there was nonetheless a strong underlying admiration, from the earliest years of Idealism, for the more radical aspect of Liberal politics. By the Edwardian era, this led, in some cases, to a direct sympathy and qualified support for the parliamentary democratic socialism of the Independent Labour Party.[1]

In 1882, Arnold Toynbee – a student of T.H. Green – gave a speech in Newcastle entitled 'Are Radicals Socialist?'. The theme of the speech was addressed largely to British Liberals concerned about the rising tide of state growth. As Toynbee noted, for many in the Liberal Party 'startling legislative measures ...have been defended by arguments in sharp contrast to the ancient principles [of liberalism]'. However, the gravest of the charges was that some form of socialism underpinned such liberal measures – socialism being 'a system which in the past [liberals] strained every nerve to oppose'.[2] Toynbee was referring here to a range of measures, such as the Irish Land Bill (1881), The Ground Game Act (1880) and The Employers' Liability Act (1880). For Toynbee, the Liberal radicals were using the same vocabulary as older Liberals, but they were subtly modifying it from within. Such Acts, for Toynbee, demonstrated that radicals were not socialists in the sense advocated by Robert Owen, but they were nonetheless advocating a subtly different form of socialism. One essential aspect of this new radicalism was that there could not be genuine *freedom of contract* between unequals. Toynbee's key point here was that the social and moral principles defended by earlier Liberals were being extended by radicals in the 1880s, through richer readings of social equality and freedom. Liberal radicals were now cognizant of the argument that 'under certain conditions the people cannot help themselves, and that then they should be helped by the state representing directly the whole people'.[3] The flexibility of the principles of Liberalism for Toynbee was such as to give rise to new understated forms of political interpretation. As T. H. Green commented, in a similar vein:

> 'The immediate object of reformers and the form of persuasion by which they seek to advance them, vary much in different generations. To the hasty observer they might even seem contradictory, and to justify the notion that nothing better than a desire for change selfish or perverse is at the bottom of all reforming movements. Only those who think a little longer about it can discern the same old cause of social good against class interests, for which under altered names, liberals are fighting now as they were fifty years ago'.[4]

The problematic socialism that Toynbee had in mind here was initially associated with what is now called Utopian socialism, that is, the work of, for example, Charles Fourier and Robert Owen. Marxian socialism, although having an impact in France and Germany from the 1870s, initially had little significant role in British political thought and practice. It was first embodied in Britain, in an eccentric form, in the 1880s Social Democratic Federation, whose effect was minimal. Marxism, as such, did not really "take off" until the 1920s in Britain, and even then tended to remain at one remove from the mainstream of British socialist thought. It was also rejected by the

British tradition of democratic socialism, beginning with the Fabians and early Independent Labour Party in the 1890s. Many British Idealists were clearly aware of the existence of Marxian socialism from the 1890s, but took it to be relatively inconsequential.

There was a definite community of views among British Idealists on socialism, which echoed Toynbee's distinction between acceptable and unacceptable readings. In effect, British Idealists focused on *two* broad forms of socialist thought. The first was (in their view) instrumental and mechanistic. It maintained that public ownership and the imposition of rigid material equality through the state sufficed. In other words, it placed heavy reliance on the collectivized administered vision of the state. Idealists tended to associate this form with the administrative statism of the Fabians, particularly the work of Sidney and Beatrice Webb, as well as some of the earlier Utopian and materialistic socialisms. Thus, Edward Caird noted – like J. S. Mill in *Chapters on Socialism* – a distinction between a more "dogmatic socialism", which he associated with Robert Owen and Charles Fourier, and a "new socialism", which was "ethical" in character. Caird mentioned the Fabian socialist, Sidney Ball, as an exemplification of the latter. This "truer" socialism was seen to provide a more effective opposition to the individualistic tendencies of classical Liberalism.[5]

A similar distinction was drawn by J. S. Mackenzie, in his *Introduction to Social Philosophy* (1895), between "ethical socialism" and "scientific socialism". Mackenzie associated the latter quite explicitly with Marxism. However, Mackenzie did admit that 'socialism is a term of great elasticity of meaning, and it covers a variety of proposals'. Bernard Bosanquet, in a contemporaneous and well-respected article, also made a similar distinction, although his categories are "economic" as against "ethical" socialism.[6] Bosanquet had his own long-running acrimonious disputes with the Webbs over the reform of the Poor Law in the first decade of the 1900s. Henry Jones also tended to think of the Fabians as a key point of critical reference for one sense of socialism. Although agreeing with Caird on the valuable ethical dimension of Sidney Ball's work, Jones also felt that the Webbs' emphasis on "administrative statism" was socially destructive. The indistinct sense of Fabianism within these debates was due largely to the fact that Fabianism itself embodied a wide diversity of beliefs about socialism. One should also recall, for example, that the Idealist D. G. Ritchie was a member of the society for a number of years.

Consequently, in sum, for the majority of British Idealists *one* form of socialism was regarded as preferable and "truer". Thus Jones, for example, drew a sharp distinction between what he referred to as "true" and "false" socialisms, rejecting what he called "authoritarian socialism". Alternatively, he praised the true socialism as one that was ultimately compatible with a radical Liberalism; it stressed the "ethical" dimension over the material, economic or scientific issues. Characteristically, though, both types of socialism were associated with the *growth* of the state. In other words, there were both enabling and disabling forms of "statism".

LIBERALISM

Liberalism, like socialism, was a movable feast for the British Idealists, characterized by a distinction – parallel to socialism – between two distinct forms. This has been variously categorized as a distinction between classical and social or New Liberalism. Idealists saw undoubted benefits within nineteenth-century classical Liberalism. It enshrined the rights to private property and individual liberty. It allowed individuals room to develop, giving maximum space to self-help and thrift. It also embodied commitments to the rule of law and constitutional government. The Idealist critique was not so much therefore to abandon classical Liberalism as to reinterpret it and transform it from within. This implied neither a seismic shift of thought, nor a simple amalgamation, rather a fluid development of interpretation around formal conceptual themes. Arguments and ideas were seen to evolve. In fact, Idealists traded on this latter idea. There were therefore no sudden transitions between these types of Liberalism.

The term "New Liberal" itself appeared in public discussion in Britain in the 1890s. Other terms were employed to denote the purported change of liberal perspective. "Radical", "progressive" or "social liberal" denoted roughly the same idea. As we saw, none of these terms were meant to indicate a total revolutionary change of view, but rather an evolution of ideas. There is still, like the "New Right" in the 1980s, some ambiguity as to who should be associated with the New Liberalism and about the character of its ideology.[7] An immense amount of scholarly debate still surrounds this issue.[8]

Formally, the New Liberalism was committed to a "social individualism": the good of the individual was seen as tied to the good of the whole community. The atomism of the formal classical view came to be regarded as morally and sociologically naive. Poverty, unemployment and illness were not just the concern of the single individual, but were social issues and dealing with them transcended individual capacities. Further, liberty was not just leaving individuals alone, but was identified with the fuller life of genuine citizenship. Freedom was a fundamentally important value. Yet, for Idealists, freedom equated with the common good, not civil privatism. Preventing humans from performing socially harmful actions was, in itself, no restraint on the individual. Finally, many advocated a modified conception of a market economy and a more responsive, sensitive and ethical conception of the state. The upshot of the increasing stress, which some classical Liberals at the time placed on the commercial mentality was, for Idealists and many New Liberals, socially, morally and politically destructive. It was thus common among progressive Liberals to acknowledge the considerable debt the New Liberalism owed to ethical socialism.

T. H. Green's essay 'Liberal Legislation and Freedom of Contract' is invaluable for understanding the inception of this New Liberalism. Green's essay, like Toynbee's cited earlier, was written to reassure the Liberals, in the early 1880s, over the gradual shifting character of their legislative programme. He constructed an historical picture of Liberal concerns. First, Liberalism had struggled for political freedoms against aristocratic privileges. Secondly, with figures such as Cobden and Bright, it had struggled for economic freedoms against protectionism. However, Liberalism was moving into a third phase, characterized by social freedoms. For Liberals concerned about freedom of contract, Green asked:' What is freedom?' He answered that freedom was a 'positive power of doing or enjoying something worth doing or enjoying'.[9] Positive freedom was identified with rational and moral action, a reconciliation of the objects of will and the objects of reason, that is, willing the common good. Such a principle was coincidental with self-realization, developed character and genuine citizenship. The progress of society was thus measured by the growth of this freedom. Simply being left alone – negative freedom – was what Green called the primitive sense of the term and was of little or no assistance to a citizen's moral development. Thus, when Liberals spoke of freedom of contract it was not just freedom from restraint, but rather the maximum power of all citizens of a community to make the best of themselves.

The New Liberal minister and British Idealist, R. B. Haldane, using Green's lecture as a template to understand the New Liberalism, extended the above argument into considering the role of the Labour Party (which he finally joined after the First World War and became its first Lord Chancellor). Haldane argued that one should not judge the democratic socialist movement, *prima facie*, by their overt policy proposals, but rather through their view that all 'should have something approaching to equality of choice in life'. Thus, one should not become obsessed (as many critics had) with certain socialist policies, such as nationalization. What really lies behind the socialist movement is a change (as both Toynbee and Green had argued) in the ideas of human freedom and equality. Haldane also suggested that this is one key reason why Liberalism failed so dismally from the 1920s onwards, namely, that many Liberals 'failed to realize in the beginning of 1906 that the spirit was rapidly changing, and that the outlook of Victorian Liberalism was not sufficient for the progressive movement'.[10] Haldane felt there was clear evidence of these subtle ideational changes among the mass of working people and their support for democratic socialist policies. He added that this change of "spirit" was also present among 'more enlightened and less prejudiced representatives of the Universities'. He contended that the 'teaching of Idealists such as Thomas Hill Green was penetrating deeply, and that turned on much more than laissez-faire'. Thus, although the actual policies of the New Liberalism, particularly in the period 1906–1914, were regarded by Haldane as immensely important, and he supported the large majority of them, nonetheless, what was more significant for him was the deep 'organising historical themes or ideas', which transcended both the New Liberal project and indeed democratic socialism.[11] Organizing fundamental ethical ideas (or colligating ideas, to use Jones' terminology) thus had their own inner momentum and logic.

CLASS

One concept, however, did draw a distinction between socialism and Liberalism, and that was class. Socialists were often deeply concerned about the unequal character of classes highlighted under Liberal capitalism. In this context, many saw democratic socialism focusing critically on the selfishness of *one* property-owning class. For the British Idealist, this analysis conflicted with the centrality of equal citizenship. For the Idealists, membership of a community came prior to any notion of class. Furthermore, we are all equally citizens and this was the first loyalty. Writing in 1898, Bosanquet's wife Helen commented that many socialists were still trying to enunciate Marx and Engels' principle of class struggle 'but the cry has found a faint echo, and the policy of direct warfare [of classes] has been almost entirely abandoned for one of compromise and permeation'.[12] The allusion to "permeation" is to the Fabian socialists, who also rejected class-based analysis.

Henry Jones reflected the same basic logic in an essay entitled 'The Corruption of the Citizenship of the Working Man'. He remarked: 'If I had the power, as I have the will, I would arraign the Labour Party before the national conscience and ask it to show cause why it should not be condemned for corrupting the citizenship of the working man'.[13] The basic contention was familiar, namely, that the Labour Party's analysis of society was both morally and intellectually flawed insofar as it appealed to factional interests over and against the common good and citizenship. However, it would also be true to say that many democratic socialists at the time, even Ramsay MacDonald (who was the target for Jones's article), rejected the idea of class. Basically, the Idealist argument was that the class analysis of society was unhelpful, if not destructive. Idealists were not, however, naïve about class divisions. They were clearly aware of a problem. Bernard Bosanquet, for example, commented on this in despondent tones, namely: 'We are not sensitive and awake to each other's needs, wants and feelings. The minds of classes are not in thorough reciprocal contact; and while this is so, the fully developed class-consciousness can hardly mean anything but the war of classes'.[14] British Idealists thus argued for a revitalization of active citizenship, that is, the encouragement for the population to realize their common will and purpose, in order to supplant both individualistic and sectional concerns.

Citizenship, it should be recalled, was not just a political or legal category. It was regarded as a state of mind. Individual citizens were seen to be rational and moral agents able to advance arguments and to deliberate and judge. The realization of citizenship denoted a change of ideas and will – and as argued in the previous chapter, for Idealists, *will* not *force* was seen as the basis of the state. Further, the breadth and character of a citizen's life were determined by the nature of the embedded purposes or colligating ideas. Human conduct was ultimately dependent on the nature of the purposes and ideas adopted by the agent and citizen. Thus, as Henry Jones put it, 'the petty life has petty and secluded interests', whereas, 'the interests of [the] neighbourhood, [the] city ... thud in the arteries of the good man'.[15] The most comprehensive ideas are communal in nature and thus express common values and a common sense of identity. All the British Idealists had a contiguous powerful sense of the role of ideas in reforming social reality through citizenship.

EDUCATION

The question arises how this idea of citizenship was to be cultivated. It is here that we find a complex range of practical ideas within the British Idealist movement. One of the primary practical motifs, which underpinned this process, was education. The Idealist interest in education was integral to their whole philosophy. Idealism, in fact, as a more general philosophical movement, took a passionate interest in both educational theory and practice. This included British, German and Italian Idealism. In each case there were clear examples of sophisticated educational theorizing as well as, in some cases, direct engagement with educational practices. For example, both Green and Haldane in Britain and Giovanni Gentile in Italy were directly involved in educational policy formulation.[16] British Idealists developed ideas on education, particularly in the period between 1870 and the 1920s. The philosophical background to these ideas lay largely in the writings of G.W.F. Hegel. It is not often fully appreciated that Hegel himself had started life as a schoolmaster and later headmaster (for a number of years) and carefully designed his own educational teaching curriculum, which had quite explicit Idealist philosophical principles supporting it.[17] In fact, in more general terms, the German model of educational practice (as well as the philosophic underpinnings) served as a formidable inspiration for British Idealist educationalists, well into the early twentieth century.

There were various linked senses of education at work in most Idealists writers, particularly in the British case. First, education was regarded as premised on a collection of sciences, which required communication and instruction. Knowledge was embodied abstractly in all the various disciplines, with the one proviso that in the final analysis all the sciences found their unity and were resolved in philosophy. There was, in other words, a systematic connection between all the various sciences or disciplines. They formed a coherent systematic unity of mind. This held for all the Idealists. However, in more substantive terms, Idealists also believed that the whole process of formal education itself was intrinsically philosophic, insofar as it was concerned with the act of thinking and thus the life of mind. Furthermore, this philosophic educational process was seen to be linked to the overall ethical and social development of the individual person; more significantly it was seen as an essential prerequisite for the development of genuine citizenship of a modern state. As human beings progressed further through a systemically organized curriculum, they could develop and grow in both knowledge and character.

Education was seen to facilitate the absorption of deep organizing ethical ideas, which enabled individuals not only to take more effective control of their own lives, but also to find common ground with their fellow citizens. The assimilation of civilizing capacious ideas meant that individuals could also be freed 'from the depressing effect of circumstance for which they were not responsible'.[18] This whole argument hearkens back to those we have already encountered in earlier chapters, concerning the will and social purpose. For Haldane – a British Idealist intensely focused on education – higher education in particular, in major civic centres, was viewed as generating a reflective unity of ideas within key cities.[19] Universities would not just be centres of research and training, but also opinion-formers in local communities, that is, bringing the grand formative, if often implicit, ideas of human thought into everyday civic practice. As he insisted, in an address to students, 'nothing is so expansive as the train of thought suggested by an idea that is really great', in effect, it 'transforms the whole outlook'. All significant higher level teaching should be guiding individuals to this "large outlook".[20] This, he thought, could also be facilitated through adult education in all civic centres.[21] He described universities, in this context, as the brain and intelligence of the educational system, permeating ideas to all other educational institutions. More recently, Michael Oakeshott reflected upon university education, espousing a view that has become anathema to the contemporary predominance of the idea that universities are training institutions preparing students for the workforce. A university education, in Oakeshott's view, is an intellectual endeavour, and the subject matter is something of an irrelevance. What a university education imparts is the ability to understand and converse in different languages of explanation. In his view, any subject matter may be studied philosophically, historically or scientifically. The practical mode was an inappropriate idiom at the university level, but not necessarily for other educational institutions. Education, then, is for its own sake, released from considerations of government goals and targets for training accountants, doctors, lawyers and engineers. A university is not a vocationally oriented education. Instead, one becomes adept at conversing in the different languages of explanation.[22]

The early British Idealist interest in education can be found in the ideas and practice of T. H. Green. For example, in 1864, Green was appointed an assistant-commissioner in the Midlands to the Schools Inquiry Commission chaired by Lord Taunton. His main responsibility, until 1866, was to inspect the endowed schools of Warwickshire and Staffordshire and later Buckingham, Leicester and Northampton. The final report of the commission, with Green's contribution, was published in 1868. The Endowed Schools Act of 1869, however, nowhere lived up to Green's vision for the reconstitution of society through education. After his commission work, Green was elected as a teachers' representative on the governing body of King Edward's School in Birmingham. Contrary to many classical Liberals, Green and the majority of British Idealists believed intensely in making education compulsory through the state. Idealists argued that this compulsion did not entail any real encroachment on the liberties of parents. On the contrary, to compel parents to educate their children removed an obstacle to the effective growth of the capacity in the next generation to exercise their rights and freedom beneficially. Insofar as compulsion was sensitive to the particular ecclesiastical or other preferences of the parents, there was no interference with the moral duty of the parent. Green also believed robustly in extending access to higher education to poorer students and working men. With the support of Benjamin Jowett, Balliol Hall – an annex to the main Oxford College – was provided for students with limited finances. Green in fact presided over the Hall. Green was also a keen supporter of the early University Extension Movement, which began in the 1870s, and of the education of women.

In fact, it is worth noting that virtually all the early pre-1914 generation of British Idealists were eager to extend educational opportunities broadly, supporting the university extension movement, ethical societies and later the workers' educational movement. This educational belief included a mix of both state- and voluntary-based organizations. Haldane was probably the most successful British Idealist in the domain of educational development.[23] He pursued educational policy throughout his working life from the 1880s up to the late 1920s and regarded education as the most important of all reform efforts. His master plan for education in Britain was: first, to establish a network of regional civic universities across Britain supported by a University Grants Committee (an idea that he initially introduced); second, to develop primary and secondary education; and, finally to facilitate the development of adult education structures. His most noteworthy work lay in the development of higher education policy.[24] His first foray into education policy was in the Universities in Scotland Bill and the University of London Bill in the 1890s. Haldane became deeply involved with Sidney Webb in the negotiations over the University of London Act. This was, in effect, to give the University both teaching and examining functions. He was also closely engaged in the establishment of Birkbeck College (University of London), guiding it through to university status. He remained president of Birkbeck College until his death in 1928. The passing of the University of London Bill was followed by a period of fruitful cooperative work with Sidney Webb, and others, in setting up the London School of Economics and Political Science. It is unlikely that it would have seen the light of day so soon without Haldane's networking skills.[25] He also became, at this time, preoccupied with the German *Technische Hochschule* system, largely based upon his visits to one particularly famous institution in Germany in Charlottenburg. He regularly campaigned on the need for a 'London Charlottenburg for South Kensington'. Although it did not come to fruition for a number of years, it eventually was established as Imperial College of Science and Technology. Haldane was quite directly involved in organizing the financial backing for its creation. He was also directly and indirectly involved the setting up of the first wave of civic universities in England and Wales, including, for example, the Universities of Liverpool, Birmingham, Leeds, Bristol, Nottingham, Southampton and Sheffield.

Haldane's other passion was adult education. In combination with Albert Mansbridge, R. H. Tawney and Harold Laski, he helped establish the Workers' Education Association (WEA) in 1921. He became a staunch supporter and for many years lectured for the Association. The WEA movement quickly extended to most of the new civic university centres across Britain. Many of the original themes behind this had already been aired in some of T. H. Green's writings and in University Settlements, such as Toynbee Hall, and the early Ethical Society movement (both of which Haldane had lectured to).[26] In summary, as one scholarly study has put it, Haldane's Idealist achievement lay 'in the foundations of our [the British] whole system of education'.[27]

Another example of this practical direction of Idealist philosophy was Henry Jones, who was one of the Commissioners on University Education in Wales prior to the First World War. He was instrumental in setting up the so-called "penny rate scheme" for Wales, that is, helping (in aim) to abolish university fees, such as to allow ordinary Welsh working men and women to enter into university education. It was a scheme subsequently adopted by many counties in England. University education, however, had to be integrated into a comprehensive policy, making education at all levels, including elementary, free and available to all children. He was a passionate supporter of the federal principle in the University of Wales, and when in Australia campaigned for the establishment of a new University in Brisbane, as well as the more widespread study of sociology to help us understand better the social problem and how education could contribute to solutions. He was in harmony with the desire among many Australian Idealists, such as William Mitchell in Adelaide, and Francis Anderson in Sydney, in expanding the educational system. Like T. H. Green, they all believed in the capacity of education as the great social leveller, delivering equality of opportunities, if not of outcomes. He also, like others such as his mentor Caird, was involved extensively on extra-mural teaching development and the WEA. This pattern, as indicated, can be seen in many of the pre-1914 generation of Idealists.

Education was not something isolated from the rest of social policy, or civic duties. The purpose of society and of education was to develop capacities and provide the opportunities for flourishing and self-realization. In this respect, education permeated all aspects of society, and no feature of it could absolve itself of the responsibility to remove the obstacles to the cultivation of character. Every workshop and factory should be a school of virtue.[28]

POVERTY: MORAL AND MECHANICAL REFORM

It was acknowledged by the British Idealists that education was not a panacea for developing citizenship *in toto*. As indicated earlier – on the question of class – inequality of resources was an unequivocal social problem facing Idealism. One particular concern that arose in this context was poverty; poverty was seen as an obstacle to good citizenship.

The situation was complex. Idealists, beginning with Green, affirmed to a greater or lesser degree aspects of the Liberal free economy. Green, following the lead of his hero John Bright – one of the leading figures in the Manchester School of Economics – defended free trade, the market economy, the development of industry and the unavoidability of some unequal resources.[29] Nonetheless, as Green was aware, any close study of the conditions of the urban working classes, as revealed in the various royal commissions and government blue books of the late nineteenth century, painted a disturbing picture. Conditions of extreme poverty and social deprivation prevailed in many urban centres. Green commented that 'the labour market is constantly thronged with men who are too badly reared and fed to be efficient labourers; who for this reason, and from the competition for employment with each other, have to sell their labour very cheap'.[30] Green's own response to the issue of poverty was peculiar. In effect, although committed to facets of state intervention, he also blamed aspects of poverty not so much on lack of resources, as on deficiencies in character. This was combined with the idea of the original conquest and ownership of large tracts of land by aristocratic families (consequently preventing the diffusion of land ownership), which in turn generated a class of itinerant landless labourers, susceptible to every flux in the free market economy and thus to periodic poverty.

Despite this partial affirmation of the role of the classical Liberal economy, the British Idealist response to the issue of poverty was nonetheless divided. We might see this division in terms of moral and mechanical reformism, although the two sides were not wholly exclusive. One argument embodied Green's suggestion that an aspect of poverty refers to character failure. Thus, poverty indicates, to an extent, moral failings in the individual. Certain Idealists had their own specific response to this. The other argument was that poverty could only be addressed systematically through more mechanistic actions by the state. The issue then became a matter of resource allocation and social justice.

The terminology "mechanical" is not wholly precise. The core of the British Idealist argument (which unified all sides of Idealism) concerned a delicate balance between individual and collective responsibility. J. H. Muirhead remarked that both he and his fellow Idealists all followed Green in believing that the 'ultimate source of social betterment lay in the individual's power of responding to improved social conditions by utilising them for social self-improvement as a member of a civilized society'.[31] The state was there to remove hindrances. The two main hindrances for Muirhead were lack of educational opportunities and poor conditions at home and work. As long as the actions by the state or municipality underpinned individual independence of mind, then they were permissible. Self-responsibility needed to be given a firmer social basis. However, the actual items of interference tended to shift among various Idealists and indeed among New Liberals.

The divisions among Idealists lay largely in the stress placed on the dimensions of individual or collective responsibility. In one reading of Green's arguments, state action on sanitation, housing, industrial conditions and education, was fully warranted, whereas taxation of unearned increments from profits was not. This argument contained various possibilities. D. G. Ritchie remarked, on the development of Liberalism, that the work of the state had grown from 'the merely negative work of removing mischievous State-action to the positive task of employing the power of the government, which is now, more or less, the real representative of the "general will" on behalf of the well being of the community'.[32] All law and enforcement by the state was acceptable for Ritchie (and this was his reading of T.H. Green's argument), insofar as it promoted freedom and the common good. As Henry Jones argued succinctly 'the liberty to do wrong is not a right, but the perversion of a right and its negation'.[33] When the state systematically addressed the social conditions of poverty, it was addressing a wrong. State action, as such, did grow markedly in the period from 1890 to 1914, but for most Idealists and indeed New Liberals, this had not diminished liberty, but rather enhanced it. Law was compatible in many contexts with liberty.

This more "mechanistic" and "circumstance-related" argument set the scene for both the New Liberalism and the later social democratic views of the Labour Party in the twentieth century. It is important to emphasize that this more mechanistic approach to poverty did not entail a rejection of the market. For both Idealists and New Liberals, markets were to be encouraged within their place. Markets were not regarded as appropriate for certain aspects of policy. As we move up to 1914, and then the 1920s and beyond, increasingly the argument concerning the circumstances of poverty moved towards the state addressing directly employment conditions, health care, education, social insurance and housing. The market was increasingly regarded, in these domains, as a crude and unpredictable device. Such areas needed sensitive state regulation. This might now be understood as an argument for a more mixed conception of the economy – involving indicative planning. The implication of the latter ideas was that the state had a more active role to play in providing the conditions for the best life of its citizens. The state was not merely a ring-holder, but an active agent. In the case of New Liberal economists, such as J. M. Keynes, the emphasis shifted to more technical economic arguments concerning the state supervision of the market system in order to increase its effectiveness in reducing unemployment and poverty. This became a major theme of New Liberalism in the 1920s, culminating in 1928 with *Britain's Industrial Future*. Known as the Yellow Book, from the colour of its cover, this was an extensive programme of Liberal state-led action involving public works, diffusion of ownership, extension of progressive taxation and encouragement to saving.

In summary, the above arguments were suggesting a form of managed Liberal capitalism. Keynes himself did not seem unduly concerned with the problem of poverty, except so far as the unemployed were an underused economic resource. Comprehensive social policies on poverty were developed by the student of the Idealist Edward Caird, W. H. Beveridge, in his 1942 *Report on Social Insurance and Allied Services*, which laid the foundations for the social security system in Britain. It is clear that many of the major policy changes in economic and social spheres in Britain during the twentieth century, until the late 1970s, were developed by New Liberals of various stripes. For one recent commentator, Liberal reformers such as Beveridge and Keynes, had a 'crucial place in defining the terms of the civic bargain that prevailed [in Britain] from 1945 to the 1970s'.[34] This bargain entailed guaranteed rights of protection against illness, old age and unemployment, as well as opportunities in education. Social rights, financed out of general taxation, provided for social citizenship.[35] This social policy development was not necessarily at odds with classical Liberalism. However, there was unquestionably a gradual extension and mutation of ideas over the nineteenth and twentieth century, which gave rise to increasing state involvement in economic and social policy.

The other dimension of the Idealist argument on poverty embodied Green's stress on character and personal moral responsibility.

The most able representative of this argument among the British Idealists was Bernard Bosanquet. The argument is largely embodied in his reflections on the work of the Charity Organisation Society.[36] The core of the argument derived from a theory of character. Bosanquet argued, in effect, for a systematic extension of Green's arguments. Character was dependent on the idea of self-maintenance. Physical and mental self-maintenance were intimately bound up with the nature of willing. The will consists in 'those ideas which are guiding attention and action'.[37] Certain ideas had a logical and systematic power to dominate and focus the mind and actions of individuals and societies. The basic logic of his case was that all the circumstances and material conditions of an individual's life were frequently created and structured by actions. Yet, all the actions of an individual were in turn structured by will and dominant ideas. The corollary was that the circumstance and material conditions of an individual's life reflect the structure of ideas and will. One key inference from this is that in order to change material conditions and circumstances, it was necessary to restructure and refocus the will and ideas of individuals.

One important consequence followed. For Bosanquet, poverty could be, in certain circumstances, as much a failure of will and ideas, as of material conditions. Human beings were not simply at the mercy of social or economic conditions. Thus, there might be work available, the agent well able to do it, and yet tried to avoid it and seek subsidies from the state or charity. In these circumstances, poverty is not a result of inevitable conditions beyond the control of individuals. If the state simply steps in here with material relief, it will have undermined the agent and reinforced weak self-interested ideas. Bosanquet therefore concluded that too much reliance upon mechanical relief via the state undermines self-maintenance and individual will. It is worth noting that the same core Idealist argument (relating to state intervention) still applied. Intervention and non-intervention had to be based on the common good. Intervention had to enhance the individual's capacity for liberty. Whereas for Ritchie or Jones this could entail much broader state intervention, for Bosanquet it was often a reason to limit state action.

Poverty was to some extent seen by Bosanquet as a failure of character, which was, in turn, a failure of self-maintenance. It was also a breakdown of will. This failure was moral since it reflected the individual's inability to look to the common good. Many become destitute due to trade cycles and changes in technique of production. This, for Bosanquet, was a non-voluntary poverty, which had to be addressed, preferably via systematic charity and state action. At points he happily admits therefore that the state or municipality could have a vital role. However, this still did not address the other dimension of poverty, which was essentially a failure of will and character. This required what Bosanquet called "social therapeutics".

British Idealists, rather like the German Idealists of the nineteenth century, tended to divide on certain key issues. Green was, in some ways, similar to Hegel in generating diverse responses to specific issues. In one sphere, figures like D. G. Ritchie and Henry Jones placed more emphasis on the material circumstances of poverty, which should be addressed by the collective responsibility of the state. On the other hand those, such as Bosanquet – although unquestionably *not* anti-state nonetheless tended to stress the role of character, will and individual responsibility in poverty arguments. This latter claim by Bosanquet, was treated with scorn by most Fabian socialists prior to 1914. The Webbs saw duties, vis-à-vis character arguments, as antiquated residues of Victoriana. This was particularly the case in the debate between the Majority and Minority Royal Commission reports on the Poor Law in 1909.[38] It also figured prominently in debates on unemployment, health insurance and old age pensions up to 1914.

SOCIAL WORK

Bosanquet thought that poverty could, in certain specific dimensions, be accounted for by showing its relation to the manner in which the individual structures his or her life (and the ideas that dominated actions and circumstances). This analysis also indicated how these circumstances could be changed. Bosanquet called this whole process "social therapeutics". The gist of social therapeutics was that if one could identify what actually motivated individuals, namely, what ideas dominated their willing, then it followed one had the possibility of intervening constructively and potentially improving a person's life. That is to say, if one could enable individuals to adopt different but ethically significant ideas, then they, in turn, would begin to restructure actions and material circumstances.

One further issue for all Idealists is that no individual functions simply on his or her own. Individualism means social individualism, even in Bosanquet. The individual grows and works in families and neighbourhoods. Only by investigating the individual's ideas and will in terms of "complex social circumstances", could one understand how he or she became poor and possibly reconfigure his or her life. This whole argument formed the basis for Bosanquet's intense interest in the practice of social work. However, this was not just individual social work, it was family- and neighbourhood-oriented social casework. The more standard terminology was family casework. Bosanquet's adoptive organization – the Charity Organisation Society – pioneered this type of social work during the late nineteenth century. For Bosanquet, family-and neighbourhood-based social work corresponded directly with his perception of the logic of Idealism. For Bosanquet, the social worker and the philosopher were both inspired and spurred by the passion and logic of reality.

One important consequence of this notion of family casework was that Bosanquet argued for the need for detailed and systematic training in social work. He also saw the new discipline of sociology as intimately linked with this training. Individuals had to be taught a strong sense of the way social collectivities work. Bosanquet's own involvement in social work training began in the late 1880s, in the context of a number of voluntary London-based groups. With Bosanquet's enthusiastic support, the Charity Organisation Society set up its own 'School of Sociology' in 1896, premised on a systematic training programme for social workers.[39] The training programme eventually assumed the title 'School of Sociology and Social Economics' in 1903. Its key task was seen as the provision of proper training in social work – something dear to the heart of Charity Organisation leaders. Bosanquet was the leading intellectual light in the new school, although E. J. Urwick, a former sub-warden at Toynbee Hall and director of the School of Ethics and Social Philosophy (which Bosanquet was also involved in), was the main organizer. The teaching of the school focused on a curriculum of sociology, social theory and practical instruction in charitable and poor law administration, all seen as a basis for the proper training of social work. The school became independent of the Charity Organisation Society within a year, although it carried on unofficially propounding the Charity Organisation Society position on social work training and sociology into the early twentieth century. Bosanquet chaired its executive from 1908 to 1912. However, the school was closed in 1912, due to financial difficulties. It was then rapidly amalgamated into the Webb's London School of Economics, much to Bosanquet's annoyance. Bosanquet retained a keen interest in developments in social work up to and beyond the First World War. The issue of social work itself and social work training was one important practical legacy of this dimension of Idealism.

TEMPERANCE

There is another important reading of the British Idealists on the practicalities of state intervention, which tries to lessen their significance. This particularly applies to the role of T. H. Green in initiating a broader role for the state. The key critical point is neatly stated by Peter Clarke when he comments 'it is certainly a mistake to hail (Green) as a collectivist or architect of the welfare state. In his lecture on 'Liberal Legislation and Freedom of Contract' (1881), Green did not go beyond an advocacy of moderate reform of the land laws and – with much more fervour – the legislative restriction of the sale of drink'.[40]

Unquestionably, Green was closely associated with the temperance movement, joining the United Kingdom Alliance in 1872 and publicly committing himself to teetotalism. He was made a Vice-President in 1878. He was also President of the Oxford Temperance Alliance and Treasurer to the Oxford Diocesan Branch of the Church of England Temperance Society; further he was President of the Oxfordshire Band of Hope and Temperance Union from 1876. His personal interest in this issue included setting up a coffee tavern for working people in St. Clements, Oxford in 1875. Apart from the fact that his brother suffered from severe alcoholism, it is also important to note that, even after the 1874 Licensing Act, child and adult drunkenness was rife in industrial and agricultural areas across Britain. Green favoured what was called the "local option" policy, which entailed local control on the sale of alcohol. In 1873, he came into direct and open dispute with a leading Liberal, Sir William Harcourt, over the latter's opposition to tighter regulation on the sale of alcohol. Green's views have been parodied here as not only out of step with the then Liberal Party, but also showing (vis-à-vis Clarke's comment) the narrowness of his approach on legislation.

Green's teetotalism did not represent his earlier views; in fact he drank socially in his early career. However, he felt that it was better to provide an example rather than to preach. It is very important to grasp the main thrust of Green's philosophical position justifying his temperance. He saw intemperance as part of a *connected pattern* of inequality and poverty, characteristic of a classical Liberal policy of laissez-faire. In addition, the justification for any state action was always premised, for Green, on the common good. His views on temperance were consistent with his more general political philosophy. Alcohol was potentially (for many people) yet another impediment to their basic development as citizens. This is as true today in the large urban centres of contemporary Britain. Citizens should be able to strive towards excellence in their characters. The state had a duty, in this context, to promote the common good via a removal of obstacles to such development. The key question was always: Does an intervention by the state actually contribute to the common good? For Green, every citizen should have the possibility of developing themselves and the state had a duty to provide the conditions to enable this. This did not mean that one could force anyone to be moral, but rather that one provided conditions for the possibility of such character development. In some cases one could restrict harmful influences on such a process. Basically if someone acts morally and responsibly, then legal intervention on, say, closing times or restriction on the sale of alcohol would have *no* effect whatsoever. Genuine liberty was not affected by law. To someone who drank moderately, restriction would only be a minor inconvenience and no actual constraint on a genuine liberty. Yet, to those who made and sold alcohol, Green felt, in essence, that no one had a right to *diminish* the rights and capabilities of others. Compulsion, in this latter case, was quite legitimate, since the agents incapacitated themselves by undermining the common good. As a matter of basic fact, for Green, too many premises selling alcohol, with longer opening hours, was in itself no contribution (in any way) to the common good and the development and liberty of citizens. It was an unnecessary and unjustifiable temptation for those who were developing as citizens. Individual responsibility needed to be underpinned by collective responsibility.

In summary, for Green, the general principle of the common good and liberty was the justification for state compulsion. This was not an abstracted sense of the common good and liberty; rather, for Green (as for all the British Idealist), the idea of the common good was derived from the existing practices of his own society. This argument embodies Green's (and other British Idealists') unique blending of

Kant's universalism and Hegelian *Sittlichkeit*. Consequently, for Idealism, to force children to school, to force employers to shield their workers from dangerous machinery or to force the restriction of alcohol, were part of the same basic pattern. State involvement in the regulation of drink, housing conditions, land ownership, employment conditions and education was all justifiable on the grounds of the common good. State interference should at all times be directed to removing barriers and providing the conditions for the realization of citizens' powers.

PROPERTY

The Idealists had a distinctive view of property, which was a practical consequence of their social theory. Private property was an exclusive idea within classical Liberalism. Communal property was seen to negate such a private value. Physical property simply could not be shared. It necessarily resists commonality. For many critics, this argument remained the stumbling block to all forms of socialism and state action. Most classical Liberals saw public ownership and nationalization in this negative light. However, the idea of a right to property in the Hegelian tradition was linked to a more general theory of rights premised on social recognition. The simple possession of an object was in itself not a right; such possession required recognition within a community, in order for it to become a property right.

There are strong parallels on the issue of property with earlier arguments in this chapter concerning, for example, poverty and state action. Thus, one near contemporary of T.H. Green remarked that his:

> 'strong sense of the necessity of property for building up of character led him, however, not so much to exalt the sacredness of property in the hands of the large owner, as to insist on the necessity of such legislation as would tend to the diffusion of property as widely as possible among the masses. A more socialist version of the Hegelian teaching is to be found in the writings of the late Professor Ritchie, while for a more individualistic interpretation the most conspicuous representative is Professor Bosanquet'.[41]

Green figures here, once again, as a seminal thinker among the British Idealists; his theory of property being subsequently interpreted in different ways. As indicated, he had clear doubts over the taxation of the unearned increment, bound up largely with the difficulty of determining the exact boundary of the earned. Green appeared to place more faith in the idea of a society of small-scale proprietors and capitalists. Yet, nonetheless, the rationale of property itself in Green's *Lectures on the Principles of Political Obligation* was fluid enough to be channelled in different directions. The basic argument was that each citizen needed property to allow him or her to realize his or her will. Property accumulation was justifiable as long as it did not interfere with the exercise of a like power by others. However, if some accumulated and deprived or restricted others, then it followed that the common good was being undermined. Given that the state's purpose was to hinder hindrances and enable citizens to realize themselves, then, if a citizen's ability to acquire property was hindered by large capital accumulations, then there was a clear necessity for state intervention in property rights, via for example, direct taxation. As Green's student Arnold Toynbee remarked: 'I do not hesitate to say that this question of the distribution of wealth is the great question of our time'.[42] Ownership of property and wealth per se could never be seen in Idealism as simply an individual achievement. It was an achievement in common with others. Property was relative to the community and thus the common good.

Henry Jones' arguments followed the same basic logic. Property was more than mere possession. It was a right held in the context of the common good. Possession per se did not entail owning. Property required more than just a private will to possess it. Something becomes mine, but more precisely, mine by right and right implies recognition. A right is something, in fact, that *'ought* to be recognized'; other wills in the organized setting of a society then recognize and respect my appropriation. Thus, my exclusive private property is not something gained or acquired *through* my privacy, rather my possession and private use are granted by society (or more precisely the organized will of society – the state). Private property is a reality, which must be respected, but we must realize its point of origin and justification.[43] For Jones – as for other Idealists – both socialists and individualist Liberals, in their different ways, embody an aspect of the truth of property. Private property is an ethical fact, but its essence 'is that it is the result of an act whereby society endows its individual members with rights against itself'.[44] On the other hand, individualists are right to insist that private property is unconditionally necessary to the individual and state. Unless its privacy and necessity are recognized by the state, it could not function as a liberating force.

Jones was fairly radical on this issue and believed the public ownership was quite clearly justifiable. He contended, for example, that 'the Post Office managed by the State enlarges the capacities of the individual. I can use its utilities… You can't send a private messenger from John of Groats to Land's End for 1d… The State does not dispossess the individual of his property. It takes his money and returns it in increased utilities'.[45] Well-financed state education, pensions for the aged, school meals, medical inspection in schools and the large viable public utilities, are, for Jones, examples of how the state can enhance the freedom of the individual. It is this form of democratic liberal socialism that carries letters, provides health care, educates children, and so forth. This does not undermine property rights; rather 'it is defending them by defining them a little more justly, which is their surest defence'.[46] Individuals are not undermined by public ownership, per se, but rather each becomes a mutual shareholder in the vast enterprise for the common good.

The question of the unearned increment, despite Green's unusual defence of it, did ultimately succumb to the logic of the Idealist argument. The distinction between the earned and unearned increment, or private and social value in wealth, could be encapsulated in a phrase used at the time of inception of the New Liberalism, that is, "property for use" and "property for power".[47] Both L.T. Hobhouse and Charles Gore, like Green, saw property as a right of control over things, which was recognized by society. It was intrinsically connected to both the rational purpose of society and individual freedom. It was thus essential to the development of citizens. The success of a state was not measured, as such, by the amount of its material wealth, but rather by the degree to which it gave all citizens the chance of making the "best of themselves". Property for use was a prerequisite to self-realization. Above this limit it became property for power. Without some property no citizen could realize himself or herself. It was thus coincidental with the common good. The state, as a repository of the common good, had a collective responsibility to ensure property for use for all its citizens and prevent or disable property for power. In the New Liberalism, the distinction between the earned and unearned increment (or private and social value) became a basis for the transformed understanding of taxation. There was thus a specific distinction drawn between property as a reward for ability, as a factor in the maintenance of industry, and property as wasteful exploitation of the market, currency speculation and the like.[48] As Hobhouse remarked, in 1911, the true function of taxation was to 'secure to society the element in wealth that is of social origin'.[49] This latter claim represented an important way in which the Idealist argument on property had evolved.

PRACTICAL LIBERTY

It is worth briefly emphasizing, once again, the point that British Idealism *was* noteworthy for translating philosophical arguments into practical prescriptions. The philosophical arguments were essential, but the practical impact of the arguments was also fundamental. This practical feature of philosophical argument can be seen in most spheres of Idealist debate. Thus, even discussion of, for example, the concept of liberty focused on its practical dimension.

There is a distinctly caricatured view of the Idealist argument on liberty, particularly in relation to the work of T. H. Green. The concept of "positive liberty", specifically in the context of Isaiah Berlin's famous essay, 'Two Concepts of Liberty', has often been used as a stick with which to beat the British Idealists. Positive liberty becomes the anteroom to a form of state oppression. What is usually not appreciated at all is the very practical and ordinary context in which Green raised the argument about positive liberty – at least in terms of one of its most succinct definitions. Thus, Green argued that freedom cannot be understood as simply the absence of restraint or compulsion, vis-à-vis contractual relations. He contended that 'we do not mean merely freedom to do as we like. We do not mean freedom that can be enjoyed by one man...at the cost of a loss of freedom to others'. Freedom, he continued, is 'a positive power of doing or enjoying, and that, too, something that we do or enjoy in common with others'.[50] Freedom is not just individual whim or desire it is something more positive. The essay in which this famous definition appears was entitled 'Liberal Legislation and Freedom of Contract' [1881]. It was written, *not* for a discerning philosophical audience, but rather for ordinary members of the Liberal Party.

As indicated, earlier in this chapter, the essay was essentially trying to persuade Liberals not to be overly worried by developments of Liberal legislation, which appeared to be intervening more in contract relations between, for example, employers and employees. It was both an explanation and justification for these legislative changes – changes in conditions of employment contracts, which we would *now* regard as perfectly normal and right, but, at that time, worried many classically minded Liberals. In a nutshell, Green's positive liberty – in a purely practical sense – corresponds exactly with our most ordinary current intuitions about law and contract. This simple fact usually evades its critics.

The core idea of Green's lecture was that law and restraint were not necessarily incompatible with liberty, an argument that has now become a republican commonplace. More controversially, Green pointed out that "free" contracts must be shown to contribute to the common good. Jones deployed a similar argument. Freedom, he argued, had often been seen as a negative principle of opposition to public authority. However, in reality, there was no opposition, 'the State itself is free, and the means of the freedom of its members'.[51] Further, for Green, the progress of society is measured by the advance of such positive freedom, which he believed was perfectly in accord with the development of Liberalism as a political movement. In addition, such freedom, because of its link to the common good, could not be premised on others' unfreedom. Freedom coincided with the common good. In this way the freedom of the individual was reconciled with society. Freedom was understood as the maximum power of *all* members of society to make the best of themselves. Thus, Green contended that it was justifiable, on grounds of freedom, to interfere in the sale and consumption of alcohol, housing, public health provisions, employment, land ownership and education. Such action, although coercive, nonetheless removed unjustifiable obstacles and so provided conditions for the genuine exercise of freedom. Law could thus contribute to the lives of the overworked, underfed, ill-housed and undereducated.

These arguments on positive freedom are echoed in many New Liberal writings through the 1890s and early 1900s. As the New Liberal Herbert Samuel remarked: 'There could be no true liberty if a man was confined and oppressed by poverty, by excessive hours of labour, by insecurity of livelihood…To be truly free he must be liberated from these things also. In many cases, it was only the power of law that could effect this. More law might often mean more liberty.'[52] Similar points are put by New Liberal figures such as Hobhouse, Winston Churchill and H. H. Asquith.[53] It is this understanding of social freedom that underpins the policy work of the New Liberal administrations of 1906–1914 and their welfare legislation. It is also this line of thought that has carried on into many aspects of the social democratic tradition to the present day.

Haldane, for example, followed the same line of thought as Samuel. He argued that Liberalism had strived to develop aspects of freedom through franchise and other such reforms during the nineteenth century. However, he contended that the New Liberalism had refocused freedom on the "social question". In explaining this development, Haldane moves immediately to quote what he referred to as a 'great master of political concepts' who 'seems to me to have expressed the necessities of our generation in the matter of social progress better than anyone else'. The individual concerned was T. H. Green (from the above cited lecture). Green's language for Haldane 'may be taken as defining generally the aim and tendency of a party which looks as much to distribution as to production, and which claims that only so can the liberalism of today be true to its mission'. Green's Idealist language can thus be taken as 'the main basis of the Liberalism of the future'. This was a language that was attuned to social freedom, the broader use of the state, a more interventionist role in the economy, and so forth. He also thought it was a language that was very close to that of many Fabian socialists. Thus, he commented, 'The New Liberals I take to be those who esteem a progressive policy in social matters more highly than anything else at present in Liberalism'.[54]

In trying to indicate a broad progressive alliance, focused on enhancing social freedom through a more imaginative use of the state and local government, Haldane gave his whole discussion a speculative gloss. This New Liberalism was really, as he put it, 'an affair of spirit... the form of its activity is moulded by the requirements of successive generations'. He suggests that the serious question that actually identifies New Liberalism is not so much the specific social programme or policies, as a "proper frame of mind". This "frame of mind" is identified by certain core colligating ideas. The New Liberalism, in other words, "coheres", "makes sense", or, is internally organized by certain historically developed ethical "ideas". In this case, it is the concept of "social freedom". Freedom (as suggested in Green's lecture) is a developing idea, which represented a 'fight for emancipation from the condition which denies fair play to the collective energy for the good of society as a whole'.[55] In concluding, Haldane suggests that this idea underpinned the whole thrust of the New Liberal policy.

CONCLUSION

This chapter has focused on the theme of Idealism as a practical creed. The philosophical arguments of Idealism were obviously crucial to their writings, as we have shown. However, one of the important facets of Idealist political philosophy was its attempt to address the political and social world in a very practical and creative manner. The ideas developed on Liberalism, socialism, education, poverty, social work practice and citizenship, and the like, were all intended to engage subtly with the realities of late Victorian and Edwardian Britain. This was a more complex matter than critics suggest because not all Idealist argument bridged or even intended to bridge theory and practice. Although some critics have inveighed against, for example, Hegel for the practical implications of his political philosophy, Hegel himself was clear, in his own mind, that philosophy had little contribution to make to practical life. In *The Philosophy of Right*, for example, he maintained that philosophy always arrives too late to offer any practical advice.[56] However, for many British Idealists, with a few key exceptions – notably Bradley, McTaggart and Oakeshott – philosophy *was* integrally related to practical life and should be directed to improve the condition of society. Henry Jones, for example, thought that the most important work of the philosopher was always to improve the condition of ordinary working people.[57]

This bridging of theory and practice was particularly evident in the work and life of T.H. Green. Green acted as an initial powerful stimulus on the whole Idealist school in the domain of moral, social and political philosophy. He was often seen therefore to have had a significant effect on generations of students, including many academics, churchmen, politicians and public servants, for example, men such as H. H. Asquith, Edward Grey, Alfred Milner, Arthur Acland, A. C. Bradley, Arnold Toynbee, Bernard Bosanquet, R. L. Nettleship, J. H. Muirhead, Charles Gore and Henry Scott Holland. It was in this context that Collingwood noted in his *Autobiography* that Green's major effect was to send out into public life 'a stream of ex-pupils who carried with them the conviction that philosophy ...was an important thing, and their vocation was to put it into practice ... Through this effect on the minds of its pupils, the philosophy of Green's school might be found, from 1880 to about 1910, penetrating and fertilizing every part of the national life'.[58] It is difficult to think of any later twentieth-century British philosophical movement that has had any comparable positive effect on practical affairs as British Idealism.

CHAPTER SIX

NATIONALITY, IMPERIALISM AND INTERNATIONAL RELATIONS

INTRODUCTION

The events that surround the period during which British Idealism was in the ascendancy encompass what Hobsbawm has called the Age of Imperialism, running in effect from the Crimean War to Second World War.[1] Many of these key events constituted the substantive international political matters to which British Idealists contributed in a sustained manner. It is, as such, surprising that very little scholarly attention has been devoted to the theories of international relations of the British Idealists in the secondary literature. In general, the British Idealists have been wrongly characterized as Realists in international relations with a purported exalted view of the state; exponents of bounded communities; and finally, understanding notions of international law and morality as mere metaphors. They have also been criticized for being pro-Imperialist and subscribers to a "German Philosophy" that was responsible for the militarism precipitating the First and Second World Wars.[2] It will be impossible to cover the full range of arguments used by the British Idealists to respond to and resolve the above issues. This chapter will focus on some key interventions surrounding Nationality and Patriotism: The second Boer War (1899–1902), Imperialism and the extension of the moral community.

WAR AND IDEALISM

It is true that Hegel sometimes provided ammunition for critical assessments, in suggesting, for example, that the state was the march of God on earth, and in his idea that the development of consciousness lay in the identification of one's real will with the collective entity higher than individual wills. There appeared to be no greater ethical sacrifice than laying one's life down for the state. Hegel also saw a role for war in regenerating an ethically moribund state. In a purple passage, he suggested that war could blow away the stagnant air from the surface of a still pond. Risking one's life for the state in war serves the purpose of confronting the person with the higher unity to which he belongs and upon which his own family, civil and economic life depends. War also serves to retard internal unrest and reinforces loyalty to the institutions of the state.[3] Hegel believed that the state logically entails the existence of other states, among which there is a struggle for recognition. The rights of states are not embedded in a universal will, but are manifest and actualized in the particular will of each. He argues that its own welfare 'is the supreme law for a state in its relations with others'.[4] War, then, is necessary for external security and the internal health of the nation. Its conduct may be regulated but not eradicated.

However, the British Idealists, in general, departed from Hegel in believing that conflict and warfare were *not* natural to mankind, and the key to the resolution of conflict was the Kantian vision of democratic republican states. The inevitability of conflict, in Green's view, is a mistake. Occasions for conflict disappear when the states perfectly achieve their objective of providing the conditions for the self-realization of the capacities of all individuals.[5] The British Idealists, as such, followed Green rather than Hegel in their views on war. For Green, wars are always wrong irrespective of the ends pursued. Blame may always be attributed to the conditions that prevented the desired end being attained by other means. Those who can genuinely plead that they resorted to war as the only available instrument to maintain the conditions for the moral progress of humanity may be absolved of complicity in what nevertheless remains a wrong. Nevertheless, few wars could claim to be fought for such high moral motives. Dynastic ambition, superseded by national conceit, had been the major cause of war over the previous four centuries.[6] Peter Nicholson has demonstrated, contrary to prevailing views, that Bosanquet is faithful to Green understanding of war.[7] Yet, Bosanquet argues that instead of denouncing it, we must try to understand war better as part of the moral life that is "liable to err".[8] We are all complicit in what he terms the "crowning stupidity" of war, but like all evils we must do our best to remove it.[9]

Ritchie is probably closer to Hegel than any of the other British Idealists in his attitude to war. He maintains that there are often irreconcilable opposites in the ideals of nations opposed to each other. War thus comprises a rough form of dialectic by which right is determined. The judgement of whether a war is right or wrong cannot be made in isolation. Our judgement is contingent on the general progress of mankind towards constitutionalism and social welfare. Reactionary rulers of nations who resist such progress and acknowledge no argument but the point of a sword deserve to be swept aside. Ritchie contended that the Turks, for example, responded much more positively to a display of force than to any argument based on principles.[10] This, in fact, is no more than what L. T. Hobhouse, a critic of the Idealist metaphysical state, was saying at the same time. It is not a question of the use of force as such, but of the occasions on which it is permissible. For Hobhouse, as for Ritchie, force is legitimate against such reactionary tendencies as "Turkish barbarity".[11]

All this is mitigated, however, by the fact that Hegel talked not of any particular state, but on the idea of the state whose purpose was not only the security of its citizens, but also their spiritual development, that is, the promotion of philosophy, the arts and sciences. Furthermore, for him, as for Edmund Burke, the emergence of conventions and customs, as a common European heritage, or common law of Europe, made war less of a war in the European context. While law requires the state to create and sustain it, in the international context the "so-called" international law did nevertheless impose prudential constraints.[12]

Critics of the international relations theory of the British Idealists have generally failed to appreciate the fundamentals of the philosophy. Philosophy somehow has to give a rational account of what is, and war and international relations were certainly evident in the consciousness of the times in which they lived. As Caird suggests: 'Men have come to see the necessity of realising the nature of the universe in which they live, and of dealing with the facts as they are, and not as they would like them to be.'[13] It is, therefore, important to distinguish between the explanations they gave for why wars occurred, and why international relations were as they were, and their arguments and beliefs for how these relations may become in the future. Green, along with all of the other British Idealists, denies the inevitability of conflict between states. Bosanquet, for example, maintains that 'the normal relations of states is co-operative'.[14] The cause of war, they suggest, is not the state as such, but states insofar as they fail to fulfil their purpose. As Muirhead suggests: 'War is a feature of states not as such but in so far as they fail to be states'.[15] The true purpose of the state is undermined by sinister and special interests, which promote and protect privileged classes and inhibit the development of civic equality, preventing the common exercise of civil rights. Privilege is maintained by the class that propagates the belief that the state's interest is furthered by the pursuit of an external policy and not by internal reform.[16] The British Idealists generally believe that war is the result of insufficient socialization.

To attain the sort of ideal relations that pertain within the state, and the moral community upon which they depend, in their interactions with other states would require the extension of the moral community beyond the borders of the state. We see in the writings of the British Idealists an emphasis upon the "Nation" as the bearer of the ideals, the hopes, morality and community of a people whose ethical lives have been formed in their mutual relations. The Idealists differ in the extent to which they acknowledge the actual achievement of a wider international community. None denied the desirability, nor the possibility of such a wider moral community developing, and indeed saw the Empire and the League of Nations as the vehicles through which further progress could be made. The crucial issue in question was how international society could be extended? By what mechanisms could narrow national self-interest be transcended to extend our moral community?

In the view of the Idealists, and indeed of many of their critics, the starting point had to be actual moral communities, that is nations or states, out of which broader principles of humanity arise. [17] On the issue of Imperialism, different Idealists supported it with differing degrees of enthusiasm, but none endorsed the sort of "social Imperialism" that Cecile Rhodes advocated, and which relied upon the exploitation of colonized people to raise and ameliorate the living standards of the working classes at home, largely in order to stave-off social unrest. The Idealists in general condemned the brutality of Imperialism, but it was a fact of history, and could be mitigated by the active promotion of the ideals of the higher civilizations in assisting the lower to achieve self-government and advanced social relations. It has gone little noticed that even their most severe critics – L. T. Hobhouse and J. A. Hobson – agreed with many of the British

Idealists on the issue of a right kind of Imperialism, one which is not exploitative, but which prepares countries for development and emancipation from enslavement to nature.

NATIONALISM, PATRIOTISM AND IDEALISM

Both Nationalism and Patriotism had a somewhat unresolved status in British Idealist thought. First, although there was some acknowledgement that the two ideas were, to a degree distinct, nonetheless there was little attempt by the Idealists *systematically* to differentiate them. There was also little attempt to try to pin down a precise definition of either of the terms. Hetherington and Muirhead did suggest that nationality was something that could be dependent on a wide range of divergent issues, such as 'race, on language, on tradition, on religion, on political or economic ideas and institutions'.[18] In consequence, they argued that there was neither any single precise way to define nationality, nor any process by which a state could meet or accommodate such diverse demands with any exactness. Some Nationalists might be happy with their own church, others with their language as part of the educational curriculum, some with a degree of legal autonomy and so forth. The concepts and the way one addressed them in practice remained open-ended and wholly contingent upon circumstances.

Secondly, there was a strong sense among the British Idealists that the concepts of nation and state nonetheless overlapped. Thus, Muirhead and Hetherington argued that 'the State can hardly become in fact what we have said it is in idea, until it takes the form of a National State'.[19] For these authors it is only 'when a State becomes a Nation that it wins for itself this feeling of personal devotion on the part of its citizens. ... the boundaries of the nation then become the boundaries of sentiment'.[20] However, despite the optimistic reverberation of these remarks, the match between the State and Nation (or *Patria*) was not always regarded as either precise or wholly clear. As Hetherington and Muirhead admit, some states may include many sub-national groups. Henry Jones, as a keen Welsh patriot and someone who spent almost all of his adult life in Scotland, was aware of the resonance of this particular argument. However, Jones did not advocate Welsh separatism, nor independence from the United Kingdom. He felt that loyalty to the Welsh nation did not preclude a broader loyalty to Britain, or indeed to the Empire.

Patriotic loyalty could thus be multi-layered. The Welsh language, poetry, prose and music would always keep a distinctive character, which was perfectly compatible with wider loyalties. Like Jones, Hetherington and Muirhead also argued that the existence of sub-national groups and sub-national loyalties was not necessarily an insuperable problem. They cite the case of the British Empire as an example, where "imperial loyalty" can combine with the "warmest of local patriotism".[21] Despite the above argument, they also acknowledge that if there was a wide divergence among nationalities, it could potentially be a source of weakness within a state. The danger was even greater if the sub-national groups felt greater kinship or affinity with the nationality of another state. This, for the authors, was a common cause of conflict between states.

Thirdly, for most of the British Idealist school there was a central distinction, which appeared in many commentaries on nationalism and patriotism, between a more positive or acceptable version and an unacceptable or negative version. The origin of this distinction can be found in T. H. Green. Green clearly sensed that there was a vital contrast. The negative theme is, in fact, quite strongly present in his work. As he observed, "national vanity" often masquerades under the rubric of Patriotism. Nationalism has thus often proved to be a 'more serious disturber of peace than dynastic ambition'.[22] A state, understood as a nation, will often have its own specific narrow passions 'which inevitably lead it to judge all questions of international right from its own point of view'.[23] Nations, in this sense, for Green, are rather like individuals judging their own causes from a self-interested perspective.

The same basic argument is echoed in the work of Bosanquet. He contended that both patriotism and nationalism were frequently a source of 'brainless and often fraudulent clamour, or at best a dangerous fanaticism'.[24] This theme underpinned much of the Idealist's scepticism over the Boer War and militaristic imperial expansion.

One of the overall more negative assessments of nationalism can be found in Ritchie's work. He expressed strong reservations on the themes of national self-determination and patriotism. He argued that nations are only metaphorically organisms and that we should not be blinded by the positive evaluative connotations of such words as national freedom and independence. Such empty ideas were often tied to reactionary causes. However, he did admit that nations could exist for the benefit of a people. But he added that we should not make a fetish of such claims in support of national independence or national distinctiveness. This is at the heart of his lukewarm view of the claims of the Boers for independence. In a similar way to J. S. Mill, Ritchie maintained that often smaller or more ineffective nationalities actually profit from being absorbed into larger states. Smaller nationalities progress under such conditions. Thus, absorption by a larger entity may be for their ultimate betterment. It is clear that Ritchie had no truck with the exclusive rights of any nation, large or small. He therefore argued (in an evolutionary mode) that if a nation does not benefit its people, 'it has no absolute moral right to block the onward movement of human progress'.[25] National rights claims were thus severely qualified by Ritchie.

Despite the Idealist critique of the negative properties of nationalism and patriotism, Green, like Muirhead and Hetherington, takes as a matter of historical fact that nations are almost inevitably prerequisites for states.[26] An underlying social unity was identified, which could not be sidestepped. As Bosanquet noted, in vivid prose, 'when we read John of Gaunt's praises of England in Shakespeare's Richard II, we feel ourselves at once in contact with the mind of a social unity'.[27] Edward Caird put it forcefully when he contended: 'a nation ought to be composed of men who, however numerous, can feel the throb of one emotion and one impulse of life, and who by such community are at once differentiated from other nations and brought into living and organic unity with one another.'[28]

Green also suggested that there could be a more acceptable form of Patriotism. He argued that to feel that sense of social unity as a "good patriotism", the state needed to be more than just a negative protector of property rights. He comments that the citizen if 'he is to have a higher feeling of political duty, ... must take part in the work of the state. He must have a share, direct or indirect.... in making or maintaining the laws which he obeys'.[29] In this sense, he sees some link between good patriotism and democratic growth. The citizen must thus take 'an active interest in the service of the state'. In addition, for Green, there need to be underlying ties, a common memory, traditions and customs (in a strongly Burkean sense). This whole process is, of course, premised for Green on the state in its policies and actions embodying the common good.

It is no surprise that Green suggested that a good patriotism could be found in a state organized in a specific manner. If the state aimed to accord rights to its own citizens and acted in harmony with the common good, then conflict could be minimized, not only within the state but, as argued in the previous section, also *between* such states. Bosanquet, like Green, was also convinced that there was a reasonable form of Patriotism, which could be harnessed to the service of the good life of citizens. Everything depended on the way the state was constituted. For Green, if states were "thoroughly formed", then the diversion of Patriotism or Nationalism into conflict was thereby diminished.

Edward Caird is thus typical among the Idealists in suggesting British "National Patriotism" could justifiably celebrate its achievements, 'not with false pride, but rather with the sobering consciousness of a great vocation'.[30] It should not be in a spirit of boastfulness we remember the deeds of our great forefathers, but in acknowledgement this is how the nation helped me, and in asking how may I help the nation? The recent misadventures of the nation, by which he alludes to Imperialism and the Boer War, had justifiably invited hostile feelings directed at Britain by other countries. Patriotism for Great Britain therefore had the added international dimension of social responsibility:

'Help England to maintain the spirit of justice in all her dominions, to labour for the liberation of mankind from the heavy yokes that still oppress them, to smite down cruelty and wrong throughout all the vast sphere of her influence, to maintain the cause of the poor, and make them sharers in all the benefits of human existence from which they have been shut out ...'[31]

The core argument to be found in Idealists such as Haldane, Caird, Green, Bosanquet, Jones, Muirhead and others, is that good civil states, which actively seek the common good for their membership, will have very little risk of international conflict among themselves. Indeed, Bosanquet argues explicitly that for a state to revert to war is evidence in itself of its failure to be the sort of state it ought to be.

Further, for Green and other Idealists, a patriotism (or nationalism) that focuses predominantly on conflict and military supremacy was more akin to that of the followers of a feudal chief, than to a proper civil state, and thus needs to be completely repudiated or reformed. For Green, one could not be genuinely obligated to such a state. Further, following Green, Hetherington and Muirhead argued: 'No nation and no State can claim either that the last devotion of its members or that its own supreme duty is to itself alone. As every right within the State has to be justified by its efficacy for the welfare of the whole, so every claim to national existence must be vindicated by reference to the whole community of mankind'.[32] In this sense, the Idealists argued for a bottom-up mode of cosmopolitanism, something that would arise out of the customary structures of properly formed civil states. We will return to this below in discussing the expansion of the moral community.

IDEALISM, IMPERIALISM AND THE BOER WAR

It is important to make a number of initial distinctions, on the one hand, within the British Idealist conception of Empire and Imperial policy and, on the other, the assessment of the 1899 Boer War. There were some direct overlaps between these two issues; however, in many instances, arguments diverged. The situation was complex. First, many British Idealists who were sympathetic or indeed enthusiastic about Imperial policy and the Empire were nonetheless hostile to the second Boer War (1899–1902). Secondly, there was a marked separation among British Idealists over their understanding of the nature of the Boer War itself. Thirdly, there were further divisions over the status and nature of Imperialism. Fourthly, the British Idealists were not alone in these rancorous internal divisions. They reflected the more general state of British civil society at the time and indeed contentions within the British Liberal Party, Independent Labour Party and the various socialist groups, such as the Fabians. Even within significant groups inside the Liberal Party, such as the New Liberals, there were further severe splits over these issues.

The term Imperialism developed in public usage within Britain during the 1890s, largely supplementing the term Empire as part of a justification for extending British possessions abroad. British imperial policy remained an odd mixture of political, legalistic and economic motivations. The older colonies, in particular, had often taken on a vocabulary of political liberty and constitutionality; by the late nineteenth century they were largely at liberty to determine their own futures. However, the manner in which the Empire developed was still both complex and messy. Empire had become, by the nineteenth century, a rich forest of types of government, usually still animated, at root, by a common interest in both commercial growth and constitutional rule. Canada, Australia and South Africa formally became states in 1867, 1900 and 1909, respectively. This constitutional movement was later enshrined in the statement of the Imperial Conference of 1926, which defined dominions as 'autonomous communities within the British Empire, equal in status, in no way subordinate to one another in any aspect of their domestic or external affairs, though united by a common allegiance to the crown and freely associated as members of the British Commonwealth of nations'.[33]

Muirhead, writing at the height of the Boer War, saw four phases in terms of British nineteenth century attitudes to Imperialism: enthusiasm, indifference, hostility and then avid jingoism, exemplified in the initial phase of the Boer War. Ironically, the periods of indifference and hostility did unexpectedly see significant acquisitions of territories and markets. Yet the period of enthusiasm for Empire, from the 1880s to 1890s, saw the final phase of such acquisition. Thus, the scramble for Africa (embodied in the 1883 Berlin conference) was merely the last of the phases of acquisition made during the nineteenth century. What has not often been grasped about these latter discussions is the quite subtle but marked differences in those who reflected on Imperialism. *Social Imperialism* was largely justified on the grounds of the gains abroad, which could then be used to fund the growing demands (from various groups) for expensive social welfare reforms on the domestic front. For some this was a business proposition, since welfare spending could help to mollify class antagonisms and blunt social radicalism. Controversially, at the time, for Joseph Chamberlain (a liberal-conservative by inclination), Social Imperialism was linked directly to Tariff reform and a system of imperial preferences. Many in the Liberal Party opposed Chamberlain, yet there was also a group of *Liberal Imperialists*, including Lord Rosebery, who gave Chamberlain's policy some qualified support. R. B. Haldane, H. H. Asquith, Edward Grey and Herbert Samuel, all joined together in a Liberal League in 1902 supporting a conception of Imperial policy. This group of Liberal Imperialists – commonly known as the "Limps" – led a vigorous campaign for extending liberal state activity into the Empire. It is important to underline the point that many of these figures, such as Haldane, Samuel and Asquith, were also key supporters of the New Liberalism. However, whereas Chamberlain coupled Social Imperialism with social reform, financed out of tariffs and increased charges on commodities, the Liberal Imperialists saw the finance for social reform arising from taxation of profits derived from imperial ventures.

There were a number of British Liberals who felt ambivalent about Imperial policy. During the period of the Boer War, this unease became pronounced in many of the so-called "little Englanders", such as David Lloyd George and Henry Campbell-Bannerman – who fiercely opposed to Chamberlain's policies. Liberalism, for these latter figures, signified constitutional self-determination. Imperialism, on this reading, denoted arbitrary control by an external power. Liberalism was seen to be incompatible with Imperialism. From a more economic perspective, the New Liberal writer J. A. Hobson delivered what is now regarded as the most significant attack on the exploitative character of Imperialism, in his book *Imperialism* (1902). The argument, in a nutshell, was that financial interests in Britain were drawn together by a common resistance to attacks on property and privilege. The attacks arose in the context of growing pressure, in the 1890s, for social reform and thus expanding public expenditure. In order to meet this issue head-on, such vested financial groups gave their support to Imperialism, which enabled new resources to be channelled into domestic policy, without unduly affecting profits and property interests. Raucous jingoism tended to dominate the sphere of social reform. In commentators such as Lenin and Luxemburg – influenced by Hobson – the motif of economic exploitation figured even more prominently, explaining Imperialism as a higher stage of capitalism itself. However, the New Liberals Hobson and Hobhouse, both adamantly opposed Social and Liberal Imperialism. They tried – contrary to the views of both – to sever the connection between genuine social reform and Imperialism. Hobson largely saw Imperialism as a conspiracy of selfish financial interests. For Hobhouse, like Lloyd George, Imperialism stood for the undemocratic and arbitrary subordination of peoples and the advocacy of racial supremacy. Thus, for them, there could be no such thing as democratic or constitutionally motivated Imperialism.

Significantly, for Hobhouse, British Idealism was seen to have paved the way for Imperialism. He argued that the Idealists' exalted view of the state had encouraged jingoism, militarism and imperial arrogance, at the expense of morality. Thus, Hobhouse tried to dismiss British Idealism as largely on par with conservative instincts and anti-reformism.[34] Hobhouse was clearly either dissimulating, or was carried away by the passion and rhetoric of the moment. He quite clearly knew of T. H. Green's own radical and anti-imperial views, which he had learnt from Bright and Cobden. Hobhouse, in fact, remained an admirer of Green throughout his life, and must also have been aware that Idealists, such as Edward Caird and Bernard Bosanquet, opposed the Boer War. Caird, for example, took part in a protest against honouring Cecil Rhodes with a degree at Oxford University. Further, both Hobson and Hobhouse were alert, vis-à-vis their opposition to the Liberal Imperialists, to the fact that New Liberals themselves were also at odds over the issue. As knowledgeable social commentators, they would also have known that analogous divisions of judgement were reflected in socialist groups. Whereas, there was unease in some socialist circles concerning the capitalist exploitation of native populations in the Empire, a group of Fabian socialists nonetheless actively promoted Imperialism, particularly in the book *Fabianism and the Empire: A Manifesto* (1900), edited by George Bernard Shaw, and vigorously supported by Sidney and Beatrice Webb.[35] The choice that such Fabians perceived was simple. The globe, as a matter of fact, was being gradually partitioned between great European powers. If Britain wished to remain a global power, she should actively pursue Imperialism. If certain countries allowed themselves to be taken over, it was more than likely a sign of their *social inefficiency*. As long as the expansion of Empire was conceived on "collectivist", and not liberal "individualist" lines, and the aim was greater social efficiency, then the Empire could, they argued, be transformed into a socialist commonwealth. This would be exploited for the collective public good and not private gain. The intellectual background to such socialist-inspired imperialist expansionism, in Webbs and Shaw was, more than likely, the social Darwinism of figures such as Karl Pearson and Benjamin Kidd. Primitive races would evolve to higher levels via bureaucratically organized Socialist Imperialism. Ultimately, they envisaged the Empire as one large collectivized state-like entity. This form of analysis led later Fabians, such as Leonard Woolf, to toy with the notion of world government – deriving from the imperial argument.[36]

Yet, clearly Hobhouse was nonetheless still, in small part, correct in his judgement of Idealism. There were other British Idealists, such as J. H. Muirhead, R. B. Haldane, D. G. Ritchie and Henry Jones, who accepted a form of ethically motivated and socially responsive Imperialism. The key question for these latter Idealists was: Had Imperialism enhanced the capacities for self-government and liberty or was it merely exploiting them for economic profit? As Muirhead observed, the imperial administration must aim at 'what is best in the instincts and traditions of these races themselves'. It must not destroy the local customs and faiths. It must let the local peoples 'know through education and example what good government means'.[37] The arguments on Imperialism paralleled directly those on the domestic state front. The object of all state interference was to enhance the common good and liberty. Lawful constraints could be used here to augment the life of people by providing greater social guarantees and enabling opportunities. Thus, initial legal restraint, associated with imperial control, could be justified by the extent to which it contributed towards both the basic protection and enhancement of greater opportunities for development and ultimately self-governance among colonized peoples.

However, it was unquestionably the second Boer war (1899–1902) that really focused the painful and jarring discussion on Imperialism in Britain. The Boer War was, as Hobhouse testifies, 'the test issue of [his] generation'.[38] Among the British Idealists, there was clearly an intricate discordance. On one level all British Idealists, irrespective of their view of the Boer War, condemned aggressive Imperialism. However, as argued above, some accepted the idea of a socially and ethically motivated Imperialism. One optimistic expression of this impulse can be seen in the work of the Liberal Imperialist, New Liberal and Idealist, R. B. Haldane. Haldane's enthusiasm for education could, he thought, be extended to the Empire, particularly via the medium of university education. As he asked in 1902: 'How far off are we from the realisation of the idea of a great postgraduate teaching centre for the Empire?'[39] This became his great scheme for the idea of an Imperial university, which would act as the *mind* of the Empire. It is here his Idealist vision is at its most expansive. He thought that the British Empire could become stronger if the various peoples voluntarily subscribed to it. He advocated, for example, Home Rule in Ireland on the same grounds, and was, in fact, a committed "Home-Ruler" for the whole of his political career. As Haldane noted, 'There is a larger conception of Imperialism than that which forms a party cry at elections. This larger conception of Imperialism is less controversial, but not less far-reaching'. [40] What could unify the Empire? For Haldane, the answer again lay in the sphere of education, specifically in his vision of an Imperial University.

However, in terms of the Boer War, anxieties and division still divided the British Idealists. D. G. Ritchie, in some writings, was a lot less condemnatory of the British war in South Africa than other Idealists. As a

Fabian on the more socially radical side of the Idealists, he nonetheless attributed much pro-Boer and anti-Imperial sentiment in Britain to the propaganda of Afrikaners and the sensationalism of journalists. He thought the nature of Empire and Imperialism was seriously misunderstood by critics. It was inevitable, he argued, on evolutionary grounds, that 'vigorous and enterprising white races should overflow into other lands as it is that water should run down hill'.[41]

The Boer War, in his view, was justified. It was a war between two incompatible types of society and as inevitable as the conflict between the Northern and Southern states in America. There may have been much in the Southern states that attracted Englishmen, and much in the North that repelled them. For Ritchie, though, everyone admitted that 'the cause of the union was the cause of true democracy, of civilisation, of progress'.[42] The Boer War was, for him, analogous to the civil war in America.

On the other hand, matters were not straightforward in this domain. Henry Jones – who despite aligning himself with the Liberal Imperialists and being active in the Liberal League – nonetheless applauded many of Hobhouse's criticisms of Imperialism and Boer War policy. He suggested that Hobhouse's criticisms were a reasonably accurate account of the political climate during the war itself, although he dissented from their shrill self-righteous tone. Further, moral progress for Idealists, such as Jones, was still possible in this darker scenario. The ultimate destiny, for most pre-1914 Idealists, of either the state or the Empire, lay not in the particulars of tariff reform, free trade or protectionism, but rather in the overall moral development of citizens. Green, Bosanquet, Jones and most other pre-1914 Idealists argued that improvements in the international sphere were largely dependent on moral improvements within the domestic state sphere. Political institutions were a reflection of the will and purposes of their membership. Thus, the Boer War, for all Idealists, undoubtedly reflected strong components of greed and brutality (even for Ritchie), yet at the same time, for Jones, it was still a war that aimed, however ineffectually, to restore basic liberties and was intended ultimately to reinstate the moral and legal bonds of Empire. What was needed, as Haldane, Muirhead and Jones argued, was a more "far-sighted Imperialism", which would address directly the pernicious behaviour of business interests and prevent cruel exploitation of native peoples.

Muirhead was not as publicly vociferous in his opposition to the Boer War as he might have liked to have been. As a Professor at

Birmingham University, he was aware of the presence of Joseph Chamberlain – Birmingham University's founder and then Chancellor. However, Muirhead expressed himself robustly in private. Although critical of the Boer War, Muirhead remained sympathetic to the idea of Imperialism, acknowledging that it was a historical fact and therefore needed to be addressed and dealt with in as humane and supportive a way as possible. He argued that irrespective of how Britain had come to gain an Empire, the existing circumstances nonetheless imposed ethical responsibilities, which could not be sidestepped. To disown these responsibilities 'would be a crime outweighing all we have committed in creating it'.[43] Muirhead, like Jones and Haldane, stressed the moral and spiritual foundations of Empire and Imperial policy, as necessary to promote the unity of sentiment, which would bind the whole together organically. This was a vision of Empire, which other Idealists, like Bosanquet, Haldane, Hetherington and Ritchie, shared. Its core components, not unusual for the time, given the widespread acceptance of the theory of stages of human development from savagery to barbarism and then civilization, were an explicit ranking of races and nations, according to their degree of civilization. It acknowledged that different forms of government were appropriate at different stages of development. However, whatever government prevailed, it had to be *for* the people, even if it was not *by* the people. Such rule had to be in accord with the rule of law. Reason of state and arbitrary rule were completely unacceptable. The ultimate aim of Empire (and a proper Imperial policy) was to educate people to a level where they could ultimately exercise self-rule. As Jones and other Idealists argued, the Empire could not be developed or maintained by financial inducement or trade preferences. If its unity depended on such a cash nexus, then the Empire was already lost. Government of the colonies, for Idealists who supported Empire, had to be for the sake of the governed. Such sentiments were echoed by Edward Caird in an address to students at Balliol College. He reminds them of how great a colonizing nation England had become, showing the might of its power in 'gaining mastery over the uncivilised races'. Despite their initiation in greed and violence, the British government had opened up those countries to the privileges of the governed, ensuring that commerce went hand in hand with civilization.[44]

Muirhead and Hetherington, like Caird, Jones and Haldane, acknowledged that Britain could not pretend that it had exercised anywhere near the same degree of vigilance in protecting the rights of indigenous peoples, as it had for the security and material benefits of the "civilized" white peoples. They suggested, however, that Britain had to adopt a more honourable attitude to the less developed races, and in regulating the relations between the civilized and uncivilized, the interests of the latter should predominate.[45] Muirhead and Hetherington did not minimize the difficulties of preparing a people for self-rule, but nevertheless believed that this must be the aim of all ruling imperial powers.

Freedom, as the British Idealists well knew, is not a gift that can be endowed upon one person by another. An advanced nation, such as Great Britain, had a duty to create the conditions for indigenous people by their own endeavours to attain freedom. The moral principle employed was essentially that espoused by Edmund Burke. It was a kind of maternalism, which later became articulated in a doctrine of trusteeship. The Imperial powers would act as guardians, imparting to those in their care the skills and principles to guide them to the age of reason, with a view to untying the colony from its mother's apron strings. British Idealists did not want to absolve the mother country of her responsibilities in this regard. Social or economic Imperialism was simply ruled out because, as MacCunn observes, all peoples have 'the capacity for a good life', and it is this principle that 'forbids us to treat them as brutes or chattels'.[46] In summary, Idealists rejected the form of Imperialism that Hobhouse and Hobson attributed to them. The irony is that even Hobhouse and Hobson acknowledged that given the fact of Imperialism that Britain had to accept its ethical responsibilities in assisting countries towards self-rule. Furthermore, despite the more popular understanding of Hobhouse and Hobson's critique of Imperialism, it is worth underscoring the point that neither of the latter thinkers was completely opposed to ethical Imperialism. For example, as Hobhouse noted, 'if Imperialism means a sense of the honour of the Empire and of its duties to subject races, then we cannot have too much Imperialism'.[47] This was precisely the Idealist point. Such an Imperialism and Empire would be compatible with morality and democracy. An Empire founded on the aim of ethical self-government would be as acceptable to Hobhouse and Hobson as to Jones, Haldane or Muirhead.

Thus, Hobhouse was therefore clearly mistaken in his attempt to caricature Idealism as simply Imperialist and conservative in its political instincts. The situation, as we have seen, was much more complex and nuanced. Many Idealists were highly critical of both Imperialism and the Boer War; some supported an ethical Imperialism, but were profoundly critical of the Boer War. Some were sympathetic to a grander conception of Empire, and rejected alternative conceptions of Imperialism, such as those based on social and economic grounds of exploitation. In general terms, *all* the British Idealists, regardless, opposed an aggressive, economic or militaristic sense of Imperialism, particularly one that did not take into consideration the interests and customs of colonized peoples. If they were sympathetic to Imperialism, they were disposed generally to a nobler ethical conception premised on education and ultimate self-rule. However, a minority of Idealists, such as Ritchie, could see some virtue in both Imperialism, in general, and the second Boer War, in particular.

It is though still worth underlining the point that Ritchie's support for the Boer War was nonetheless subtle. He was aware of the injustices and atrocities, but saw beneath all that a much wider principle than national self-interest or colonial domination. His justification was based upon a sense of cosmopolitan and humanitarian duty. He contended that he saw in the second Boer War a spirit of solidarity, a willingness to sacrifice personal advantage and convenience, 'and even life itself to the cause, not of an isolated nation, but of free institutions, civilisation, and progress'.[48] Such causes were premised on the belief that nations and states were temporary communities that may be transcended and transformed into wider ethical entities, gradually encompassing the whole world. Ritchie passionately denounced those who accused apologists of the war for embracing a false Patriotism, which elevated the nation above the higher ends of humanity. It was to the Boers to whom these words should be directed, Ritchie contended, 'and not to those who hold that the British Empire and the wider and wider federation to which it will lead the way – a federation of many States of mixed and diverse races ... – is a far healthier "organ of humanity" than the independent domination of a backward race'.[49]

EXPANDING THE MORAL COMMUNITY

We have seen that for the Idealists morality, justice and rights are firmly grounded in the nation state, which is the embodiment of a bounded ethical community comprising the requisite solidarity for a common purpose or common good. Edward Caird forcefully expresses this view when he maintained: 'the highest really organic society, the greatest actual ethical union that exists is the national state. Cosmopolitan charity is still in the main an individualistic thing, a thing that shows itself in the relations of individual man to man, and not in the creation of a real society of mankind'.[50] Despite this apparent rejection of the existence of a wider social and moral community beyond the nation state, Caird reminds us of Green's words and aspirations that the road to a genuine enthusiasm for humanity is the same highway that reason takes us on the journey from good neighbour, to honest citizen and further, until the whole world is my neighbour.[51]

We saw in Chapter 1 how pervasive evolutionary theory had become in the Victorian era, and how it coloured all aspects of life. Evolution lent itself to naturalistic conceptions of international relations and justifications of war and Imperialism. Evolution was also invoked to justify peaceful relations, and not only by those who subscribed to the distinction between cosmic evolution and ethical evolution, or the evolution of morals. It was nevertheless the case that A. R. Wallace and T. H. Huxley were at the forefront in denying the right of biology untrammelled access to the realm of social behaviour and values.[52] Discussions of both kinds often explicitly or implicitly assumed a theory of stages of evolutionary development, and depending upon which stage people may inhabit, relations between them and the civilized nations may differ.

It was quite common among later nineteenth-century theorists, influenced by evolutionary ideas, to extend the struggle for existence beyond individual competition to groups or communities, particularly nations. Natural Selection was deemed to be a mechanism of evolution that operated not only at the individual level, that is what Karl Pearson called intra-group competition, but also among groups ranging from small communities to nations, which compete against each other in the struggle for survival. In Bosanquet's view, the division of labour and exchange of services mitigate nature's competition (red in tooth and claw), and make the group itself 'the primary unit in the struggle for existence'.[53] In Karl Pearson and Benjamin Kidd, and also to a lesser extent in David Ritchie, the idea of group selection led to a justification of Imperialism in which the favoured races had a right to exploit the lower in the competition for existence. The most extreme and uncomplicated of these was Kidd. History, for him, exemplified the remorseless spectacle of competition, selection and survival. In agreement with Weissman, he contended where there is progress it is the result of selection and rejection. Both individuals and societies were subject to the same natural laws in this respect, that is, the survival of the fittest. Rationality and reason could not stem the flow of such a tidal force. Only religion, in Kidd's view, could provide the ultra-rational constraint on unmitigated competition.[54]

Darwin and Spencer themselves gave little ammunition in support of naturalistic theories of war, Imperialism and international relations. Spencer rejected any such conclusions by suggesting that in the evolution from militant to industrial society, physical competition is replaced by commercial competition and co-operation. He was, for example, appalled at British policy during the Boer War condemning it as a blatant struggle for mastery, and thus reacted critically to the potential erosion of traditional freedoms posed by wartime government constraints.[55] In *The Descent of Man*, Darwin attempted to discern human-like consciousness, morality, aesthetics as well as reasoning ascending the evolutionary scale from animals, to lower primates, savages, barbarians and children. He also tried to discover animal senses and instincts, as well as habits in humans. In this latter book, Darwin was more inclined to talk about natural sociability and cooperation than natural aggression. Social cohesiveness, military discipline and skilled organization in technology and weaponry had led to success in overcoming threats from other groups. People, so endowed, were able to reproduce in numbers in a safe environment, potentially advancing social and moral qualities throughout the world by diffusion.[56] Darwin suggested that ethical values would be inculcated into the young by example through education. Darwin identified the same instinct or feeling as Jean Jacques Rousseau in mitigating the brutality of nature, namely sympathy or compassion. Modern warfare may, at the very least, be retrogressive in exposing young healthy men to the perils of battle and the travails of sexually transmitted diseases, much more prevalent in the forces than among the civilian population. There is much equivocation in Darwin on the issues of higher and lower civilizations, the tendency to warfare, as well as upon the way that sentiments and morals are passed on to progeny, but there is little denying the optimistic overall framework within which his speculative history of the ascent of man is set. He indicates that gradually our instinctive sympathy, or what he sometimes calls our virtue of sympathy, one of the noblest of man's endowments, will lead to the transcending of smaller group loyalties such as those to the nation, and extend to 'men of all nations and races' and even to all sentient things.[57] In this respect, Darwin and the British Idealists are in agreement. The issues relate to the way the moral community may be expanded, and for the Idealists it is more of a rational than an emotional mechanism, but both are necessary for the solidarity required to sustain a moral community beyond the state.

As we saw, the British Idealists positioned themselves in the evolutionary debate with the naturalists by asserting the unity of nature and spirit, but sided more with the ethical evolutionists, such as Huxley and Wallace, in maintaining that nature, however refined it may be in the theories of Darwin and Spencer, could not act as the guide to morality. They subscribed to Hegel's version of evolution, or emanation, in which the higher explains the lower in the evolutionary process. They nevertheless developed their own views on international relations and the enlargement of the moral community beyond the state, which exhibited a greater degree of optimism than Hegel was willing to concede. The differences here were though partly due to what had happened subsequently since Hegel's days.

The British Idealists were basically more optimistic than Hegel in believing that the organization of sovereign states would be superseded by a gradual extension of the moral community, embodying the common good. However primitive a community may be, Green contends, consciousness of a good and participation in it are never absent. Rational consciousness of the unfulfilled potential of a common reason impresses upon us a consciousness of wider circles of people who have claims upon us and upon whom we may justifiably make claims. Rights belong to the moral person who has a capacity for conceiving of a good that is common and of acting in such a way as to attain it. These rights or powers do not depend on the state, but upon social relations. Even slaves, insofar as they have social relations, both with other slaves and with the families who own them, have this capacity for conceiving a common good and for acting upon it.[58]

The important point is this: insofar as membership of any community is in principle membership of all communities, each person has a right to be treated as a free person by all other persons, and not to be subjected to force unless it is to prevent force. Recognizing anyone as human acknowledges they are capable of participating in the common good. Green argues: 'It is not the sense of duty to a neighbour, but the practical answer to the question Who is my neighbour?

that has varied'.[59] The road to a cosmopolitan morality begins at home, in the family, neighbourhood, nation and beyond to international morality. It is not the idea of a cosmopolitan humanity that requires explanation, but the retreat from it by sectional interests and privileged classes anxious to give their support to any counter-theory that furthers their exclusive and privileged ends.[60]

There were differences among the Idealists over the extent to which the international community was merely nascent or something of much more moral substance. Bosanquet, Caird and Bradley, for example, were sceptical but not pessimistic. They believed that the unifying process of individuals in organized wholes, such as the nation, would in time be superseded and pass beyond the boundaries of the state. They believed, however, that the process had hardly begun. Bradley conceded that while right exists between states, it did not comprise a "visible community", and to take moral rules applicable to citizens and transform them into abstractions by applying them everywhere was indefensible.[61] An organism requires consciousness of its connections, Bosanquet contends, and no such consciousness has yet been attained in the international sphere, nor was likely to develop in the foreseeable future. There is no international moral tradition comparable with that sustained within a state. Bradley and Bosanquet thus maintained that before humanity could be regarded as an organic whole, a consciousness of it must exist. There must be a communal mind expressive of a general will. Nothing more existed, however, than "mere reciprocal influence", or "external convention".[62] In addition, Jones suggests that '*international ethics*, measured in any recognized and ordinary moral terms, are crude, confused, uncertain, and extra-ordinarily feeble'.[63] Like Hegel, however, Bosanquet acknowledges that the relations among states are nevertheless 'mitigated by humane conventions and usages'.[64]

Such conventions and usages have a more concrete existence as constraining forces for such British Idealists as Sorley, MacKenzie, MacCunn, Jones, Watson, A. C. Bradley, Haldane and Collingwood. Constant interaction among nations, especially in the context of the common heritage of Europeans, has given rise to a common morality and even, for example, a common law of Europe. Morality, they maintain, does not require or rest upon legal enforcement, and the performance of one's moral duty does not require legal sanction. Much of morality falls outside of the scope of law, such as compassion, decency and humaneness, which do not require enforced obedience.[65] The classic statement of this point of view among British Idealists has already been alluded to, namely, Lord Haldane's 'Higher Nationality: A Study in Law and Ethics'.[66] Between civil states there are few hindrances to prevent an international customary body of rules developing what Haldane called an international *Sittlichkeit*. *Sittlichkeit* for Haldane is 'the system of habitual or customary conduct, ethical rather than legal, which embraces all those obligations of the citizen'. These customs were basic and assumed in civil conduct.[67] It therefore represented a 'habit of mind and action'.[68] Another way of describing it is as the system of dominant "organizing ideas" embodied in international customary rules. Haldane sees this subtle body of obligations present in all the institutions of civil society and the state. The central question he puts is: Can there be *Sitte* that surpasses particular states? His answer is quite direct. Sociologically and legally there is nothing to prevent this. Once states are educated and rational enough, they will begin inevitably begin to consider the opinions of other states. With common civilizing ideas gradually evolving, Haldane thus envisages a developing global system of legal and moral norms. He refers explicitly to this as an "international *Sittlichkeit*". However, such *Sitte* would nonetheless be embedded constitutively in all genuinely civil states. The only hindrance to this is 'the absence of a clear conception of principle'.[69]

More recently, R. G. Collingwood had criticized those – and some Idealists like Hegel, Ritchie and Caird would be among them – who have a narrow conception of international law, proclaiming it as a pseudo-law, or not law at all, because it lacks an international sovereign and collective enforcement. Such a conception, he contends, shows an unawareness of modern European history. Customary law, both civil and international, was the rule rather than the exception in later medieval early modern Europe. In the international sphere, it resembles the condition of law in the Icelandic sagas, a form of customary law which was never formally enacted, but was articulated by the Law-Speaker and comes about as a result of the everyday business of interaction, commerce and communication. No group of people was charged with its execution, but some may form alliances to crush those who disregard it.[70]

The British Idealists, on the whole, favoured the view that law was the expression of the will of an organized sovereign community, enforceable by its agents. Therefore, international agreements could be extended the title of law only as a matter of courtesy. In this respect, when compared with classic international relations theory, they are closer to Pufendorf than to Grotius. Bradley remarks that 'it is doubtful if international law can be said to exist', and Ritchie calls it a convenient fiction.[71] In this respect, they follow Hegel who maintains that the "so-called *international law*" is not, strictly speaking, law at all because it lacks a sovereign to enforce it.[72] This was also a view common to Thomas Hobbes and John Austin. Even though international law is predicated on the principle that it ought to be obeyed, universal right, the basis of such an obligation, is not actual. This is why Ritchie argued that resort to arbitration between nations remains purely voluntary, but: 'Everything that helps towards the ideal of a federation of the world (not in a mere sentimental sense but in the stricter political sense of the term "federation") or of greater portions of it, seems to me a genuine movement for durable peace'.[73]

Morality and the higher ideals of humanity do not pre-exist in a realm outside of the state awaiting apprehension and application. We cannot force or contrive them and impose them on an unfertile ground by means of a legal framework. A legal framework may promote a common sympathy, but the sympathy is itself a prerequisite of success.[74] The British Idealists believe our conception of the good life and of the highest ideals of civilization are derived from our participation in a community, which is itself a partial realization of these ideals. Our nation provides and sustains for us the standards we project upon humanity. A nation's sense of honour, decency and propriety is taken by it and projected onto the wider world as humanitarian principles.[75] This does not mean that one ideal is as good as another. Each state may travel a different path, and all seek to emulate the best that they find in the representatives of civilization they admire most. The conception of freedom, human dignity, mutual recognition and self-realization precludes certain ideals gaining purchase, and in this respect Idealism rejects relativism.

CONCLUSION

We have seen that Patriotism and humanitarianism are not for the British Idealists' incompatible principles. The nation or state is the vehicle through which we contribute to humanity. It is being a good citizen and ensuring that the state is genuinely committed to its purpose that facilitate what is best in the state being translated into the cosmopolitan ideal. Sectional interest and privilege, the causes of external and internal antagonism, will wither away in the face of the

Patriotism of the good citizen. In general, then, the British Idealists are suggesting that the cause of humanity is furthered by putting one's own house in order, and this requires moralizing the institutions and relations of the state as they stand. [76]

The issues of Imperialism and the Boer War were divisive among all sections of society, and likewise the British Idealists differed in their views and the degree to which they were prepared to support either. The bottom line was that Imperialism was a fact and Britain, the more humanitarian critics believed, could not absolve itself of the responsibility of preparing the "backward" peoples for self-government and assisting them in their quest to join the community of more developed states. They acknowledged that grave injustices had been perpetrated against less advanced peoples, but believed that a more humane and sensitive Imperialism could deliver them from subjugation. This ethically orientated Imperialism was generally acceptable even to some of the more severe critics of Imperialism, such as Hobhouse and Hobson. Whatever one's attitude to Imperialism, there was no necessary conclusion determining the stance one took towards the Boer War. There were genuine principled disagreements, often resting on the imputation of motives and interpretations of the steady flow of information, often contradictory, about local atrocities. In general, views were divided along two lines. There were those who opposed the war because they believed that Britain was caught up in jingoistic nationalism, wanting to assert its military might over the Boers and rule South Africa in its own interests. Supporters of the war often saw wider issues of principle, such as the honouring of the duty to include black South Africans in a democratic process, achieving the wider cosmopolitan ideals of justice and humanity and eliminating racial discrimination and bigotry.

However, the carnage of the First World War transformed even the most sceptical of the British Idealists towards internationalism. The aftermath of the war provided the occasion to support a federation of states as the salvation of mankind. A League of Peace, or League of Nations, was enthusiastically supported by many Idealists. Bosanquet, for example, welcomed the establishment of the League of Nations as 'the hope and refuge of mankind'.[77] He was still concerned, however, that any such experiment in international organization preserved the individual national contributions to mankind.[78] The general enthusiasm for international cooperation, following the 1914–1918 war, demonstrated to the British Idealists the existence of a will stronger than they had envisaged. They were still cautious in their enthusiasm for the League of Nations, mainly because the moral will – by which alone success could be guaranteed – was still emerging and fragile. Formal structures and mere agreements would not transform international relations, without the foundation of a common community spirit.[79] Yet, they nonetheless retained what might be considered their trademark optimism about what could be achieved in future international cooperation.

What again stands out from these protracted British Idealists reflections on war, Imperialism, international organization and international law is the thoughtful and subtle adaptability of British Idealist thought in the way it responded to events. As we have seen in prior chapters, despite internal conflicts within the school, British Idealism did contain immensely sophisticated and yet often understated moral and philosophical resources, enabling it to respond in creative and constructive ways to changing circumstances. The arguments we see within Idealism concerning international events are still, in general terms, pertinent to our own day, particularly to our current judgements on war, humanitarian intervention and international law. We have neither outgrown their problems, nor, as yet, actually completely surpassed, in any lasting or meaningful way, the systematic thoroughness and intellectual substance of their rich and complex answers.

NOTES

INTRODUCTION

1. Oakeshott, M. 'Beyond Realism and Idealism'. A review of W. M. Urban, Beyond Realism and Idealism in Michael Oakeshott, *The Concept of a Philosophical Jurisprudence*, L. O'Sullivan (ed.), Exeter: Imprint Academic, pp. 321–22, 2006.
2. Sorley, W. R. *Recent Tendencies in Ethics*, Edinburgh: Blackwood, p. 87, 1904.
3. Green, T. H. *Prolegomena to Ethics* [original publication 1883], London: Longmans, Green, § 183, 1907.
4. Bradley, F. H. *Ethical Studies,* second edition [original publication 1876], Oxford: Clarendon Press, p. 116, 1962. Cf. Green, *Prolegomena to Ethics*, § 184.

CHAPTER 1

1. Kant, I. *Critique of Pure Reason*, London: Dent, p. 12, 1946. Karl Reinhold in developing the ideas of the *Critique* on representation and J. G. Fichte on self-consciousness sought to give Kant's work a firmer foundation. These thinkers formulated methods and ideas that were to result in radical and novel methodologies, such as phenomenological description. See Scott Jenkins, 'Self-Consciousness, System and Dialectic' in D. Moyer (ed.), *The Routledge Companion to Nineteenth Century Philosophy*, London: Routledge, p. 3, 2010.
2. Cited in Muirhead, J. H. *Coleridge as Philosopher*, London: George Allen and Unwin, p. 49, 1930.
3. Cited in Davie, G. *The Democratic Intellect*, Edinburgh: Edinburgh University Press, p. 276, 1961. Davie argues that Ferrier continues of the Common Sense school, occupying its rationalist end as opposed to the intuitionist middle.
4. See Ferrier, J. F. *The Institutes of Metaphysic: The Theory of the Knowing Mind: The Theory of Knowing and Being*, Edinburgh: Blackwood, pp. 91–2, 1856, first edition 1854.
5. Andrew Seth later changed his name to Andrew Seth Pringle-Pattison in order to satisfy the terms of a bequest.

NOTES

6 Haldane and Seth had also tried unsuccessfully to establish a journal that aimed at giving more attention to metaphysics than the preeminent philosophical journal *Mind*.
7 It became received wisdom to discuss the idea of 'My Station and Its Duties' as Bradley's communitarian theory of ethics. Peter Nicholson, however, has convincingly shown that Bradley's own position is articulated in the chapter on 'Ideal Morality'. Peter Nicholson, *The Political Philosophy of the British Idealists*, Cambridge: Cambridge University Press, pp. 1–53, 1990.
8 Edward Caird, 'Preface', in *Essays in Philosophical Criticism*, A. Seth and R. B. Haldane (eds), London: Longmans Green, pp. 2–3, 1883.
9 Seth, A. 'Philosophy As Criticism of Categories' in *Essays in Philosophical Criticism*, pp. 8–40. Also see J. H. Muirhead, *The Platonic Tradition in Anglo-Saxon Philosophy*, London: Allen and Unwin, pp. 174–75, 1931.
10 Carlyle, T. *The Works of Thomas Carlyle*, H. D. Traill (ed.), London: Chapman and Hall, Vol. 27, p. 59, 1896–1899.
11 Muirhead, J. H. *The Platonic Tradition*, p. 146.
12 See Hamilton, W. 'On the Philosophy of the Unconditioned (1829)' in *Discussions on Philosophy and Literature, Education and University Reform, Chiefly from the Edinburgh Review; Corrected, Vindicated, Enlarged, in Notes and Appendices*, London, Brown Green and Longmans, 1853. For a clear statement of his basic position see, Phillip Ferreira, 'Ferrier, James Frederick' in *Dictionary of Nineteenth Century British Philosophers*, W. J. Mander and P. F. Sell (eds), Bristol: Thoemmes, pp. 382–86, 2002.
13 Sorley, W. R. *A History of English Philosophy*, Cambridge: Cambridge University Press, p. 284, 1937.
14 James Frederick Ferrier, *Institutes of Metaphysics*, p. 495.
15 See Bradley, J. 'Hegel in Britain: A Brief History of British Commentary and Attitudes', *Heythrop Journal*, XX, p. 7, 1979.
16 Davie, G. *Democratic Intellect*, p. 299.
17 Ferrier, F. *Institutes of Metaphysics*, p. 80.
18 McKillop, A. B. *A Disciplined Intelligence*, Montreal and Kingston: McGill Queen's University Press, p. 173, 2001.
19 Ferrier, F. *Institutes of Metaphysic*, p. 536. For a clear statement of his basic position see, Phillip Ferreira, 'Ferrier, James Frederick', pp. 382–86.
20 Ferrier, *Institutes of Metaphysics*, p. 522.
21 Cited in Davie, G. *Democratic Intellect*, p. 335. Ferrier is reputed to have said that he turned Hegel's book *Science of Logic* upside-down in the hope that it would become clearer.
22 He authored the book on him in the Blackwood Philosophical Classics series. A. Campbell Fraser, *Berkeley*, Edinburgh: Blackwood, 1881. Fraser also edited Berkeley's *Works* in four Volumes, 1901.
23 We will return to the dispute between Absolute and Personal Idealism in the next chapter.

24 Fraser, A. C. *Berkeley and Spiritual Realism*, London: Constable, p. 82, 1908.
25 Fraser, A. C. *Berkeley and Spiritual Realism*, p. 84.
26 Barbour, G. F. 'Memoir' in Andrew Seth Pringle-Pattison, *The Balfour Lectures on Realism*, London and Edinburgh: Blackwood, pp. 8–11, 1933.
27 See the Introduction to Boucher, D. 'The Scottish Idealists', Exeter: Imprint Academic, 2004; Muirhead, J. H. *The Platonic Tradition*; James Hutchison Stirling, *The Secret of Hegel: Being the Hegelian System in Origin, Principle, Form, and Matter*, Edinburgh: Oliver and Boyd, 1898, second edition; first edition 1865.
28 Stirling, J. H. *The Secret of Hegel*, p. 85.
29 Muirhead relating Andrew Seth's comments in *The Platonic Tradition*, p. 170.
30 Greenleaf, W. H. *Oakeshott's Philosophical Politics*, London: Longmans, p. 1, 1966.
31 Ferreira, P. 'Stirling, James Hutchinson' (1820–1909), *Dictionary of Nineteenth Century British Philosophers*, W. J. Mander and Alan P. F. Sell (eds), Bristol: Thoemmes, Vol. 2, p. 1082, 2002.
32 Flint, R. *Vico*, Edinburgh: Blackwell, p. 3, 1891.
33 Jones, H. and Muirhead, J. H. *The Life and Philosophy of Edward Caird*, Glasgow: Maclehose, Jackson and Co., p. 23, 1921.
34 Jones, H. *Old Memories*, London: Hodder and Stoughton, p. 94, 1922.
35 Richter, M. *The Politics of Conscience: T. H. Green and his Age*, Bristol: Thoemmes, p. 71, 1996.
36 Green, T. H. *The Works of T. H. Green*, Vol. III, London: Longmans, Green, 1888, pp. i, 371 and W. R. Sorley, *A History of English Philosophy*, Cambridge: Cambridge University Press, p. 288, 1937.
37 Muirhead, J. H. (ed.), *Contemporary British Philosophy*, London: Macmillan, dedication page, 1925.
38 See Muirhead, J. H. (ed.), *Bernard Bosanquet and his Friends: Letters Illustrating the Sources and the Development of his Philosophical Opinions*, London: George Allen and Unwin, 1935.
39 Smith, J. A. 'Philosophy as the Development of the Notion and Reality of Self-Consciousness' in *Contemporary British Philosophy* (second series), J. H. Muirhead (ed.), London: George Allen and Unwin, pp. 225–44, 1925.
40 Gibbins, J. and Grote, J. *Cambridge University and the Development of Victorian Thought*, Exeter: Imprint Academic, p. 410, 2007.
41 Sorley, W. R. 'The Historical Method', in A. Seth and R. B. Haldane (eds), *Essays in Philosophical Criticism*, p. 125.
42 Sorley, W. R. *The Moral Life*, Cambridge: Cambridge University Press, pp. 126–40, 1911.
43 Oakeshott, M. *Rationalism in Politics*, Indianapolis: Liberty Press, p. 45, 1991.
44 See, for example, Sorley, W. R. *On the Ethics of Naturalism*, Edinburgh and London: Blackwood, 1885, and *Recent Tendencies in Ethics*, Edinburgh and London: Blackwood, 1904.

NOTES

45 McTaggart, J. M. E. 'Introduction to the Study of Philosophy', Syllabus of a course of lectures delivered in Trinity College in Cambridge, second edition 1906, reprinted in 1911 and 1920. It is 29 printed pages with the argument of each topic presented in numbered paragraphs. Michael Oakeshott's copy is heavily annotated by him. Also see J. M. E. McTaggart, 'Introduction to the Study of Philosophy', in *Philosophical Studies* by McTaggart and edited by S. V. Keeling, New York: Books for Libraries, 1966: first edition, 1934.
46 Oakeshott, M. Notes Volume III, August 1922, Oakeshott Papers, The British Library of Political Science, 29, quoting page 242 of Jones, H. *A Faith That Enquires*, London, Macmillan, 1922.
47 Oakeshott, M. Notebook IV, 2 July 1923, Oakeshott Papers, The British Library of Political Science, 1617.
48 Review of *The Life and Philosophy of Edward Caird in the Hibbert Journal*, October 1922.
49 See, for example, Podoksik, E. *In Defence of Modernity: Vision and Philosophy in Michael Oakeshott*, Exeter: Imprint Academic, p. 10–16, 2003. Collingwood, R. G. *An Essay on Philosophical Method*, Oxford: Oxford University Press, 1933; Oakeshott, M. *Experience and its Modes*, Cambridge: Cambridge University Press, 1933; and Collingwood, R. G. *Speculum Mentis: or the Map of Knowledge*, Oxford: Clarendon Press, 1924.
50 Ritchie, D. G. 'Ethical Democracy: Evolution and Democracy' in D. Boucher (ed.), *The British Idealists*, Cambridge: Cambridge University Press, pp. 68–93, 1997.
51 Wittgenstein, L. *Tractatus Logico-Philosophicus*, London: Routledge, Kegan Paul, 1960, pp. 4, 112.
52 Sorley, W. R. *Recent Tendencies in Ethics*, p. 83. Sorley suggests: '...according to it the facts dealt with by the natural sciences are the only reality which is knowable; man's nature is part of these and has to be adapted to them, and there is nothing further with which it can be brought into relation.'
53 See Ruse, M. *The Darwinian Paradigm: Essays on Its History, Philosophy and Religious Implications*, London: Routledge, p. 11, 1993.
54 Ruse, M. 'Natural Selection in The Origin of Species', *Studies in History and Philosophy of Science*, 1, pp. 311–51, 1972.
55 Burrow, J. W. *Evolution and Society: A Study in Victorian Social Theory*, Cambridge: Cambridge University Press, pp. 20, 100, 1966.
56 Darwin added an historical sketch of his precursors to the third edition of *The Origin of Species*, 1862. He expanded upon the sketch in subsequent editions.
57 Baillie, J. B. 'The Individual and his World', in J. H. Muirhead (ed.), *Contemporary British Philosophy*, first series, London: George Allen and Unwin, p. 17, 1924.
58 Sorely, W. R. *Recent Tendencies in Ethics*, Edinburgh: Blackwood, p. 34, 1904.
59 Spencer, H. *The Principles of Ethics*, Indianapolis: Liberty Press, Vol. 1, p. 7, 1978, [first published in 1893].

NOTES

60 Modern opponents such as F. de Waal, basing their arguments on Kant, want to argue that nature and humanity are different in kind and that different forms of explanation are applicable. *Primates and Philosophers: How Morality Evolved*, New Jersey: Princeton University Press, pp. 116–17, 2006.
61 See Howard, J. *Darwin*, Oxford: Oxford University Press, p. 6, 1982; and George, W. *Darwin*, London, Fontana, p. 7, 1982.
62 In *The Descent of Man and Selection in Relation to Sex*, London: Murray, 1888, Darwin describes the Feugians in the following terms: 'They possessed hardly any arts, and like wild animals lived on what they could catch; they had no government, and were merciless to everyone not of their own small tribe'. p. 619.
63 Desmond, A. and Moore, J. *Darwin*, London: Michael Joseph, pp. 468–69, 1992.
64 Hull, D. L. 'Darwin's Science and Victorian Philosophy of Science' in M. J. S. Hodge and G. Radick (eds), *The Cambridge Companion to Darwin*, Cambridge: Cambridge University Press, 2003. Barry G. Gale has argued that when Darwin published *The Origin of Species* his evidence in support of his theories was no more substantial than that of the Creationists. *Evolution Without Evidence: Charles Darwin and the Origin of Species*, Albuquerque: University of New Mexico, 1982. Darwin, C. *The Origin of Species by Means of Natural Selection: Or the Preservation of Favoured Races in the Struggle for Life*, edited by J. W. Burrow, Harmondsworth: Penguin, 1985: First published by John Murray, 1859.
65 Richards, R. A. 'Darwin's Philosophical Impact' in D. Moyar (ed.), *The Routledge Companionto Nineteenth Century Philosophy*, London: Routledge, p. 471, 2010.
66 Clark, R. E. D. *Darwin: Before and After*, Exeter: Paternoster, p. 39, 1971.
67 Darwin, C. *Origin of Species*, pp. 458–59.
68 Dawkins, R. *The Blind Watchmaker*, London: Penguin, new edition, 2006.
69 Paley, W. *Natural Theology*, Vol. IV, *Works*, London: George Cowie, 1837. The volume was first published in 1802.
70 Hofstadter, R. 'The Vogue of Spencer' from Chapter 2 of *Darwinism in American Thought* (1955). Reprinted in *Darwin* (Norton Critical Edition), P. Appleman (ed.), New York: Norton, pp. 389–410, 1979.
71 Jones, H 'The Misuse of Metaphors in the Human Sciences' in *Working Faith of the Social Reformer*, London: Macmillan, p. 44, 1910. Pringle-Pattison, A. S. 'Life and Philosophy of Herbert Spencer', *The Quarterly Review*, 200, pp. 241–42, 1904; and Bosanquet, B. 'Socialism and Natural Selection' in D. Boucher (ed.), *The British Idealists*, pp. 50–67.
72 Ritchie, D. G. *Darwin and Hegel With Other Philosophical Studies*, London: Swan Sonnenschein, pp. 32–7, 1893.
73 Ritchie, D. G. 'Ethical Democracy: Evolution and Democracy' in D. Boucher (ed.), *The British Idealists*, Cambridge: Cambridge University Press, p. 73.

NOTES

74 Ritchie, D. G. *Darwinism and Politics*, London: Swan Sonnenschein, pp. 100–101. Also see pp. 131–32, 1901.
75 Kuhn, T. S. *The Structure of Scientific Revolutions*, Chicago: University of Chicago Press, 1996, third revised edition.
76 See Boucher D. and Vincent, A. *A Radical Hegelian: The Political and Social Philosophy of Henry Jones*, Cardiff: University of Wales Press, Chapter 4, 1992.
77 Darwin, C. *Origin of Species*, p. 458.
78 Spencer, H. *The Principles of Ethics*, Indianapolis: Liberty Press, Vol. I, p. 40, 1978 [first published 1893].
79 In maintaining that all the races of man are descended from a common stock, for example, Darwin refers us to Huxley for substantiation. Darwin, C. *The Descent of Man*, p. 176.
80 Huxley, T. H. 'Natural Rights and Political Rights', *The Nineteenth Century*, 25, pp. 179–80, 1890.
81 Huxley, T. H. 'Evolution and Ethics', in *Evolution and Ethics: T. H. Huxley's Evolution and Ethics with New Essays on its Victorian Sociobiological Context*, J. Paradis and G. C. Williams (eds), New Jersey: Princeton University Press, p. 132, 1989.
82 Sorley, W. R. Recent Tendencies in Ethics, p. 47.
83 Huxley, T. H. 'Evolution and Ethics', note 20.
84 Jones, H. *Faith That Enquires*, p. 95.
85 Jones, H. *Idealism as a Practical Creed*, Glasgow: Maclehose, p. 29, 1909. Elsewhere he argues that the power of the idea of evolution has 'transfigured the world'. Jones, H. *The Working Faith of the Social Reformer*, London: Macmillan, p. 36, 1910.
86 Bosanquet, B. 'Socialism and Natural Selection', p. 57.
87 Jones, H. 'Is the Order of Nature Opposed to the Moral Life?' An Inaugural Address, Glasgow: Maclehose, pp. 26–30, 1894.
88 Ritchie, D. *Darwinism and Politics*, p. 115.
89 Seth, G. *Hegelianism and Personality*, p. 89.
90 See Ritchie, D. *Darwin and Hegel*, p. 47.
91 Caird, E. *The Evolution of Religion*, Glasgow: Maclehose, Vol. I, p. 45, 1899.
92 Ritchie, D. G. *The Principles of State Interference*, second edition, London: Swan Sonnenschein, p. 44, 1896.
93 Caird, E. *The Critical Philosophy of Kant*, Glasgow: Maclehose, Vol. I, p. 35, 1889.
94 Caird, E. *Evolution of Religion*, Vol. 1 p. x. Cf. 24–5 and 27.
95 Jones, H. *A Faith that Enquires*, p. 98.
96 See, Williams, B. *Ethics and the Limits of Philosophy*, London: Harper Collins, p. 174, 1993. This argument forms an important theme of his whole book.
97 Green, T. H. *Prolegomena to Ethics*, § 317.
98 Murdoch, I. *Metaphysics as a Guide to Morals*, Middlesex: Penguin Books, p. 47, 1993.
99 Sidgwick, H. *Methods of Ethics*, 7th edition preface, London: Macmillan, pp. xix–xx, 1907.

NOTES

100 The term 'sleek and tame' comes from D. G. Ritchie. Ritchie commented in his review of Sidgwick's *Elements of Politics* (although it applies equally to the *Methods of Ethics*) that it was 'much more than we might expect from an end of the century Blackstone, or from an English Hegel, showing the rationality of the existing order of things, with only a few modest proposals of reform'. Ritchie, D. G. 'A Review of *The Elements of Politics*', *International Journal of Ethics*, 2, p. 255, 1892.
101 See Collini S. et al., *That Noble Science of Politics*, Cambridge: Cambridge University Press, p. 294, 1983. Sidgwick would, in fact, probably still be partly right today about utilitarianism.
102 See Collingwood, R. G. *The New Leviathan*, revised edition, D. Boucher (ed.), Oxford: Oxford University Press, 1993.
103 Bernard Williams comments on this that utilitarianism assumes 'the mind, before any experience is empty ... it involves elaborate and implausible explanations about evolution and human learning', Williams, B. *Ethics and the Limits of Philosophy*, p. 106.
104 Bradley, F. H. 'Mr Sidgwick's Hedonism', in *Collected Essays* Vol. 1, Oxford: Clarendon, p. 95, 1935.
105 Bradley obviously enjoyed this quote from Sir James Fitzjames Stephens: 'If I wanted to make you happy, which I do not, I should do so by pampering to your vices, which I will not'. *Ethical Studies*, p. 105.
106 Stephen, L. 'Ethics and the Struggle for Existence', *Contemporary Review*, 64, p. 165, 1893.
107 See Mulhall, S. and Swift, A. second edition, *Liberals and Communitarians*, Oxford: Blackwell, 1996.
108 Bradley, F. H. *Ethical Studies*, p. 171.
109 Hegel, G. W. F. *Philosophy of Right*, § 146, p. 190.
110 Hegel, G. W. F. *Philosophy of Right*, § 148, p. 191.

CHAPTER 2

1 Jones, H. 'Idealism and Politics', in two parts, part II, *Contemporary Review*, 42, p. 743, 1907.
2 Jones, H. 'Idealism and Politics', p. 749.
3 Joachim, H. H. *The Nature of Truth*, second edition, edited by R. G. Collingwood, London: Oxford University Press, 1939.
4 Collingwood, R. G. *An Autobiography*, with an Introduction by Stephen Toulmin, Oxford: Oxford University Press, pp. 29–43, 1978. Also see Collingwood, R. G. *An Essay on Metaphysics*, new revised edition edited by Rex Martin, Oxford: Clarendon Press, part I, Metaphysics, 1998.
5 Bradley, F. H. *Appearance and Reality: A Metaphysical Essay*, Oxford: Clarendon Press, 9th edition, p. 127, 1969.
6 Oakeshott, M. *Experience and its Modes*, p. 26.
7 Collingwood, R. G. *The Idea of History*, revised edited by W. J. van der Dussen Oxford: Clarendon Press, p. 215, 1993.
8 Bradley, F. H. *Appearance and Reality*, p. 321.

NOTES

9 Bradley, F. H. *Essays on Truth and Reality*, Oxford: Clarendon Press, p. 239, 1968, first published 1914.
10 Oakeshott, M. *Experience and its Modes*, p. 59. Also see Bradley, *Truth and Reality*, p. 215; and T. H. Green, *Prolegomena to Ethics*, Oxford: Clarendon Press, pp. 16–60, 1907.
11 Bradley, F. H. *Appearance and Reality*, p. 434.
12 Bradley, F. H. *Truth and Reality*, p. 235; and *Appearance and Reality*, pp. 439–40.
13 Hegel, G. W. F. *Elements of the Philosophy of Right*, A. W. Wood, (ed.) and translated by H. B. Nisbet, Cambridge: Cambridge University Press, 1991.
14 Jones, H. *Idealism as a Practical Creed*, Glasgow: Maclehose, 1909.
15 Collingwood, R. G. *An Autobiography*, pp. 146–67.
16 Hobhouse, L. T. *The Metaphysical Theory of the State*, London: Allen and Unwin, 1951. First published in 1918.
17 See Vincent, A. 'The Individual in Hegelian Thought' *Idealistic Studies*, XII, 2, pp. 156–68, 1982.
18 Bradley, F. H. *Appearance and Reality*, pp. 464–65.
19 Bradley, F. H. *The Principles of Logic*, second edition with commentary and terminal essays, Oxford: Clarendon Press, 1932, p. 656. Cf. Sweet, '"Absolute Idealism" and Finite Individuality', *Indian Philosophical Quarterly*, Vol. XXIV, No 4, 1997.
20 Bradley, F. H. *Ethical Studies*, second edition, Oxford: Clarendon Press, pp. 166–67 and 173, 1928.
21 Bradley, F. H. *Appearance and Reality*, p. 217. Cf. Bernard Bosanquet, *The Value and Destiny of the Individual*, London: Macmillan, p. 69, 1912.
22 Bosanquet, B. *Psychology of the Moral Self*, London: Macmillan, p. 95, 1897.
23 Jones, H. *The Philosophy of Martineau*, London: Macmillan, pp. 20–1, 1905.
24 Jones, H. *Idealism as a Practical Creed*, p. 263.
25 Published as H. Wildon Carr (ed.), *Life and finite individuality: Two symposia. I and II*, London: Williams and Norgate, 1918.
26 Oakeshott, M. *Experience and its Modes*, pp. 268–74.
27 Seth, for example, objected to Absolute Idealism's 'unification of consciousness in a single Self'. Seth, A. *Hegelianism and Personality*, Edinburgh: Blackwood, p. 215, 1888.
28 Seth, A. *Scottish Philosophy*, p. 221.
29 Seth, A. *Hegelianism and Personality*, p. 215.
30 Pringle-Pattison, A. S. *The Idea of God in the Light of recent Philosophy*, Oxford: Oxford University Press, p. 189, 1917. [In 1898, to meet the condition for inheriting an estate, Andrew Seth changed his name to Andrew Seth Pringle-Pattison].
31 Seth, A. *The Idea of God*, p. 259. Cf. G. Watts Cunningham, *The Idealistic Argument in Recent British and American Philosophy*, New York: Century, pp. 162–63, 1933.
32 Sturt, H. 'Preface' to *Personal Idealism*, H. Sturt (ed.), London: Macmillan, p. vi, 1902.

NOTES

33 Cunningham, G. W. *The Idealistic Argument*, p. 165.
34 Seth, A. 'Philosophy as Criticism of the Categories', *Essays in Philosophical Criticism*, A. Seth and R. B. Haldane (eds), London: Longmans Green, p. 38, 1883.
35 Pringle-Pattison, A. S. *The Idea of God in the Light of Recent Philosophy*, Oxford, Clarendon Press, p. 266, 1920. Also see, Rashdall, H. 'Personality, Human and Divine', *Personal Idealism*, H. Sturt (ed.), London: Macmillan, p. 372, 1902.
36 Seth, A. 'A New Theory of the Absolute', in *Man's Place in the Cosmos*, Edinburgh: Blackwood, pp. 129–225, 1897.
37 Boyce Gibson, W. R. 'A Peace Policy for Idealists', *The Hibbert Journal*, 5, p. 409, 1906–1907.
38 Sturt, H. (ed.), *Personal Idealism: Philosophical Essays*, London: Macmillan, p. x, 1902.
39 McTaggart, J. M. E. 'An Ontological Idealism' in *Philosophical Studies*, p. 273.
40 McTaggart, J. M. E. 'The Individualism of Value' in *Philosophical Studies*. Also cited in Coates, Jr., *Oakeshott and his Contemporaries*, p. 108, from the copy found among Oakeshott's unpublished papers. McTaggart differs from fellow Personalists such as Pringle-Pattison and Rashdall in that he had very little sympathy for religion.
41 See Jones, H. and Muirhead, J. H. *The Life and Philosophy of Edward Caird*, Glasgow: Maclehose, Jackson and Co., Chapter viii, 1921.
42 Caird, E. 'Idealism and the Theory of Knowledge' (1903), in *Collected Works of* Edward Caire, C. Tyler (ed.), Vol. 12, *Miscellaneous Writings*, Bristol: Thoemmes, p. 101, 1999.
43 Caird, E. *Hegel*, Edinburgh: Blackwood, p. 138, 1903.
44 See Collingwood, R. G. *An Essay on Metaphysics*.
45 Caird, E. *Hegel*, p. 55.
46 Caird, E. 'Metaphysics', *Essays on Literature and Philosophy*, Vol. 2, Glasgow: Maclehose, p. 442, 1892.
47 Seth, A. *From Kant to Hegel*, p. 81.
48 Seth, A. *Scottish Philosophy*, p. 203.
49 See for an exemplification Mitchell, W. 'Moral Obligation' in *The Scottish Idealists: Selected Philosophical Writings*, D. Boucher (ed.), Exeter: Imprint Academic, pp. 141–58, 2004.
50 Oakeshott, M. *Hobbes on Civil Association*, Oxford: Blackwell, p. 78, 1975. Also see D. Boucher, 'Oakeshott and the History of Political Thought', *Collingwood and British Idealism Studies*, Vol. 13:2, 2007.
51 Oakeshott, M. *Hobbes on Civil Association*, pp. 147–8. Also see Tregenza, I. *Michael Oakeshott on Hobbes*, Exeter: Imprint Academic, 2003.
52 Jones, H. 'Aims of Philosophy', p. 162.
53 Quoted in Kluback, W. *Wilhelm Dilthey's Philosophy of History*, New York: Columbia University press, p. 27, 1956.
54 Collingwood, R. G. *Philosophical Method*, p.11.
55 Bosanquet, B. *The Essentials of Logic*, London: Macmillan, p. 166, 1903.

NOTES

56 Oakeshott, M. 'The Concept of a Philosophical Jurisprudence', *Politica* 3, p. 346, 1938.
57 Stebbing, L. S. 'The Method of Analysis in Metaphysics', *Proceedings of the Aristotelian Society*, 33, p. 93, 1932–1933.
58 Take McTaggart, for example, who maintained that metaphysics rests upon certain assumptions, but unlike the natural sciences, does not make them uncritically, see McTaggart, J. M. E. 'Introduction to the Study of Philosophy', p. 184.
59 Moore, G. E. 'The Nature and Reality of Objects of Perception', in *Philosophical Studies*, London: Routledge and Kegan Paul, p. 31–96, 1922.
60 Moore, G. E. 'Proof of an External World', *Proceedings of the British Academy*, 25, pp. 272–300, 1939.
61 Joachim, H. H. *Nature of Truth*, p. vii.
62 Joachim, H. H. *Nature of Truth*, p. 176.
63 Oakeshott, M. *Experience and its Modes*, p. 11.
64 Bosanquet, B. *The Meeting of Extremes in Contemporary Philosophy*, London: Macmillan, 1921.
65 For an excellent account of Collingwood's engagement with Realism see Junichi Kasuga, *The Formation of R. G. Collingwood's Early Criticism of Realism*, unpublished Ph.D., Cardiff University, 2010.
66 Collingwood, R. G. *An Essay on Metaphysics*, pp. 162–71.
67 Boyce Gibson, W. R. 'A Peace Policy for Idealists', *The Hibbert Journal*, 5, p. 407, 1906–1907.
68 McTaggart, J. M. E. 'Dare to Be Wise', in *Philosophical Studies*, 38.
69 Russell, B. *Our Knowledge of the External World*, 17. Cf. 26, London: George Allen and Unwin, 1914.
70 McTaggart, J. M. E. 'Dare to be Wise', 40.
71 Bradley, F. H. *Ethical Studies*, second edition, Oxford, Clarendon Press, p. 193, 1927: first edition 1874.

CHAPTER 3

1 Bradley, F. H. *The Presuppositions of Critical History* (1874), reprinted in *Collected Essays*, Vol. I, p. 17, 21 and 45, Oxford: Clarendon Press, 1935.
2 Bradley, F. H. *Presuppositions*, p. 13,
3 Bradley, F. H. *Presuppositions*, p. 45. Collingwood accuses Bradley of undermining his Idealism by introducing an element of naturalism in positing his criterion of historical truth. See R. G. Collingwood, *The Idea of History*, revised edition, W. J. van der Dussen (ed.), Oxford: Clarendon Press, pp. 134–41, 1993.
4 Bosanquet, B. *Philosophical Theory of the State*, London: Macmillan, p. 2, 1899.
5 Oakeshott, M. *Experience and its Modes*, Cambridge: Cambridge University Press, p. 2, 1933.
6 Jones, H. *A Faith That Enquires*, London: Macmillan, p. 95, 1922.

NOTES

7 Notes taken by Thomas Jones of Henry Jones' Moral Philosophy Lectures (Pass), Vol. II, p. 3. National Library of Wales, Aberystwyth, 1897–1898.
8 Jones, H. *Faith That Enquires*, p. 93.
9 For a brief summary in his own words see Popper, K. *Unended Quest: An Intellectual Autobiography*, London: Routledge, 2002.
10 Jones, H. *Faith That Enquires*, p. 82.
11 Jones, H. *Faith That Enquires*, p. 82. T. S. Kuhn, *The Structure of Scientific Revolutions*, Chicago: Chicago University Press, pp. 111–35, 1970; R. G. Collingwood, *An Essay on Metaphysics*, revised edition, Martin R. (ed.), Oxford: Clarendon Press, p. 48, 1998.
12 Bosanquet, B. *The Philosophical Theory of the State*, London: Macmillan, p. 77, 1965.
13 Caird, E. 'The Problem of Philosophy' in D. Boucher (ed.), *The Scottish Idealists: Selected Philosophical Writings*, Exeter: Imprint Academic, pp. 26–7, 2004.
14 McTaggart, J. M. E. 'Introduction to the Study of Philosophy', p. 183.
15 McTaggart, J. M. E. 'Introduction to the Study of Philosophy', p. 184.
16 Collingwood, R. G. *Speculum Mentis: or the Map of Knowledge*, Oxford: Clarendon Press, p. 36, 1924.
17 Collingwood, R. G. *Speculum Mentis*, p. 15.
18 Collingwood, R. G. *Speculum Mentis*, p. 316.
19 Bosanquet, B. *Philosophical Theory of the State*, p. 2.
20 Oakeshott, M. *Hobbes on Civil Association*, Oxford: Blackwell, p. 5, 1975.
21 Hegel, G. W. F. *The Philosophy of Mind*, trans. William Wallace, Section 377, *Zusatz*, Oxford, Clarendon Press, 1971.
22 Bosanquet, B. *Philosophical Theory of the State*, pp. 2–3.
23 Gentile, G. *The Theory of Mind as Pure Act*, translated by H. Wildon Carr, London: Macmillan, p. 33, 1922.
24 Harris, H. H. 'Introduction' to G. Gentile, *The Genesis and Structure of Society*, Urbana: University of Illinois Press, p. 18, 1960.
25 Gentile, G. *Theory of Mind as Pure Act*, p. 215.
26 Collingwood, R. G. 'Can the New Idealism Dispense with Mysticism?' in *Faith and Reason: Essays in the Philosophy of Religion* L. Rubinoff (ed.), Chicago: University of Chicago Press, p. 275, 1968.
27 Collingwood, R. G. 'Can the New Idealism Dispense with Mysticism?' in *Faith and Reason*, p. 274.
28 Collingwood, R. G. 'Notes Towards a Metaphysic' (1933–4) in *The Principles of History and other writings in the philosophy of history*, W. H. Dray and W. J. van der Dussen (eds), Oxford: Oxford University Press, p. 127, 1999.
29 Collingwood, R. G. 'Notes Towards a Metaphysic', p. 128–29.
30 See Croce, B. *What is Living and What is Dead of the Philosophy of Hegel*, translated by D. Ainslie, New York: Russell and Russell, 1969, and *Logic as the Science of the Pure Concept*, translated by D. Ainslie, London: Macmillan, 1917.

NOTES

31 Collingwood, R. G. *An Essay on Philosophical Method*, Oxford: Clarendon Press, p. 46–51, 1977.
32 Collingwood, R. G. *Speculum Mentis*, p. 84.
33 Collingwood, R. G. *Essay on Philosophical Method*, p. 173.
34 Collingwood, R. G. *Essay on Philosophical Method*, p. 89.
35 Collingwood, R. G. *Outlines of a Philosophy of Art*, reprinted in *Essays in the Philosophy of Art*, A. Donagan (ed.), Bloomington, Indiana: Indiana University Press, p. 50, 1964.
36 Collingwood, R. G. *Speculum Mentis*, pp. 102–107, 134–38, 169–76, 221–31, and 304–305. He was later to modify his views positing Greco-Roman scientific thinking as the theoretical basis of utilitarian action; Renaissance scientific thinking as the basis of regularian action; and nineteenth and twentieth-century historical thinking as the theoretical reason unpinning the practical reason of duty. See *The New Leviathan*.
37 Collingwood, R. G. *Outlines of a Philosophy of Art*, pp. 145–46.
38 Bradley, F. H. *Appearance and Reality*, Oxford: Clarendon Press, p. 441, 1930.
39 Bradley, F. H. *Appearance and Reality*, pp. 439–40.
40 Bradley, F. H. *Appearance and Reality*, pp. 404–405, 429.
41 Bradley, F. H. *Essays on Truth and Reality*, Oxford: Clarendon Press, p. 235 and pp. 252–54, 1914. Cf. Bradley, J. review of *On History and Other Essays*, by Oakeshott M. in *The Heythrop Journal*, XXVII, p. 361, 1986.
42 Bradley, F. H. *Appearance and Reality*, p. 433 and 440.
43 Bradley, F. H.*Appearance and Reality*, p. 404.
44 Bradley, F. H.*Appearance and Reality*, p. 6.
45 Oakeshott, M. *Experience and its Modes*, p. 84 and 87.
46 Oakeshott, M. *Rationalism in Politics and Other Essays*, new and expanded edition, T. Fuller (ed.), Indianapolis: Liberty Press, 1991.
47 Oakeshott, M. *Experience and its Modes*, pp. 86–168.
48 Oakeshott, M. *On Human Conduct*, Oxford: Clarendon Press, p. 17, 1975.
49 Oakeshott, M. *Experience and its Modes*, pp. 31–2.
50 Oakeshott, M. 'The Concept of a Philosophical Jurisprudence' *Politica III*, p. 204, 1938. Cf. Oakeshott, M. 'History and the Social Sciences', The Institute of Sociology, *The Social Sciences*, London: Le Play House Press, p. 72, 1936. See Oakeshott, M. *Experience and its Modes*, p. 5 and Oakeshott M. , *On History and Other Essays*, Oxford: Basil Blackwell, p. 2 and 26, 1983.
51 Oakeshott, M. *Experience and its Modes*, p. 324.
52 See Oakeshott, M. 'The Voice of Poetry in the Conversation of Mankind', in *Rationalism in Politics*, pp. 488–541.
53 Rorty, R. *Philosophy and the Mirror of Nature*, Oxford: Blackwell, pp. 156–57, 159, 163, 170–171, 318, 322, 371–73, 377–78, 386 and 389–94, 1980.
54 Oakeshott, M. *Experience and Its Modes*, pp. 297–98.

NOTES

55 All of the modes are now different ways of imagining rather than of experiencing, which conveyed too passive a view of understanding.
56 Oakeshott, M. *Rationalism in Politics*, Indianapolis: Liberty Press, p. 503, 1991.
57 Oakeshott, M. *Rationalism in Politics*, p. 527.
58 Collingwood, R. G. *The Principles of Art*, Oxford: Clarendon Press, 1938.
59 Oakeshott, M. *Rationalism in Politics*, p. 514. Oakeshott clearly thought the *Principles of Art* a remarkable book. In a letter to Collingwood, dated, 18 May, 1938, Oakeshott wrote: 'I have just finished your *Principles of Art* and I would like to tell you with what excitement, delight and admiration I have read it. Sense at last in the philosophy of art; you have performed a miracle. Please accept my deepest thanks.' Letter in the possession of Mrs Teresa Smith, Collingwood's daughter.
60 Collingwood, R. G. 'Notes on Historiography written on a voyage to the East Indies'. Collingwood MS., DEP 13, 21, Bodleian Library, Oxford University. Cf. Collingwood, R. G. *The Idea of History*, p. 218 and Collingwood, R. G. *An Autobiography*, Oxford: Clarendon Press, p. 107, 1939.
61 Skinner, Q. 'The Rise of, Challenge to and Prospects for a Collingwoodian Approach to the History of Political Thought' in D. Castiglione and I. Hampsher-Monk (eds), *The History of Political Thought in National Context*, Cambridge: Cambridge University Press, p. 185, 2001 and 'Interpretation, Rationality and Truth', in Skinner, Q. *Visions of Politics*, I, *Regarding Method*, Cambridge: Cambridge University Press, p. 47, 2002.
62 Collingwood, R. G. *Autobiography*, p. 114. Cf., p. 106. This is not to suggest that re-enactment is a passive process; 'it is a labour of active and therefore critical thinking'. *Idea of History*, p. 215.
63 Oakeshott, M. *On History*, p. 28.
64 Oakeshott, M. *On Human Conduct*, p. 57.
65 Oakeshott, M. *On History*, p. 24.
66 Oakeshott, M. *Rationalism in Politics*, p. 154. Cf. 'The historian is the maker of events; they have a meaning for those who participated in them, and he will not speak of them in the same way as they spoke of them'. M. Oakeshott, 'Mr. Carr's First Volume', *Cambridge Journal*, IV p. 347, (1950–1951).
67 Oakeshott, M. *On History*, p. 64 and 93; and Oakeshott, *Rationalism in Politics*, p. 164.
68 Oakeshott, M. *Experience and its Modes*, p. 334.
69 See for example, Grant, R. *Oakeshott*, London: Claridge Press, pp. 65–70, 1990; Gerencser, S. *The Skeptic's Oakeshott*, London: Macmillan, especially pp. 33–51, 2000; Nardin, T. *The Philosophy of Oakeshott*, Pennsylvania: Penn State University, pp. 44–5, 2001; Franco, P. *Michael Oakeshott: An Introduction*, New Haven: Yale University Press, p. 125, 2004.
70 Oakeshott, M. *On Human Conduct*, pp. 25–6 and 33.

NOTES

CHAPTER 4

1. In more recent years, since the 1980s, there has been a recovery of the negative stance in various forms of libertarianism and neo-liberalism.
2. Green, T. H. *Works of Thomas Hill Green*, Vol. III, London: Longmans, Green, p. 375, 1888.
3. On Bosanquet's work see Vincent, A. 'The Poor Law Reports of 1909 and the Social Theory of the Charity Organization Society', *Victorian Studies*, Vol. 27, No. 3, 1984.
4. Ritchie, D. G. *The Principles of State Interference*, London: Swan Sonnenschein, p. 138, 1888.
5. Green, T. H. *Lectures on the Principles of Political Obligation: and other writings*, Cambridge: Cambridge University Press, § 143, 1986.
6. Hobbes, T. *Leviathan* C. B. Macpherson (ed.), Middlesex: Penguin, p. 225, 1968.
7. Hobbes, T. *Leviathan*, Macpherson (ed.), pp. 227–28.
8. In his *Lectures on the Principles of Political Obligation*.
9. Green, T. H. *Lectures*, § 102.
10. Green, T. H. *Lectures*, § 84.
11. Green, T. H. *Lectures*, § 68–9.
12. Bradley, F. H. *Collected Essays*, Vol.II, pp. 444–45, Oxford: Clarendon Press, 1935.
13. Hegel, G. W. F. *Elements of the Philosophy of Right*, translated by E. B. Nisbet, A. W. Wood (ed.), Cambridge: Cambridge University Press § 4, addition, 1991.
14. Bosanquet, B. (ed.) 'Reality of the General Will', *Aspects of the Social Problem*, London: Macmillan, p. 322, 1895.
15. Bosanquet, B. 'Reality', p. 324.
16. Bosanquet, B. 'Reality', p. 325.
17. Collingwood, R. G. *New Leviathan*, p. 13, 25.
18. See Nicholson, P. 'Collingwood's New Leviathan Then and Now', *Collingwood Studies*, I, p. 164, 1994.
19. Collingwood, R. G. *New Leviathan*, 20. pp. 49–53.
20. Hegel, G. W. F. *Philosophy of Right*, § 146 and § 148.
21. Bradley, F. H. *Ethical Studies*, p. 166, Oxford: Clarendon Press, 1962.
22. Bradley, F. H. *Ethical Studies*, p. 193.
23. Bradley's view here reflects closely Hegel's own conception of philosophy, see for example, Hegel, *Philosophy of Right*, preface, pp. 10–11. The next clear and forceful statement of this position, in the British Idealist tradition, can be found in Michael Oakeshott (no doubt influenced by Bradley, as much as by Hegel), who also argued unequivocally that philosophy, or any theoretical mode such as history or science, is incapable of offering injunctions for practical conduct, see Oakeshott, M. *Experience and Its Modes*, Cambridge: Cambridge University Press, 1933.
24. Bosanquet, B. in his ethical writings, argues that moral values are to be realized in and through lived experience. One *must* live and become aware of the problems and intricacies of living before making any full sense of ethics. As he comments, if you 'cut yourself loose' from the

NOTES

lived process 'you would be nothing'. The process of living is one of self-moulding 'whose being shall incorporate what it can of value'. To work with values and to mould oneself is not a deductive process from ethical first principles. This squares with Bradley's argument. A moral life, if anything, is inductive. No rules precondition one's actions. The more precise analogy for ethics, for Bosanquet, is with art, which sounds mysteriously like Foucault's 'care of the self'. The self-moulding and the role of ethics are thus conceived as 'artistic creation ex nihilo', see Bosanquet, B. *Some Suggestions in Ethics*, London: Macmillan, p. 158, 1918.

25 Lamont, W. D. in articulating Green's conception of the role of moral philosophy, states the point quite precisely: for Green the moral philosopher 'is not to create – not even to advocate – moral ideals, but simply to understand them, analysing their nature and demonstrating their implications', Lamont, W. D. *Introduction to Green's Moral Philosophy*, London: George Allen and Unwin, p. 20, 1934. Green does however give a much stronger emphasis to the 'guiding' role of philosophy than Bradley.
26 Green, T. H. *Prolegomena to Ethics*, Oxford: Clarendon Press, § 310, 1907.
27 Green, T. H. *Prolegomena*, § 311.
28 Green, T. H. *Prolegomena*, § 317.
29 This idea is also central to Green's historical writing, for example his 'Four Lectures on the English Commonwealth', Green, *Works*, Vol. III, pp. 277–364.
30 Green, T. H. *Prolegomena*, § 317.
31 Green, T. H. *Prolegomena*, § 328.
32 Green, T. H. *Prolegomena*, § 311.
33 Oakeshott, M. *On Human Conduct*, Oxford: Clarendon Press, p. 63, 1975.
34 Oakeshott, M. *Human Conduct*, p. 64.
35 Oakeshott, M. *Human Conduct*, p. 65.
36 Oakeshott, M. *Human Conduct*, p. 70.
37 Sidgwick, H. 'Critical Notice of Ethical Studies', *Mind*, Vol. 1, p. 548, 1876.
38 See, for example, Vincent, A. 'Metaphysics and Ethics in the Philosophy of T. H. Green' in Cookson M. D. and Mander B. (eds), *T.H Green Ethics, Metaphysics and Political Philosophy*, Oxford, Clarendon Press, 2006.
39 Green, T. H. *Prolegomena*, §§ 285 and 286.
40 As Green comments 'the only good which is really common to all who may pursue it, is that which consists in the universal will to be good' *Prolegomena*, § 244.
41 Green, T. H. *Prolegomena*, § 270.
42 See Carter, M. *T.H. Green and the Development of Ethical Socialism* (Exeter: Imprint Academic, 2003).
43 Green, T. H. *Lectures*, § 26.
44 Green, T. H. *Lectures*, § 21.
45 Green, T. H. *Lectures*, § 25.
46 Green, T. H. *Lectures*, § 26.

NOTES

47 Ritchie, D. G. *Natural Rights*, London: Swan Sonnenschein, p. 270, 1894.
48 Ritchie, D. G. *Natural Rights*, p. 103.
49 Such individualism was also seen as potentially dangerous since ultimately its sheer vacuity provided no limitations to conduct. It appeared innocuous, but it was not. As Hegel indicated, the terror of the French Revolution, which 'rent asunder every political and social bond', was rooted in such a thin individualism, see for example, Jones, H. 'The Social Organism', in A. Seth and R. B. Haldane (eds), *Essays in Philosophical Criticism*, London: Longmans, p. 192, 1888.
50 Jones, H. 'The Present Attitude of Reflective Thought Towards Religion', *Hibbert Journal*, I and II, I, p. 229, (1902–1903 and 1903–1904).
51 See Green, T. H. *Prolegomena*, § 234ff. For studies of Green's overall contribution, see Vincent A. and Plant, R. *Philosophy Politics and Citizenship*, Oxford: Blackwell, 1984, Carter, T. H. *Green and the Development of Ethical Socialism*, Wempe, B. *T. H. Green's Theory of Positive Freedom*, Exeter: Imprint Academic, 2004, Leighton, D. P. *The Greenian Moment: T. H. Green and Political Argument in Victorian Britain*, Exeter: Imprint Academic, 2004, de Sanctis, A. *The 'Puritan' Democracy of Thomas Hill Green*, Exeter: Imprint Academic, 2005 and Colin Tyler, *The Metaphysics of Self-Realisation and Freedom: Part 1 of The Liberal Socialism of Thomas Hill Green*, Exeter: Imprint Academic, 2010.
52 Bosanquet, B. (ed.) 'The Duties of Citizenship', in *Aspects of the Social Problem*, pp. 5–6.

CHAPTER 5

1 See Jones, H. 'The Ethical Demand of the Present Political Situation', *The Hibbert Journal*, p. 539, 1909–1910.
2 Toynbee, A. 'Are Radicals Socialist?' in *Lectures on the Industrial Revolution in England, Popular Addresses, Notes and Other Fragments*, Newton Abbott: David and Charles Reprint, p. 203, 1969.
3 Toynbee, A. 'Are Radicals Socialist?' p. 219.
4 Green, T. H. *Works*, Vol. III, London: Longmans, p. 367, 1888.
5 Caird E. 'Individualism and Socialism: Inaugural Lecture to the Civic Society of Glasgow', Glasgow: Maclehose, p. 9, 1897.
6 See Mackenzie, J. S. *An Introduction to Social Philosophy*, Glasgow, Maclehose, p. 323, 1985. Bosanquet, B. 'The Antithesis between Individualism and Socialism Philosophically Considered', in *The Civilization of Christendom*, London: Swan Sonnenschein, pp. 304–57, 1899.
7 See Vincent, A. 'New Ideology for Old?' *Political Quarterly*, 69, No. 1, 1998.
8 See Vincent, A. 'The New Liberalism in Britain 1880–1914', *The Australian Journal of Politics and History*, 36, 3, 1990; A. Simhony and D. Weinstein (eds), *The New Liberalism: Reconciling Liberty and Community*, Cambridge: Cambridge University Press, 2001.

9   Green, T. H. 'Liberal Legislation and Freedom of Contract', in *Works of T. H. Green*, Vol. III, 371.
10 Haldane, R. B. *An Autobiography*, London: Hodder and Stoughton, p. 213, 1929.
11 All quotations from Haldane, R. B. *Autobiography*, pp. 213–14.
12 Bosanquet, H. *The Standard of Life*, London: Macmillan, p. 90, 1898.
13 Jones, H. 'The Corruption of the Citizenship of the Working Man' *Hibbert Journal* X, p. 163, 1911–12.
14 Bosanquet, B. *Some Suggestions in Ethics*, London: Macmillan, pp. 239–40, 1918.
15 Jones, H. 'The Obligations and Privileges of Citizenship: A Plea for the Study of Social Science', *Rice Institute Studies*, VI, p. 176, 1919.
16 Admittedly Gentile's involvement was deeply tarnished by his link with fascism.
17 See Hegel, G. W. F. *The Philosophical Propaedeutic*, introduction M. George and A. Vincent (eds), Oxford: Blackwell, 1986.
18 Haldane, R.B. *Autobiography*, p. 301.
19 'I had convinced myself that a civic university was a possible institution, and that if called into being it would have a great moulding influence and a high standard under the impulse of the local patriotism of the great cities', Haldane, R. B. *Autobiography*, p. 140.
20 Quotes from Haldane, R. B. *Universities and National Life: Three Addresses to Students*, London: John Murray, pp. 12–13, 1910. There is something of Thomas Carlyle's heroes and hero-worship here. Universities count for Haldane for what is the 'highest' in any state. 'And it is in the Universities, with their power over the mind, greater in the end than the power of any government or any church, that we see how the soul of the people at its highest mirrors itself', Haldane, R. B. *Universities and National Life*, London: Murray, p. 31, 1910.
21 'Knowledge is of many kinds, and what we have to do is to bring together what is inherent in knowledge and the unity of its grasp .... It was upon adult education, based on this principle, that we should rely as a foundation on which we could appeal to men and women, irrespective of their creeds or positions in society, to seek to develop this quality that was latent within them', Haldane, R. B. *Autobiography*, p. 302.
22 Oakeshott, M. 'The Study of Politics at a University', *Rationalism in Politics and other essays*, new and expanded edition, T. Fuller (ed.), Indianapolis: Liberty Press, pp. 184–218, 1991.
23 See Vincent, A. 'German Philosophy and British Public Policy' *Journal of the History of Ideas*, 68, 1, pp. 157–79, 2007.
24 See Andrew Vincent's 'German Philosophy and British Public Policy'. Haldane's 'prime educational interest was in the promotion of universities. But he wanted universities to be an integral part of a coherent system of education such as is only now ... beginning to develop in Britain. His vision was of a national education system with universities at the pinnacle, permeating (as he used to say) the whole education beneath them and, through adult education, beyond them', Ashby E. and Anderson, M. *Portrait of Haldane at Work on Education*, London, Macmillan, p. xv, 1974.

NOTES

25 See Sir Logan, D. *Haldane and the University of London* 1st March 1960, London: Haldane Memorial Lecture, University of London, 1960.
26 Haldane was a friend of Canon Barnett the first warden of Toynbee Hall, see Vincent A. and Plant, R. *Philosophy Politics and Citizenship*, Chapters 7 and 8.
27 Ashby, E. and Anderson, M. *Portrait of Haldane*, p. 173.
28 For a fuller discussion see Boucher D. and Vincent, A. *A Radical Hegelian: The Political and Social Philosophy of Henry Jones*, Cardiff: University of Wales Press, pp. 10–11, 17–20, and 99–109, 1993.
29 Green, T. H. *Lectures*, § 227.
30 Green, T. H. *Lectures*, § 228.
31 Muirhead, J. H. *Reflections of Journeyman in Philosophy on the Movements of Thought and Practice in his Time*, London: George Allen and Unwin, pp. 160–161, 1942.
32 Ritchie, D. G. *Principles of State Interference*, London: Swan Sonnenschein, p. 138, 1891.
33 Jones, H. *The Working Faith of the Social Reformer*, London: Macmillan, p. 10, 1910.
34 Ignatieff M. 'The Myth of Citizenship' in R. Beiner (ed.), *Theorizing Citizenship*, New York: State University of New York Press, p. 67, 1995.
35 Social citizenship, for Marshall, was the phase which developed after the civil and political citizenship, see Marshall, T. H. *Citizenship and Social Class*, Cambridge: Cambridge University Press, 1950.
36 See Vincent A. and Plant, R. *Philosophy Politics and Citizenship*, Chapter 7.
37 Bosanquet, B. (ed.) 'Reality of the General Will', in *Aspects of the Social Problem*, London: Macmillan, p. 322, 1895.
38 See Vincent A. 'The Poor Law Reports of 1909 and the Social Theory of the Charity Organisation Society' *Victorian Studies*, 27, 3, 1984.
39 See Urwick, E. J. 'A School of Sociology' in C. S. Loch (ed.), *Methods of Social Advance*, London: Macmillan, 1904 and Bosanquet, H. 'Methods of Training' in *The Charity Organisation Review*, p. 44, 1904.
40 Clarke, P. F. *Liberals and Social Democrats*, Cambridge: Cambridge University Press, p. 15, 1978. For a very scholarly corrective view of Green on temperance, see Nicholson, P. 'T. H. Green and Liquor Legislation' in A. Vincent (ed.), *The Philosophy of T. H. Green*, Aldershot: Gower, 1986.
41 Rashdall H. in C. Gore (ed.) *Property: Its Rights and Duties, Historically Philosophically and Religiously Considered*, London: Macmillan, p. 57, 1915.
42 Toynbee, A. 'Wages and Natural Law', in *Lectures on the Industrial Revolution*, p. 156.
43 As Jones says: 'whenever it becomes a right, [it] is due not alone nor primarily to his having said *Mine*, but to the State having said *Thine*', Jones, H. *The Working Faith of Social Reformer*, London: Macmillan, p. 97.
44 Jones, H. *Working Faith of Social Reformer*, p. 98.
45 Jones letter to Fisher 1916, Fisher Papers MS, Bodleian Library, Oxford, pp. 259–60, 7. In another work Jones writes, 'It is quite true that common

NOTES

ownership and common enterprise turns us into limited proprietors; but they make us limited proprietors of indefinitely large utilities', *Working Faith of Social Reformer*, p. 110.

46 Jones, H. 'The Ethical Demand of the Present Political Situation', *Hibbert Journal*, p. 537, 1909–10.
47 See Gore, C. (ed.), introduction and essay by L. T. Hobhouse in *Property: Its Rights and Duties*.
48 An idea, which seems as relevant today in 2011 – after the 2008 banking crisis – as it was in 1911.
49 Hobhouse, L. T. *Liberalism*, London: Thornton Butterworth, p. 202, 1911.
50 See Green, T. H. *Works*, Vol. III, pp. 370–71.
51 Jones, H. *Idealism as a Practical Creed*, Glasgow: Maclehose, p. 100, 1909.
52 See Samuel, H. *Memoirs*, London: Cresset Press, p. 25, 1945. J. A. Hobson also commented that 'Free land, free travel, free power, free credit, security, justice and education, no man is "free" for the full purposes of civilized life today unless he has all these liberties', see Hobson, J. A. *The Crisis of Liberalism: New Issues of Democracy*, London: P. S. King, p. 113, 1909.
53 See Vincent, A. and Plant, R. *Philosophy Politics and Citizenship*, pp. 73–6.
54 Haldane, R. B. 'The New Liberalism', *The Progressive Review*, Vol.1, No. 2, pp. 135–39, November 1896.
55 Haldane, R. B. 'New Liberalism', pp. 141–2.
56 Hegel, G. W. F. *The Philosophy of Right*, § 7.
57 Jones, H. *The Working Faith of the Social Reformer*, p. x.
58 Collingwood, R. G. *Autobiography*, Oxford, Oxford University Press, pp.15–7, 1951.

CHAPTER 6

1 Thus incorporating the Crimean War (1854–1856); the unification of both Germany (1871) and Italy (1867); the Boer Wars (1880–1881 and 1899–1902); the Russian Revolution (1917); the rise of German Militarism and the First World War (1914–1918), the rise and fall of liberal internationalism; the creation of the League of Nations (1919); and ultimately the Second World War (1939–1945).
2 See Boucher D. and Vincent, A. *A Radical Hegelian: The Political and Social Philosophy of Henry Jones*, Cardiff: University of Wales Press, 1992, Chapters 7 and 8. Also see Boucher, D. 'British Idealism, the State and International Relations', *Journal of the History of Ideas*, p. 55, 1994.
3 Hegel, G. W. F. *Elements of the Philosophy of Right*, Translated by E. B. Nisbet and edited by A. W. Wood, Cambridge: Cambridge University Press, § 324, 1991.
4 Hegel, G. W. F. *Philosophy of Right*, § 336.
5 Moorefield, J. *Covenants Without Swords: Idealist Liberalism and the Spirit of Empire*, New Jersey: Princeton University Press, pp. 99–100, 2005.

NOTES

6 Green, T. H. *Lectures on Principles of Political Obligation*, Cambridge: Cambridge University Press, § 1606, 1986.
7 Nicholson, P. *Political Philosophy of the British Idealists*, Cambridge: Cambridge University Press, pp. 227–28, 1990.
8 Bosanquet, B. 'Function of the State in Promoting the Unity of Mankind', in *Social and International Ideals: Being Studies in Patriotism*, London: Macmillan, p. 301, 1917.
9 Bosanquet, B. *Some Suggestions in Ethics*, London: Macmillan, p. 242, 1918; 'Functions of the State in Promoting the Unity of Mankind', p. 301.
10 Ritchie, D. G. 'War and Peace', *International Journal of Ethics*, XI, p. 138, 141, 149, 1900–1901.
11 Hobhouse, L. T. 'Foreign Policy of Collectivism, *The Economic Review*, 9, p. 215, 1899.
12 The authors have independently defended Hegel against the more extreme views, which have attributed all of the ills of the twentieth century to him, including German Militarism. Vincent, A. 'The Hegelian State and International Politics', *Review of International Studies*, 9, 1983; and Boucher, D. *Political Theories of International Relations*, Oxford: Clarendon Press, Chapter 14, 1998.
13 Caird, E. *Lay Sermons and Addresses*, Glasgow: Maclehose, p. 193, 1907.
14 Bosanquet, B. 'Function of the State in Promoting the Unity of Mankind', *Social and International Ideals*, p. 277.
15 Muirhead, J. H. *Reflections by a Journeyman in Philosophy on the Movements of Thought and Practice of his Time*, London: Murray, p. 179, 1942. Cf. Bosanquet, Patriotism in a Perfect State, p. 145.
16 See Green, T. H. *Lectures*, Lecture K, § 157ff, Watson, J. *The State in Peace and War*, Glasgow: Maclehose, pp. 249–50, 1919. Bosanquet says: 'Now states are dangerous to each other by reason of their biased consciences, and biased consciences come of inequality. No State can exhibit an unperverted conscience abroad which is not bent on making itself an equal instrument of the best life for all its members'. Bosanquet, B. 'Wisdom of Naaman's Servants', Bosanquet, B. *Social and International Ideals*, p. 309.
17 This is what J. A. Hobson suggests in his famous book on *Imperialism* and L. T. Hobhouse when he contends: 'All virtues are like charity in one respect – they begin at home'. Hobhouse, L. T. 'The Foreign Policy of Collectivism', *Economic Review*, 9, p. 212, 1899. Cf, J. A. Hobson, *Imperialism: A Study*, London: Nisbet, 1902.
18 Hetherington, H. J. W. and Muirhead, J. H. *Social Purpose: A Contribution to a Philosophy of Civic Society*, London: Allen and Unwin, p. 264, 1918.
19 Hetherington H. J. W. and Muirhead, J. H. *Social Purpose*, p. 261.
20 Hetherington H. J. W. and Muirhead, J. H. *Social Purpose*, p. 262.
21 Hetherington H. J. W. and Muirhead, J. H. *Social Purpose*, p. 262.
22 Green, T. H. *Lectures*, § 162.
23 Green, T. H. *Lectures*, § 170.

NOTES

24 Bosanquet, B. 'The Teaching of Patriotism' in Bosanquet, *Social and International Ideals*, p. 3.
25 Ritchie, D. G. 'The Moral Problems of War – In reply to Mr J. M. Robertson', *International Journal of Ethics*, 11, p. 494, 1900–1. Reprinted the *Collected Works of D. G. Ritchie*, Vol. 6. P. Nicholson (ed.), Bristol, Thoemmes, 1998.
26 Green, T. H. *Lectures*, § 171.
27 Bosanquet, B. *The Philosophical Theory of the State*, London: Macmillan, p. 12, 1899.
28 Caird, E. 'The Nation as an Ethical Ideal' in *Lay Sermons and Addresses*, Glasgow: Maclehose, p. 100, 1907.
29 Green, T. H. *Lectures*, § 122.
30 Caird, E. 'Address on Queen Victoria's Jubilee' in *Lay Sermons and Addresses*, Glasgow: Maclehose, p. 91, 1907.
31 Caird, E. 'On Queen Victoria's Jubilee', p. 95–6.
32 Hetherington H. J. W. and Muirhead, J. H. *Social Purpose*, p. 264.
33 This was then reinforced by the Statute of Westminster (1931). Other colonies in India, Africa and the Far East had a more ambiguous status.
34 Hobhouse, L. T. *Democracy and Reaction*, London: T. Fisher Unwin, 1904.
35 Shaw, G. B. (ed.), *Fabianism and the Empire: A Manifesto*, London: G. Richards, 1900.
36 Variants of such arguments appeared again in the Fabian colonial bureau (1940) and Arthur Creech Jones's *Fabian Colonial Essays*, (1945).
37 Muirhead, J. H. Service of the State Four Lectures on the Political Teachings of T. H. Green, London: John Murray, p. 110, 1908.
38 Cited by Collini, S. *Liberalism and Sociology: L. T. Hobhouse and Political Argument in England 1880–1915*, Cambridge: Cambridge University Press, p. 82, 1979. For a brief account of the issues see Shannon, R. *The Crisis of Imperialism 1865–1915*, London: Harper Collins, pp. 323–37, 1976.
39 Haldane, R. B. *Education and Empire: Addresses on Certain Topics of the Day*, London: Murray, p. 37, 1904.
40 Haldane, R. B. *Education and Empire*, p. 160.
41 Ritchie, D. G. 'War and Peace', *International Journal of Ethics*, 11, p. 164, 1900–1901.
42 Ritchie, D. G. 'Another View of the South African War', *The Ethical World*, p. 20, January 13, 1900. Reprinted in *Collected Worked of D. G. Ritchie*, Vol. 6.
43 Muirhead J. H. 'What Imperialism Means' *Fortnight Review*, 404, n.s., 183, 1 August 1900.
44 Caird, E. 'The Nation as an Ethical Idea', p. 114.
45 Muirhead J. H. and Hetherington, H. J. W. *Social Purpose*, pp. 278–9.
46 MacCunn, J. 'Cosmopolitan Duties', *International Journal of Ethics*, Vol. IX, p. 155, 1898–9.
47 Hobhouse, L. T. 'The Foreign Policy of Collectivism', *Economic Review*, 9, p. 215, 1899.
48 Ritchie, D. G. 'Another View of the South African War', p. 20.
49 Ritchie, D. G. 'The South African War', *The Ethical World*, February 3, p. 71, 1900. Reprinted in *Collected Works of D. G. Ritchie*, Vol. 6.

NOTES

50 Caird, E. *'The Nation as an Ethical Ideal'*, p. 110.
51 Caird, E. *'The Nation as an Ethical Ideal'*, p. 110.
52 Crook, P. *Darwinism, War and History*, Cambridge: Cambridge University Press, p. 3, 1994.
53 Bosanquet, B. 'Socialism and Natural Selection', in D. Boucher (ed.) *The British Idealists*, Cambridge: Cambridge University Press, p. 55, 1997.
54 Kidd, B. *Social Evolution*, pp. 3–5, 22, 34–35, 62–3 and 93–4, London: 1894. See Robert C. Bannister, *Social Darwinism: Science and Myth in Anglo-American Social Thought*, Philadelphia: Temple University Press, pp. 150–58, 1989.
55 Crook, P. *Darwinism, War and History*, p. 47.
56 Darwin, C. *The Descent of Man and Selection in Relation to Sex*, London: John Murray, pp. 198–200, 1871.
57 Darwin, C. *Ascent of Man*, pp. 218 and 224.
58 Green, T. H. *Lectures*, § 140.
59 Green, T. H. *Prolegomena to Ethics*, Oxford: Clarendon Press, § 207, 1899.
60 Green, T. H. *Prolegomena*, § 250.
61 Bradley, F. H. *Ethical Studies*, p. 205; and Bradley, F. H. *'Limits of Individual and National Self-Sacrifice'*, Bradley, *Collected Essays*, Vol. I, Oxford: Clarendon Press, p. 22.
62 Bradley, F. H. *Ethical Studies*, p. 342, and Bosanquet, B. 'Patriotism in a Perfect State', p. 150.
63 Jones, H. *'Moral Problems of the War'*, p. 35.
64 Bosanquet, B. *'Patriotism in a Perfect State'*, p. 149; also see in the same text, pp. 135, 137, and 150; 'Function of the State in Promoting the Unity of Mankind', pp. 288, 192, 295, and 297.
65 For a few examples see, Bradley, A. C. 'International Morality' and Sorley, W. R. 'State and Morality', both in the *International Crisis: The Theory of the State*, L. Creighton et al (eds), London: Oxford University Press, 1915; and Watson, *The State in Peace and War*, Glasgow: Maclehose, pp. 254–55, 1919.
66 Reprinted in *Selected Addresses and Essays*, pp. 49–93, London: Murray, 1928. The essay was first published in 1913.
67 See Haldane, R. B. 'The Higher Nationality: A Study in Law and Ethics', in *Conduct of Life*, p. 115, London, Murray.
68 Haldane, R. B. 'Higher Nationality', pp. 115–17.
69 Haldane, R. B. 'Higher Nationality', p. 135. It should be noted here that Haldane did give a particular emphasis to what Britain, the dominions and the USA had in common.
70 Collingwood, R. G. *The New Leviathan*, revised edition, D. Boucher, (ed.) Oxford: Clarendon Press, pp. 217, 219, and 450–51, 1992.
71 Bradley, F. H. 'Limits of International and National Self-Sacrifice', 21. Ritchie, D. G. 'Moral Problems of War', p. 494.
72 Hegel, G. W. F. *The Philosophy of Mind*, translated by W. Wallace and A. V. Miller, Oxford: Clarendon Press, § 547, 1971; Hegel, G. W. F. *Philosophy of Right*, § 333–34.

NOTES

73 Ritchie, D. G. 'The Moral Problems of War – In reply to Mr J. M. Robertson', *International Journal of Ethics*, 11, 495, 1900–1901. Reprinted in *Collected Works of D. G. Ritchie*, Vol. 6.
74 A similar view has been expressed more recently by J. E. S. Fawcett: 'Law cannot of itself create order, but emerges only where there is a minimum degree of order, which it may, however, serve to rationalise and extend'. 'The Development of International Law' in *International Relations in the Twentieth Century*, M. Williams (ed.), London: Macmillan, p. 195, 1992. Cf. Also Bosanquet, B. 'Wisdom of Naaman's Servants', p. 315; MacKenzie, J. S. *Outlines of Social Philosophy*, p. 78.
75 Hegel, G. W. F. *Philosophy of Right*, § 338–39.
76 Bosanquet, B. *'Wisdom of Naaman's Servants'*, p. 309. Also see MacCunn, J. *'Cosmopolitan Duties'*, p. 160; Caird, E. 'Nation as an Ethical Ideal', p. 110; and Hetherington H. J. W. and Muirhead, J. H. Social Purpose, p. 215.
77 Bosanquet, B. *Philosophical Theory of the State*, p. l.
78 Bosanquet, B. *'The Function of the State in Promoting the Unity of Mankind'*, p. 298. Cf. Nicholson, Political Philosophy of the British Idealists, p. 225.
79 Bosanquet, B. 'Patriotism in the Perfect State', pp. 136–40.

BIBLIOGRAPHY

Ashby, E. and Anderson, M., *Portrait of Haldane at Work on Education*. London: Macmillan, 1974.
Baillie, J. B., 'The Individual and his World', in J. H. Muirhead (ed.), *Contemporary British Philosophy*, first series, London: George Allen and Unwin, 1924.
Bannister, R. C., *Social Darwinism: Science and Myth in Anglo-American Social Thought*, Philadelphia: Temple University Press, 1989.
Barbour, G. F., 'Memoir', in A. S. Pringle-Pattison (ed.), *The Balfour Lectures on Realism*, London and Edinburgh: Blackwood, 1933.
Berlin, I., *Four Essays on Liberty*, Oxford: Oxford University Press, 1969.
Beveridge, W. H., *Report on Social Insurance and Allied Services*, HMSO, London, Command Paper 6404–6405, 1942.
Bosanquet, B., 'Reality of the General Will' in B. Bosanquet (ed.), The Duties of Citizenship', *Aspects of the Social Problem*, pp. 1–27, London: Macmillan, 1895.
—*Psychology of the Moral Self*, London: Macmillan, 1897.
—'The Antithesis between Individualism and Socialism Philosophically Considered' in B. Bosanquet (ed.), *The Civilization of Christendom*, London: Swan Sonnenschein, 1899.
—*The Philosophical Theory of the State*, London: Macmillan, 1999.
—*The Essentials of Logic*, London: Macmillan, 1903.
—*The Value and Destiny of the Individual*, London: Macmillan, 1912.
—'Wisdom of Naaman's Servants', in B. Bosanquet (ed.), *Social and International Ideals*, 1917a.
— 'The Teaching of Patriotism', in B. Bosanquet (ed.), *Social and International Ideals*, 1917b.
— 'Function of the State in Promoting the Unity of Mankind', in B. Bosanquet (ed.), *Social and International Ideals*, 1917c.
—*Social and International Ideals: Being Studies in Patriotism*, London: Macmillan, 1917d.
— *Some Suggestions in Ethics*, London: Macmillan, 1918.
—*The Meeting of Extremes in Contemporary Philosophy*, London: Macmillan, 1921.
—'Socialism and Natural Selection' [1895], in D. Boucher (ed.) *The British Idealists*, Cambridge: Cambridge University Press, 1997.
Bosanquet, H, *The Standard of Life*, London: Macmillan, 1898.

BIBLIOGRAPHY

—'Methods of Training', in *The Charity Organisation Review*, No. 44, 1904.
Boucher, D, 'British Idealism, the State and International Relations', *Journal of the History of Ideas*, 55, 1994.
—*Political Theories of International Relations*, Oxford: Clarendon Press, 1998.
—'Oakeshott and the History of Political Thought', *Collingwood and British Idealism Studies*, 13, 2, 2007.
Boucher, D., (ed.), *The British Idealists*, Cambridge: Cambridge University Press, 1997.
—*The Scottish Idealists: Selected Philosophical Writings*, Exeter: Imprint Academic, 2004.
Boucher, D and Vincent, A, *A Radical Hegelian: The Political and Social Philosophy of Henry Jones*, Cardiff: University of Wales Press, 1992.
—*British Idealism and Political Theory*, Edinburgh: Edinburgh University Press, 2000.
Boyce G. W. R., 'A Peace Policy for Idealists,' *The Hibbert Journal*, 5, 1906–7.
Bradley, A. C., 'International Morality' in E. M. Sidgwick, G. Murray, A. C. Bradley et al (eds), *The International Crisis in its Ethical and Psychological Aspects*, London: Humphrey Milford, 1915.
Bradley, F. H., *Essays on Truth and Reality* [originally published 1914], Oxford: Clarendon Press, 1968.
—*Appearance and Reality: A Metaphysical Essay* [originally published 1893], Oxford: Clarendon Press, 9th edition, 1930.
—*The Principles of Logic*, 2nd edition with commentary and terminal essays [original publication 1883], Oxford: Clarendon Press, 1932.
—'Limits of Individual and National Self-Sacrifice', in *Collected Essays* vol. I [original publication date 1894], Oxford: Clarendon Press, 1935a.
—*Collected Essays*, Vols I and II, Oxford: Clarendon Press, 1935b.
—*Mr. Sidgwick's Hedonism in Bradley*, *Collected Essays*, Vol. 1 [original publication 1877], Oxford: Clarendon Press, 1935c.
—*The Presuppositions of Critical History* [original publication 1874], reprinted in F. H. Bradley, *Collected Essays*, Vol. I, Oxford: Clarendon Press, 1935d.
—*Ethical Studies*, 2nd [original publication 1876], Oxford: Clarendon Press, 1962.
Bradley, J., 'Hegel in Britain: A Brief History of British Commentary and Attitudes (1)' *TheHeythrop Journal*, XX, 1979.
—Review of 'On History and Other Essays by Michael Oakeshott', in *The Heythrop Journal*, XXVII, 1986.
Britain's Industrial Future. The Report of the Liberal Industrial Inquiry, London, Ernest Benn, 1928.
Burrow, J. W., *Evolution and Society: A Study in Victorian Social Theory*, Cambridge: Cambridge University Press, 1966.
Caird, E., 'Preface', in A. Seth and R. B. Haldane (eds), *Essays in Philosophical Criticism*, London: Longmans Green, 1883.
—'Individualism and Socialism: Inaugural Lecture to the Civic Society of Glasgow', Glasgow: Maclehose, 1897.

BIBLIOGRAPHY

—*The Critical Philosophy of Kant* in 2 Vols, Glasgow: Maclehose, 1889.
—'Metaphysics' [original publication 1883] in Edward Caird, *Essays on Literature and Philosophy*, Vol. 2, Glasgow: Maclehose, 1892.
—*The Evolution of Religion* in 2 Vols, Glasgow: Maclehose, 1899.
—*Hegel* [original publication 1883], Edinburgh: Blackwood, 1903.
—*Lay Sermons and Addresses*, Glasgow: Maclehose, 1907a.
—'Address on Queen Victoria's Jubilee' in Caird, *Lay Sermons*, 1907b.
—'The Nation as an Ethical Ideal' in Caird, *Lay Sermons*, 1907c.
—'Idealism and the Theory of Knowledge' in *Collected Works of Edward Caird* [original publication 1903], C. Tyler (ed.), Vol. 12, *Miscellaneous Writings*, Bristol: Thoemmes, 1999.
—'The Problem of Philosophy' [original publication 1881] in D. Boucher (ed.), *The Scottish Idealists*, 2004.
Fraser, A. C. *Berkeley*, Edinburgh: Blackwood, 1881.
—*Berkeley and Spiritual Realism*, London: Constable, 1908.
Carlyle, T, *The Works of Thomas Carlyle*, H. D. Traill (ed.), London: Chapman and Hall, 1896–1899.
Carter, M, *T. H. Green and the Development of Ethical Socialism*, Exeter: Imprint Academic, 2003.
Clark, R. E. D., *Darwin: Before and After*, Exeter: Paternoster, 1971.
Clarke, P. F., *Liberals and Social Democrats*, Cambridge: Cambridge University Press, 1978.
Coates, W. J. Jr., *Oakeshott and his Contemporaries*, Selinsgrove: Susquehanna University Press, 2000.
Collingwood, R. G., *Outlines of a Philosophy of Art* [original publication 1925] reprinted in *Essays in the Philosophy of Art*, A. Donagan (ed.), Bloomington, Indiana: Indiana University Press, 1964.
—*An Essay on Philosophical Method* [original publication 1933], Oxford: Clarendon Press, 1977.
—'Notes on Historiography written on a voyage to the East Indies'. In R.G. Collingwood MS., DEP 13, 21, Bodleian Library, Oxford University, 1939.
—*Speculum Mentis: Or the Map of Knowledge*, Oxford: Clarendon Press, 1924.
—*The Principles of Art*, Oxford: Clarendon Press, 1938.
—'Can the New Idealism Dispense with Mysticism?' in R. G. Collingwood (ed.), *Faith and Reason: Essays in the Philosophy of Religion* Lionel Rubinoff [original publication 1923], Chicago: University of Chicago Press, 1968.
—*An Autobiography*, with an Introduction by Toulmin, S. [original publication 1939], Oxford: Oxford University Press, 1978.
—*The Idea of History* [original publication 1946] revised edition, W. J. van der Dussen (ed.), Oxford: Clarendon Press, 1993a.
—*The New Leviathan* [original publication 1942] revised edition, David Boucher, (ed.), Oxford: Oxford University Press, 1993b.
—*An Essay on Metaphysics* [original publication 1940] new revised edition edited by R. Martin, Oxford: Clarendon Press, 1998.
—'Notes Towards a Metaphysic' (1933–1934) in W. H. Dray and W. J. van der Dussen (eds), *The Principles of History and other writings in the philosophy of history*, Oxford: Oxford University Press, 1999.

BIBLIOGRAPHY

—'*Libellus de Generatione*', unpublished papers, Bodleian Library, Oxford University, Dep. 27.
Collini, S, Winch, D., and Burrow, J., *That Noble Science of Politics*, Cambridge: Cambridge University Press, 1983.
—*Liberalism and Sociology: L. T. Hobhouse and Political Argument in England 1880–1915*, Cambridge: Cambridge University Press, 1979.
Croce, B., *Logic as the Science of the Pure Concept*, translated by D. Ainslie, London: Macmillan, 1917.
—*What is Living and What is Dead of the Philosophy of Hegel*, translated by D. Ainslie [original publication 1915], New York: Russell and Russell, 1969.
Crook, P., *Darwinism, War and History*, Cambridge: Cambridge University Press, 1994.
Darwin, C., *The Descent of Man and Selection in Relation to Sex* [original publication 1871], London: Murray, 1888.
—*The Origin of Species by Means of Natural Selection: Or the Preservation of Favoured Races in the Struggle for Life*, edited by J. W. Burrow, Middlesex: Penguin. [First published by John Murray, 1859], 1985.
Davie, G. *The Democratic Intellect*, Edinburgh: Edinburgh University Press, 1961.
Dawkins, R. *The Blind Watchmaker*, London: Penguin, 2006.
De Waal, F., *Primates and Philosophers: How Morality Evolved*, New Jersey: Princeton University Press, 2006.
Desmond, A. and Moore, J., *Darwin*, London: Michael Joseph, 1992.
Dimova Cookson, M., and Mander, W. (eds), *T. H. Green: Ethics, Metaphysics and Political Philosophy*, Oxford, Clarendon Press, 2006.
Fawcett, J. E. S., 'The Development of International Law' in M. Williams (ed.), *International Relations in the Twentieth Century*, London: Macmillan, 1992.
Ferreira, P., 'Ferrier, James Frederick' in W. J. Mander and P. F. Sell (eds), *Dictionary of Nineteenth Century British Philosophers*, Bristol: Thoemmes, 2002a.
—'Stirling, James Hutchinson' (1820–1909), *Dictionary of Nineteenth Century British Philosophers*, W. J. Mander and Alan P. F. Sell (eds), Bristol: Thoemmes, 2002b.
Ferrier, J. F., *The Institutes of Metaphysic: The Theory of Knowing and Being*, Edinburgh: Blackwood [first edition, 1854], 1856.
Fisher Papers M.S., *Bodleian Library*, Oxford.
Flint, R., *Vico*, Edinburgh: Blackwood, 1891.
Franco, P., *Michael Oakeshott: An Introduction*, New Haven: Yale University Press, 2004.
Gale, B., *Evolution Without Evidence: Charles Darwin and the Origin of Species*, Albuquerque: University of New Mexico, 1982.
Gentile, G., *The Theory of Mind as Pure Act*, translated by H. W. Carr, London: Macmillan, 1922.
George, W., *Darwin*, London: Fontana, 1982.
Gerencser, S., *The Skeptic's Oakeshott*, London: Macmillan, 2000.

Gibbins, J., *John Grote, Cambridge University and the Development of Victorian Thought*, Exeter: Imprint Academic, 2007.
Gore, C., (ed.), introduction *Property: Its Rights and Duties, Historically Philosophically and Religiously Considered*, London: Macmillan, 1915.
Grant, R. *Oakeshott*, London: Claridge Press, 1990.
Green, T. H., *Lectures on the Principles of Political Obligation: and other writings*, Cambridge, Cambridge University Press, 1986.
—'Liberal Legislation and Freedom of Contract' in *Works*, London, Longmans Green, 1888, vol III, pp. 365–86.
—'Liberal Legislation and Freedom of Contract' [original publication 1881] in Green, *The Works of T. H. Green*, Vol. III, London: Longmans, Green, 1888a.
—*Prolegomena to Ethics* [original publication 1883], Oxford: Clarendon Press, 1907.
Greenleaf, W. H., *Oakeshott's Philosophical Politics*, London: Longmans, 1966.
Haldane, R. B., 'The New Liberalism' *The Progressive Review*, November, Vol. 1, No. 2, 1896.
—*Education and Empire: Addresses on Certain Topics of the Day*, London: Murray, 1904.
—*Universities and National Life: Three Addresses to Students*, London: John Murray, 1910.
—'The Higher Nationality: A Study in Law and Ethics' [original publication 1913] in Haldane, *Conduct of Life and Other Addresses*, London: Murray, 1914.
—*An Autobiography*, London: Hodder and Stoughton, 1929.
Hamilton, W., 'On the Philosophy of the Unconditioned [original publication 1829]' in *Discussions on Philosophy and Literature, Education and University Reform Chiefly from The Edinburgh Review; corrected, vindicated, enlarged, in Notes and Appendices*, London: Brown, Green and Longmans, 1853.
Harris, H. S., 'Introduction' to G. Gentile's, *The Genesis and Structure of Society*, Urbana: University of Illinois Press, 1960.
Hegel, G. W. F., *The Philosophy of Mind*, translated by W. Wallace and A.V. Miller, Oxford: Clarendon Press, 1971.
—*The Philosophical Propaedeutic*, introduction by George, M. and Vincent, A. Oxford: Blackwell, 1986.
—*Elements of the Philosophy of Right*, translated by E. B. Nisbet, edited by A. W. Wood, Cambridge: Cambridge University Press, 1991.
Hetherington, H. J. W., and Muirhead, J. H., *Social Purpose: A Contribution to a Philosophy of Civic Society*, London: Allen and Unwin, 1918.
Hobbes, T., *Leviathan*, C.B. Macpherson (ed.) [original publication 1651], Middlesex: Penguin, 1968.
Hobhouse, L. T., 'The Foreign Policy of Collectivism', *Economic Review*, 9, 1899.
—*Democracy and Reaction*, London: T. Fisher Unwin, 1904.
—*Liberalism*, London: Thornton Butterworth, 1911.
—*The Metaphysical Theory of the State* [original publication 1918], London: Allen and Unwin, 1951.

BIBLIOGRAPHY

Hobson, J. A., *Imperialism: A Study*, London: Nisbet, 1902.
—*The Crisis of Liberalism: New Issues of Democracy*, London: P. S. King, 1909.
Hofstadter, R., 'The Vogue of Spencer' Chapter 2 of *Darwinism in American Thought* (1955), Reprinted in *Darwin* (Norton Critical Edition), P. Appleman (ed.), New York: Norton, 1979.
Howard, J., *Darwin*, Oxford: Oxford University Press, 1982.
Hull, D. L., 'Darwin's Science and Victorian Philosophy of Science' in M. J. S. Hodge and G. Radick (eds), *The Cambridge Companion to Darwin*, Cambridge: Cambridge University Press, 2003.
Huxley, T. H., 'Evolution and Ethics' in *Evolution and Ethics: T. H. Huxley's Evolution and Ethics with New Essays on its Victorian Sociobiological Context*, J. Paradis and G. C. Williams (eds), New Jersey: Princeton University Press, 1989.
—'Natural Rights and Political Rights', *The Nineteenth Century*, 25, 1890.
Ignatieff, M., 'The Myth of Citizenship' in R. Beiner (ed.), *Theorizing Citizenship*, New York: State University of New York Press, 1995.
Jenkins, S., 'Self-Consciousness, System and Dialectic' in D. Moyer (ed.), *The Routledge Companion to Nineteenth Century Philosophy*, London: Routledge, 2010.
Joachim, H. H., *The Nature of Truth*, 2nd edition, edited by R. G. Collingwood, Oxford: Oxford University Press, 1939.
John, G. *Exploratio Philosophica*, Cambridge, Cambridge University Press, 1865.
Jones, A. C., *Fabian Colonial Essays*, London, Hogarth Press, 1959.
Jones, H., 'The Social Organism', in A. Seth and R. B. Haldane (eds), *Essays in Philosophical Criticism*, London: Longmans, 1883.
—'Is the Order of Nature Opposed to the Moral Life?' An Inaugural Address, Glasgow: Maclehose, 1894.
—'Notes taken by Thomas Jones in Henry Jones's Moral Philosophy Lectures in Glasgow', Vol. II, National Library of Wales, Aberystwyth, 1897–1898.
—'The Present Attitude of Reflective Thought Towards Religion', *Hibbert Journal* I and II, 1902–1903 and 1903–1904.
—*The Philosophy of Martineau*, London: Macmillan, 1905.
—'Idealism and Politics', in two parts, *Contemporary Review*, 42, 1907.
—*Idealism as a Practical Creed*, Glasgow: Maclehose, 1909.
—'The Ethical Demand of the Present Political Situation', *The Hibbert Journal*, Vol. XIII, 1909–10.
—*The Working Faith of the Social Reformer*, London: Macmillan, 1910.
—'The Corruption of the Citizenship of the Working Man' *Hibbert Journal*, Vol. X, 1911–1912.
—'The Obligations and Privileges of Citizenship: A Plea for the Study of Social Science', *Rice Institute Studies*, VI. 1919a.
—*The Principles of Citizenship*, London: Macmillan, 1919b.
—*A Faith That Enquires*, London: Macmillan, 1922a.
—*Old Memories*, London: Hodder and Stoughton, 1922b.
Jones, H and Muirhead, J. H., *The Life and Philosophy of Edward Caird*, Glasgow: Maclehose, Jackson and Co., 1921.

BIBLIOGRAPHY

Kant, I., *Critique of Pure Reason*, London: Dent, 1946.
Kasuga, J. *The Formation of R. G. Collingwood's Early Criticism of Realism*, unpublished Ph.D., Cardiff University, 2010.
Kidd, B., *Social Evolution*, London: Macmillan, 1894.
Kluback, W., *Wilhelm Dilthey's Philosophy of History*, New York: Columbia University Press, 1956.
Kuhn, T. S., *The Structure of Scientific Revolutions*, third revised edition, Chicago: University of Chicago Press, 1996.
Lamont, W. D., *Introduction to Green's Moral Philosophy*, London: George Allen and Unwin, 1934.
Leighton, D. P., *The Greenian Moment: T. H. Green and Political Argument in Victorian Britain*, Exeter: Imprint Academic, 2004.
Locke, J., *John Two Treatises on Government*, P. Laslett (ed.), Cambridge, Cambridge University Press, 1988.
Logan, Sir D. *Haldane and the University of London*, 1 March 1960, London: Haldane Memorial Lecture, University of London, 1960.
Lyell, C. *Principles of Geology*, being an attempt to explain the former changes of the earth's surface, by reference to causes now in operation. London, John Murray, 1830–34.
MacCunn, J., 'Cosmopolitan Duties', *International Journal of Ethics*, IX, 1989–1989.
Mackenzie, J. S., *An Introduction to Social Philosophy*, Glasgow: Maclehose, 1895.
Marshall, T. H., *Citizenship and Social Class*, Cambridge: Cambridge University Press, 1950.
McKillop, A. B. *A Disciplined Intelligence*, Montreal and Kingston: McGill Queen's University Press, 2001.
McTaggart, J. M. E, 'An Ontological Idealism' in McTaggart, *Philosophical Studies*, S. V. Keeling (ed.), [originally published 1934], New York, Books for Libraries, 1966a.
—'Dare to Be Wise' in McTaggart, *Philosophical Studies*, 1966b.
—'The Individualism of Value', in, *Philosophical Studies*, 1966c.
—'Introduction to the Study of Philosophy', in *Philosophical Studies*, 1966d.
Mills, J. S., *Principles of Political Economy and Chapters on Socialism* (*Oxford World Classics*), J. Riley (ed.), Oxford, Oxford University Press, 2008.
Mitchell, W., 'Moral Obligation' [original publication 1886] in D. Boucher (ed.), *The Scottish Idealists*, 2004.
Moore, G. E., 'The Nature and Reality of Objects of Perception', *Philosophical Studies*, London: Routledge and Kegan Paul, 1922.
—'Proof of an External World', *Proceedings of the British Academy*, 25, 1939.
Moorefield, J., *Covenants Without Swords: Idealist Liberalism and the Spirit of Empire*, New Jersey: Princeton University Press, 2005.
Muirhead J. H. 'What Imperialism Means', *Fortnightly Review*, No. 404. n.s. 1 August 1990.
—*Service of the State: Four Lectures on the Political Teaching of T. H. Green*, London: John Murray, 1908.

BIBLIOGRAPHY

—*Coleridge as Philosopher*, London: George Allen and Unwin, 1930.
—*The Platonic Tradition in Anglo-Saxon Philosophy*, London: George Allen and Unwin, 1931.
—*Reflections of a Journeyman in Philosophy on the Movements of Thought and Practice in his Time*, London: George Allen and Unwin, 1942.
Muirhead, J. H. (ed.), *Contemporary British Philosophy*, London: Macmillan, 1925.
—*Bernard Bosanquet and his Friends: Letters Illustrating the Sources and the Development of his Philosophical Opinions*, London: George Allen and Unwin, 1935.
Mulhall, S. and Swift, A., 2nd edition, *Liberals and Communitarians*, Oxford: Blackwell, 1996.
Murdoch, I., *Metaphysics as a Guide to Morals*, Middlesex: Penguin Books, 1993.
Nardin, T., *The Philosophy of Oakeshott*, Pennsylvania: Penn State University, 2001.
Nicholson, P., 'T. H. Green and Liquor Legislation' in A. Vincent (ed.) The Philosophy of T. H. Green, Aldershot: Gower, 1986.
—*The Political Philosophy of the British Idealists*, Cambridge: Cambridge University Press, 1990.
—'Collingwood's *New Leviathan* Then and Now', *Collingwood Studies*, I, 1994.
Oakeshott, M., '*Review of The Life and Philosophy of Edward Caird*' in the *Hibbert Journal*, Vol. 20, 1922a.
—*Notes* Volume III, August 1922, Oakeshott Papers, The British Library of Political Science, 1922b.
—*Notebook IV*, 2 July 1923, Oakeshott Papers, The British Library of Political Science, 1923.
—*Experience and its Modes*, Cambridge: Cambridge University Press, 1933.
— 'History and the Social Sciences', The Institute of Sociology, *The Social Sciences*, London: Le Play House Press, 1936.
—'The Concept of a Philosophical Jurisprudence', *Politica* 3, 1938.
—'Mr. Carr's First Volume', *Cambridge Journal*, IV, 1950–1.
—*Hobbes on Civil Association*, Oxford: Blackwell, 1975a.
—*On Human Conduct*, Oxford: Clarendon Press, 1975b.
—*On History and Other Essays*, Oxford: Basil Blackwell, 1983.
—*Rationalism in Politics and Other Essays*, new and expanded edition, T. Fuller (ed.), Indianapolis: Liberty Press, 1991a.
—*Rationalism in Politics and other Essays*, Indianapolis: Liberty Press, 1991b.
—'Beyond Realism and Idealism'. A review of W. M. Urban, *Beyond Realism and Idealism* in Michael Oakeshott, *The Concept of a Philosophical Jurisprudence*, L. O'Sullivan (ed.), Exeter: Imprint Academic, 2006.
Paley, W., *Natural Theology*, Vol. IV, *Works*, London: George Cowie, 1837.
Podoksik, E., *In Defence of Modernity: Vision and Philosophy in Michael Oakeshott*, Exeter: Imprint Academic, 2003.
Popper, K., *Unended Quest: An Intellectual Autobiography*, London: Routledge, 2002.

BIBLIOGRAPHY

Pringle-Pattison, A. S. 'Life and Philosophy of Herbert Spencer', *The Quarterly Review*, Vol. 200, 1904.
—*The Idea of God in the Light of Recent Philosophy*, Oxford: Oxford University Press, 1917.
Rashdall, H., 'Personality, Human and Divine', *Personal Idealism*, H. Sturt (ed.), London: Macmillan, 1902.
Richard, R. J., 'Darwin's Philosophical Impact' in D. Moyar (ed.), *The Routledge Companion to Nineteenth Century Philosophy*, London: Routledge, 2010.
Richter, M. *The Politics of Conscience: T. H. Green and his Age* [original publication 1964], Bristol: Thoemmes, 1996.
Ritchie, D. G. 'A Review of *The Elements of Politics*', *International Journal of Ethics*, 2, 1892.
—*Darwin and Hegel: With Other Philosophical Studies*, London: Swan Sonnenschein, 1893a.
—'On the Conception of Sovereignty' in D. G. Ritchie (ed.), *Darwin and Hegel*, London, Sonnenschein, 1893
—*Natural Rights*, London: Sonnenschein, 1894.
—*The Principles of State Interference*, 2nd edition [1st edition 1891], London: Swan Sonnenschein, 1896.
—'The South African War', *The Ethical World*, February 3. Reprinted in *Collected Works of D. G. Ritchie*, Vol. 6, 1900.
—'The Moral Problems of War – In reply to Mr J. M. Robertson', *International Journal of Ethics*, XI. Reprinted in *Collected Works of D. G. Ritchie*, Vol. 6, 1900–1.
—'War and Peace' *International Journal of Ethics*, XI, 1900–1.
—*Darwinism and Politics*, London, Swan Sonnenschein, 1901.
—'Ethical Democracy: Evolution and Democracy' in D. Boucher (ed.), *The British Idealists*, Cambridge: Cambridge University Press, 1997.
—'Another View of the South African War', *The Ethical World*, January 13, 1900, p. 20. Reprinted in *Collected Works*, Vol. 6, edited by P. Nicholson, 1998a.
—*Collected Worked of D. G. Ritchie*, Vol. 6, edited by P. Nicholson, Bristol: Thoemmes, 1998b.
Rorty, R. *Philosophy and the Mirror of Nature*, Oxford: Blackwell, 1980.
Ruse, M. 'Natural Selection in *The Origin of Species*', *Studies in History and Philosophy of Science*, 1, 1972.
—*The Darwinian Paradigm: essays on its history, philosophy and religious implications*, London: Routledge, 1993.
Russell, B. *Our Knowledge of the External World: As a Field for Scientific Method in Philosophy*, London George Allen and Unwin, 1914.
Samuel, H., *Memoirs*, London: Cresset Press, 1945.
Sanctis, A, de, *The "Puritan" Democracy of Thomas Hill Green*, Exeter: Imprint Academic, 2005.
Seth, A., 'Philosophy as Criticism of the Categories', *Essays in Philosophical Criticism*, A. Seth and R. B. Haldane (eds), London: Longmans Green, 1883.
—*Hegelianism and Personality*, Edinburgh: Blackwood, 1888.

BIBLIOGRAPHY

—'A New Theory of the Absolute' in Seth, *Man's Place in the Cosmos* [original publication 1894], Edinburgh: Blackwood, 1894.
Seth, A. and Haldane, R. B. (eds), *Essays in Philosophical Criticism*, London: Longmans Green, 1883.
Shannon, R., *The Crisis of Imperialism 1865–1915*, London: Harper Collins, 1976.
Shaw, G. B. (ed.), *Fabianism and the Empire: A Manifesto*, London: G. Richards, 1900.
Sidgwick, H., 'Critical Notice of Bradley's *Ethical Studies*' *Mind*, 1, 1876.
—*Elements of Politics*, London: Macmillan, 1897.
—*Methods of Ethics*, 7th edition [original publication 1874], London: Macmillan, 1907.
Simhony, A. and Weinstein, D., (eds), *The New Liberalism: Reconciling Liberty and Community*, Cambridge: Cambridge University Press, 2001.
Skinner, Q., 'The Rise of, Challenge to and Prospects for a Collingwoodian Approach to the History of Political Thought' in Dario Castiglione and Iain Hampsher-Monk (eds) *The History of Political Thought in National Context*, Cambridge: Cambridge University Press, 2001.
—'Interpretation, Rationality and Truth', in Quentin Skinner (ed.), *Visions of Politics*, I, *Regarding Method*, Cambridge: Cambridge University Press, 2002.
Smith, J. A., 'Philosophy as the Development of the Notion and Reality of Self-Consciousness' in *Contemporary British Philosophy* (second series), J. H. Muirhead (ed.), London: George Allen and Unwin, 1925.
Sorley, W. R., 'The Historical Method', in A. Seth and R. B. Haldane (eds), *Essays in Philosophical Criticism*, London: Longmans Green, 1883.
—*On the Ethics of Naturalism*, Edinburgh and London: Blackwood. 1885.
—*Recent Tendencies in Ethics*, Edinburgh and London: Blackwell, 1904.
—*The Moral Life*, Cambridge: Cambridge University Press, 1911.
—'State and Morality' in *The International Crisis: The Theory of the State* by L. Creighton et al. (eds), London: Milford and Oxford University Press, 1916.
—*A History of English Philosophy*, Cambridge: Cambridge University Press, 1937.
Spencer, H. *The Principles of Ethics* [original publication 1893], Indianapolis: Liberty Press, 1978.
Stebbing, L. S., 'The Method of Analysis in Metaphysics', *Proceedings of the Aristotelian Society*, 33, 1932–1933.
Stephen, L., 'Ethics and The Struggles for Existence', *Contemporary Review*, 64, 1893.
Stirling, J. H., *The Secret of Hegel: Being the Hegelian System in Origin, Principle, Form, and Matter*, Edinburgh: Oliver and Boyd [1st edition 1865], 1898.
Sturt, H., (ed.), *Personal Idealism: Philosophical Essays*, London: Macmillan, 1902.
Sweet, W., '"Absolute Idealism" and Finite Individuality', *Indian Philosophical Quarterly*, XXIV, 4, 1997.

BIBLIOGRAPHY

Toynbee, A., 'Are Radicals Socialist?' in *Lectures on the Industrial Revolution in England, Popular Addresses, Notes and Other Fragments* [original publication 1884], Newton Abbott: David and Charles Reprint, 1969a.

— 'Wages and Natural Law' [original publication 1884], in *Lectures on the Industrial Revolution*, 1969b.

Tregenza, I., *Michael Oakeshott on Hobbes*, Exeter: Imprint Academic, 2003.

Tyler, C., *The Metaphysics of Self-Realisation and Freedom: Part 1 of The Liberal Socialism of Thomas Hill Green*, Exeter: Imprint Academic, 2010.

Urwick, E. J., 'A School of Sociology' in C.S. Loch (ed.) *Methods of Social Advance*, London: Macmillan, 1904.

Vincent, A., 'Metaphysics and Ethics in the Philosophy of T. H. Green' in M. D. Cookson and B. Mander (eds), *T. H Green: Ethics, Metaphysics and Political Philosophy*, Oxford, Clarendon Press, 2006.

Vincent, A., 'The Individual in Hegelian Thought' *Idealistic Studies*, XII, 1982.

— 'The Hegelian State and International Politics', *Review of International Studies*, 9, 1983.

— 'The Poor Law Reports of 1909 and the Social Theory of the Charity Organisation Society' *Victorian Studies*, 27, 1984.

— 'The New Liberalism in Britain 1880–1914', *The Australian Journal of Politics and History*, 36, 1990.

— 'New Ideology for Old?' *Political Quarterly*, 69, 1998.

— 'German Philosophy and British Public Policy' *Journal of the History of Ideas*, 68, 2007.

Vincent, A., (ed.), *The Philosophy of T. H. Green*, Aldershot: Gower, 1986.

Vincent, A., and Plant, R., *Philosophy, Politics and Citizenship: The Life and Thought of the British Idealists*, Oxford: Blackwell, 1984.

Watson, J. *The State in Peace and War*, Glasgow: Maclehose, 1919.

Cunningham, G. W. *The Idealistic Argument in Recent British and American Philosophy*, New York: Century, 1933.

Wempe, B., *T. H. Green's Theory of Positive Freedom*, Exeter: Imprint Academic, 2004.

Carr, H. W. (ed.), 'Life and finite individuality: Two symposia' I / II, *Aristotelian Society*, Vol. 1, London: Williams and Norgate, 1918.

Williams, B., *Ethics and the Limits of Philosophy*, London: Harper Collins, 1993.

Wittgenstein, L., *Tractatus Logico-Philosophicus*, London: Routledge, Kegan Paul, 1960.

FURTHER READING

COLLECTED ESSAYS AND WORKS

There has been some detailed scholarly republication of the works of many of the British Idealists over the last two decades. This has been pioneered by Thoemmes Press, for example, *The Collected Works of F. H. Bradley*, C. A. Keene and W. J. Mander (eds), Bristol: Thoemmes Press, 1999; *The Collected Works of T. H. Green*, R. L. Nettleship and Peter Nicholson (eds), Bristol: Thoemmes, 1997; *The Collected Works of Bernard Bosanquet*, Will Sweet (ed.), Bristol: Thoemmes, 1999; *The Collected Works of Edward Caird*, Colin Tyler (ed.), Bristol: Thoemmes, 1999, *Bosanquet: Essays in Philosophy and Social Policy 1883–1922*, W. Sweet (ed.). Bristol: Thoemmes, 2003; Colin Tyler (ed.), *Unpublished Manuscripts in British Idealism: Political Philosophy, Theology and Social Thought*, 2 Vols, Bristol: Thoemmes and Continuum, 2005.

There has also been a series of republications of the major work of R. G. Collingwood from Oxford University Press. In addition, Imprint Academic has made major scholarly contributions with several academic series of monographs dedicated to the works of R. G. Collingwood, Michael Oakeshott and T. H. Green, many of which have been referred to in this book. There has also been since 1993, a Collingwood and British Idealist Centre, now located at Cardiff University, which produces the principal journal in the field *Collingwood and British Idealist Studies: Incorporating Bradley Studies*. More recently, the Centre for the Study of British Idealism and the New Liberalism has been established by James Connelly and Colin Tyler. Both centres contribute to the work of the British Idealism Specialist Group of the Political Studies Association of the United Kingdom.

FURTHER READING

RECENT HISTORIES OF IDEALISM

Jeremy Dunham, Iain Hamilton Grant, Sean Watson, Idealism: *The History of a Philosophy*, Durham, Acumen, 2011; W. J. Mander, *British Idealism: A History*, Oxford, Oxford University Press, 2011.

RECENT GENERAL COLLECTIONS

There have been some helpful collections of both essays and biographical information on the British Idealists: D. Boucher, J. Connelly and T. Modood (eds), *Philosophy, Politics and Civilization*, Cardiff: Wales University Press, 1995, W. J. Mander (ed.), *Anglo-American Idealism*, Westport Connecticut and London: Greenwood Press, 2000; Corey Able and Timothy Fuller, *The Intellectual Legacy of Michael Oakeshott*, Exeter: Imprint Academic, 2005; Maria Dimova-Cookson and W. J. Mander (eds), *T. H. Green: Ethics, Metaphysics and Political Philosophy*, Oxford: Clarendon Press, 2006; Will Sweet (ed.), *Bernard Bosanquet and the Legacy of Idealism*, Toronto: University of Toronto Press, 2007; Will Sweet (ed.), *The Moral, Social and Political Philosophy of the British Idealists*, Exeter: Imprint Academic, 2009; Will Sweet (ed.), *Biographical Encyclopaedia of British Idealism*, London: Continuum, 2010; J. Connelly and S. Panagakou (eds), *Anglo-American Idealism: Thinkers and Ideas* Oxford: Peter Laing, 2010.

METAPHYSICS AND RELIGION

Metaphysical, logical, epistemological and religious studies have played a significant part in recent works on the British Idealists. F. H. Bradley is often a subject of these works: Peter Robbins, *The British Hegelians 1875–1925*, New York and London: Garland, 1982; A. Manser, *Bradley's Logic*, Oxford: Blackwell, 1983; A. Manser and G. Stock (eds). *The Philosophy of F. H. Bradley*, Oxford: Clarendon Press, 1984; J. Patrick, *The Magdalene Metaphysicals: Idealism and Orthodoxy in Oxford*, Macon: Mercer University Press, 1985; Don McNiven, *Bradley's Moral Psychology*, Lewiston: Edwin Mellen, 1987; P. Hyllton, *Russell, Idealism and the Emergence of Analytic Philosophy*, Oxford: Clarendon Press, 1990; T. L. S. Sprigge, *James and Bradley: American Truth and British Reality*, Chicago and La Salle, Illinois: Open Court, 1993; W. J. Mander, *An Introduction to*

Bradley's Metaphysics, Oxford: Clarendon Press, 1994; A. P.F . Sell, *Philosophical Idealism and Christian Belief*, Cardiff: University of Wales Press, 1995; Steven Anthony Gerencser, *The Skeptic's Oakeshott*, London: Macmillan, 2000. Terry Nardin, *The Philosophy of Oakeshott*, Pennsylvania: Penn State University Press, 2001; Paul Franco, *Michael Oakeshott: An Introduction*, New Haven: Yale University Press, 2004; Stewart Candlish, *The Russell/ Bradley Dispute and its Significance for Twentieth Century Philosophy*, Basingstoke: Palgrave Macmillan, 2006; Olaf Bengtsson, *The Worldview of Personalism: Origins and Early Development*, Oxford: Oxford University Press, 2006.

ETHICS

Ethics has received some attention, although it appears along with politics: G. Thomas, *The Moral Philosophy of T. H. Green*, Oxford: Clarendon Press, 1987; Maria Dimova-Cookson, *T. H. Green's Moral and Political Philosophy: A Phenomenological Perspective*, Basingstoke: Palgrave Macmillan, 2001; David O. Brink, *Perfectionism and the Common Good: Themes in the Philosophy of T. H. Green*, Clarendon Press, Oxford, 2003; Will Sweet (ed.), *The Moral, Social and Political Philosophy of the British Idealists*, Exeter: Imprint Academic, 2009.

POLITICS

The political philosophy of the British Idealists has been one of the more busy areas of scholarly study, often combined with ethics. Some works on the Idealists are more concerned to situate them in specific ideological and historical context, others focus much more directly on the philosophical arguments: A. J. M. Milne, *The Social Philosophy of English Idealism*, London: Allen and Unwin, 1962; W. H. Greenleaf, *The British Political Tradition: The Ideological Heritage*, Vol. II, London: Methuen, 1983; Andrew Vincent and Raymond Plant, Philosophy Politics and Citizenship, *The Life and Thought of the British Idealists*, Oxford, Blackwell, 1984. Michael Freeden, *The New Liberalism: An Ideology of Social Reform*, Oxford, Clarendon Press, 1986; I. M. Greengarten, *Thomas Hill Green and the Development of Liberal-Democratic Thought*, Toronto: University of Toronto Press, 1987; David Boucher, *The Social and Political*

Thought of R. G. Collingwood, Cambridge: Cambridge University Press, 1989; David Boucher and Andrew Vincent, *A Radical Hegelian: the Social and Political Thought of Henry Jones*: Cardiff, University of Wales Press, 1991; S. M. Den Otter, *British Idealism and Social Explanation: A Study in Late Victorian Thought*, Oxford; Clarendon Press, 1996; Will Sweet, *Idealism and Rights: The Social Ontology of Human Rights in the Political Thought of Bernard Bosanquet*, Lanham MD: University of America Press, 1997; David Boucher and Andrew Vincent, *British Idealism and Political Theory*, Edinburgh University Press, 2000; James Connelly, *Metaphysics, Method and Politics*, Exeter: Imprint Academic, 2003; Colin Tyler, *Idealist Political Philosophy: Pluralism and conflict in the absolute idealist tradition*, London: Continuum, 2006, David Weinstein, *Utilitarianism and the New Liberalism*, Oxford: Clarendon Press, 2007; Richard Murphy, *Collingwood and the Crisis of Western Civilisation*, Exeter: Imprint Academic, 2008; Stamatoula Panagakou also edited a special edition of *The British Journal of Politics and International Relations, Vol. 7* (2005), devoted to the British Idealists.

INDEX

absolute idealism 1, 12–13, 16–17, 18, 38–48, 57–75
absolute presupposition 49
analytic tradition 52, 53–4
Aristotle 18, 30
art 66–7, 71
Asquith, H. H. 127, 139
Austin, John 81–2, 152
Ayer, Alfred Jules 2, 40, 52

Baillie, J. B. 14, 22
Ball, S. 103, 105
Baur, F. C. 9
Bentham, Jeremy 4, 31–4, 35, 78
Berkeley, Bishop 1, 11, 12–13
Beveridge, William 103, 117
biblical criticism 15
Birkbeck College 113
Blanshard, Brand 43
Boer War (1899–1902) 136, 138–46
Bosanquet, Bernard 7, 17, 16–17, 42, 43–4, 47, 49, 58, 63, 76, 77, 79, 84–5, 87, 89, 90, 100, 118–19, 120, 123, 129, 131, 132–3, 135, 136, 137, 144, 149, 150
Boyce Gibson, W. R. 43, 47, 54
Bradley, A.C. 150
Bradley, F. H. 7, 10, 15–16, 32, 35, 40, 41, 43–4, 46–7, 54, 55, 57, 58, 60, 67, 68, 76, 83–4, 87, 89, 90, 99, 149, 150
Brown, Thomas 11
Burke, Edmund 30–1, 145

Caird, Edward 7, 9, 10, 14, 15, 19, 44, 48, 49, 60, 98, 105, 132, 136, 137, 141, 144, 146–7, 149, 151
Cambridge realists 50–4
Campbell Fraser, Alexander 12, 13
Carlyle, Thomas 8, 9, 10, 11, 14
Carnap, R. 51
Chamberlain, Joseph 139, 144
Charity Organization Society 17, 118–19, 120–1
Churchill, Winston 127
citizenship 97–101, 109–10, 122, 125, 136
class 108–10
Coleridge, Samuel Taylor 8, 15
colligating hypothesis 49–50
Collingwood, R.G. 2, 18, 20, 40, 41, 49, 53, 58, 60, 61, 62–7, 70–5, 79, 85–6, 150, 157
common good 3, 87–94, 122, 125, 136–7
common sense 51
compulsion 78–9, 83–5, 136–7
Comte, A. 14
consequentialism 4
conservatism of 30
Cook Wilson, John 2
cosmopolitanism 147, 150, 151
Croce, Benedetto 17, 18, 62, 63, 64, 65, 70
customary law 151

INDEX

Darwin, Charles   21–2, 23–4, 26, 148
Dawkins, Richard   24
Dilthey, W.   50
disobedience   80
dualism   12, 27–8

education   110–14
emotivism   4
empiricism   10, 33, 38–9
epistemology   32–3
ethical societies   17, 113–14
ethics   19, 27–8, 87–94, 152
Eucken, R.   47
evolution   2, 7, 20–9, 147–59
experience   40–1

Fabians   105, 138, 141
family casework   120
Fergusson, Adam   11
Ferrier, Frederick James   9, 10, 11–12, 19
Fichte, J. G.   9, 10, 36
First World War (1914–18) 42–3
Flint, Robert   14
Fourier, Charles   104, 105
freedom (*see* liberty)

Gentile, G.   17–18, 57, 62–5, 67, 70, 110
German militarism   42
German philosophy   7, 8
Green, T. H.   7, 9, 10, 15, 29, 31, 40, 42, 76, 77, 79, 80, 80–96, 100, 104, 107, 108, 112, 115–19, 121–3, 123–8, 131, 135, 136, 137, 140, 143, 149
Grey, Edward   139
Grote, John   18–19
Grotius, Hugo   152

Haldane, Elizabeth   14
Haldane, Richard Burdon   9, 10, 45, 103, 108, 112–14, 128, 137, 139, 141, 144, 145, 150, 151

Hamilton, William   11, 12
Hastie, William   14
Hegel, G. W. F.   9, 10, 11–20, 26, 28, 35, 36, 42, 47, 49, 57, 62, 75, 83, 87–8, 89, 110, 123, 130, 131, 132, 149
Hershel, John F. W.   21
Hetherington, Hector   134, 135, 136, 137–8, 144
historical criticism   15, 19
historical method   39
history   39, 72–3
Hobbes, Thomas   4, 49–50, 81–2, 94–5, 152
Hobhouse, L. T.   42, 43, 80, 103, 125–6, 127, 132, 133–4, 140, 141, 142, 145
Hobson, J. A.   80, 133–4, 140, 145
Hofstadter, Richard   25
Hooker, Joseph   23
Hume, David   4, 10, 12, 15
Husserl, Edmund   17
Hutchinson Stirling, James   13–14
Huxley, T. H.   26, 147, 149

idealism
  common good   33, 87–94, 122, 125, 136–7
  conception of philosophy   48–50
  critique of utilitarianism   2, 3, 4, 10, 29–35, 39, 92–4
  dualism   27–8
  education   3, 110–14
  experience and   41
  historical criticism   15, 19, 35, 39, 72–3
  language of   5–6
  liberalism   3, 97–8, 106–8, 123
  metaphysics of   38–75
  modality   41–2
  morality   3, 19, 27–8, 87–94, 152
  naive caricature of   48
  optimism of   5

INDEX

parts and wholes 28–9
political philosophy of 76–101
realism 1, 13, 39, 40, 48–55
self-realization 3, 43–4, 125
theory and practice 42, 87–90, 98–9, 102–29
unity of nature and spirit 28–9
war 5, 130–4
imperialism 138–46
Independent Labour Party 105
individualism 43, 44, 45, 87–8, 97–101, 119–20
inequality 93
international relations 130–54

Joachim, Harold 17, 53
Jones, Henry 7, 14–15, 16, 17, 19–20, 38, 42, 47, 50, 57, 58–60, 79, 98, 103, 114, 119, 124–5, 134–5, 137, 141, 143, 144, 145
Jowett, Benjamin 15, 112

Kant, I. 8, 9, 10, 11–20, 32–3, 36, 46, 83, 90, 122
Keynes, John Maynard 51, 117
Kidd, B. 141, 147
Kuhn, Thomas 26

Lamarck, Jean-Baptiste 22, 25
Laski, Harold 80
League of Nations 133, 153–4
liberal imperialism 139, 143
liberalism 79, 80, 97–8, 106–8, 123
liberty 126–8
Lloyd George, David 140
Locke, John 10, 12
logic 2, 15, 16–17, 51–2, 53
logic of question and answer 2
logical positivists 52–3
London School of Economics and Political Science 113
Lotze, Herman 9, 16, 36, 53
Lyell, Sir Charles 22

MacCunn, S. 145, 150
MacDonald, Ramsay 109
Mackenzie, J. S. 19, 105, 150
Marxism 104–5
McTaggart, J. M. E. 19, 47, 48, 54, 55, 76
Mill, J. S. 12, 15, 31, 35, 78, 105, 136
Mitchell, William 114
modality 41–2
modes of experience 41–2
monism 39, 57–75
Moore, G. E. 2, 50, 51, 54
morality (*see* ethics)
Muirhead, J. H. 9, 16, 79, 115–16, 133, 135, 136, 137–8, 141–2, 143–4, 145
Murdoch, Iris 30

nationalism 4–5, 134–8
naturalism 7, 20–9, 48, 90–4
natural selection 23, 25
natural theology 24
neo-Kantianism 4
new liberalism 103, 106–8, 116–17, 125–8, 138–41
Nicholson, Peter 131

Oakeshott, Michael 1, 2, 17–18, 20, 40, 41, 43, 44, 50, 53, 54, 55, 57, 58, 61, 68–71, 72–5, 76, 79, 89, 92–9, 111–12
obligation 85–7
ontological unity 44–5
Owen, Robert 104

Paley, William 24
parts and wholes 38–42
patriotism (*see* nationalism)
Personal Idealism 1, 12–13, 42–8
personalists and absolutists 42–8
Plato 9, 10, 15
poetry 3, 71–2
political philosophy 76–101
Poor Law Reports (1909) 119
positivism 39

INDEX

poverty 114–19
pragmatism 57
property 123–6

Rashdall, Hastings 76
Rawls, John 80
realism 1, 13, 39, 40, 48, 50–5
recognition 94–6
Reid, Thomas 10, 11
rights 27, 94–6
Ritchie, D. G. 17, 21, 25–6, 31, 33, 76, 77, 80, 96, 98, 105, 116, 119, 132, 135, 136, 141, 142, 143, 146, 147, 151
Rorty, Richard 6
Rousseau, J. J. 83
Royce, Josiah 47
Russell, Bertrand 2, 4, 51, 52, 54–5

Samuel, Herbert 127
Schelling, F. W. J. 9, 10, 36
Schlick, M. 52
Scottish common sense philosophy 8, 9, 10, 11, 12
Secret of Hegel 13–14
self-realization 43–4, 125
Seth Pringle Pattison, Andrew 9, 10, 43, 45, 46, 49, 76
Shaw, George Bernard 141
Sidgwick, Henry 30, 32, 78, 90, 97
Sittlichkeit 16, 123, 151
Smith, J. A. 17–18
social and non-social 86
social imperialism 5, 133, 139
Sorley, W. R. 19, 23, 150
Spencer, Herbert 10, 12, 15, 22, 25, 29, 34, 35, 77–8, 98, 148

spiritual realism 12
state 77–81, 102–3, 114–19, 122–3
Stebbing, Susan 50
Stephen, Leslie 34, 35
Stewart, Dugald 11
Sturt, Henry 43, 46, 47

Tawney, R. H. 103
theory and practice 42, 87–90, 98–9, 102–29
Toynbee, Arnold 103–4, 120, 124
truth 39–40, 41–2

University Extension Movement 112–14
University settlements 103, 113–14
utilitarianism 2, 3, 4, 10, 29–35, 39, 92–4

Vico, G. 14
Vienna Circle 51–2

Wallace, Alfred Russel 23, 147, 149
Wallace, William 14
war 130–4
Webb, Sidney and Beatrice 105, 113, 119, 121, 141
Whewell, William 21
Whitehead, Alfred North 54
Williams, Bernard 29
Wittgenstein, Ludwig 2, 4, 21, 51, 52, 53–4
Wolff, F. C. 10
Woolf, Leonard 141

www.ingramcontent.com/pod-product-compliance
Lightning Source LLC
Chambersburg PA
CBHW070329230426
43663CB00011B/2260